Pink Collar Workers

Pink Collar Workers

Inside the World of Women's Work

Louise Kapp Howe

G. P. Putnam's Sons, New York

Third Impression

Copyright © 1977 by Louise Kapp Howe

All rights reserved. This book, or parts thereof, must not be reprinted in any form without permission. Published simultaneously in Canada by Longman Canada Limited, Toronto.

Portions of this book have previously appeared in *McCall's*.

SBN: 399-11588-7

Library of Congress Cataloging in Publication Data

Howe, Louise Kapp.
  Pink collar workers.

  Bibliography
  1. Women—Employment—United States.   2. Labor and laboring classes—United States.   I. Title.
  HD6095.H68   1977   331.4′0973   76-41300

PRINTED IN THE UNITED STATES OF AMERICA

Charts on pages 279–289 reprinted from *1975 Handbook of Women Workers*, U.S. Department of labor, Employment Standards Administration, Washington, D.C.

Acknowledgments

My deep appreciation to the Ford Foundation, and in particular to Robert Schrank and Susan Berresford, for the grant that enabled me to begin. And to Charles L. Howe, who provided intellectual and emotional enrichment every step of the way. And to Elaine Markson, Genevieve Stuttaford, Joseph E. Kolman, Marcia Freedman, Vivien Leone, David Pesonen and the many others who were generous with their knowledge, advice, and time. And to my insightful editor at Putnam's, Edward T. Chase, and his remarkable assistant, Gail Hochman. And most of all, to my teachers, the women whose occupational world this book explores.

Contents

Now I ask you—do I need to read about the triumphant lives of Helen Gurley Brown or Mary Wells Lawrence?. . . Most of us are clerks, secretaries, salesgirls, social workers, nurses, and—if lucky enough still to be working—teachers. For us, the superwoman who knits marriage, career, and motherhood into a satisfying life without dropping a stitch is as oppressive a role model as the airbrushed Bunny in the Playboy centerfold or That Cosmopolitan Girl.

> —Sylvia Rabiner
> "How the Superwoman Puts Women Down"
> *The Village Voice,* May 24, 1976

In the real struggle between wife-mother and career-woman each side has had its violent advocates. What few suspect is that the fluctuation back and forth serves a purpose. . .

> —Sebastian de Grazia
> *Of Time, Work and Leisure*
> Twentieth-Century Fund, 1962

1

Pink Collar

You might think it all had been said. After all the debates, after all the discussions, after all the slogans and programs and suggested solutions, the subject would appear to be exhausted. Equal pay for equal work. Affirmative action. Equal employment opportunities. Equal education. Quality child care. What more is there to add? Enough words, enough talk, just keep pushing for the necessary action. And yet if I was to learn anything at all by the end of the journey that this book records, it was that—for all the good and vitally necessary steps now being taken and proposed—the most fundamental issues concerning the female labor force in America have only begun to be addressed. Have only begun to be scratched. In many ways, have only begun to be recognized.

Certainly I hadn't recognized them fully myself, sitting at home communing with the statistics. More women in the labor force than ever before (53 percent between ages 18 and 64 in 1974). More married women in the labor force (43 percent at the time). More employed mothers of preschool children (37 percent, although only about one-fifth worked full-time the year round). A slight dip since 1970 in the proportion employed over age 55 (23 percent). Which all very clearly added up to . . . what?

When I first started out I didn't know what I would find, had no startling notions in mind, just that I wanted to be among women still working in the occupations traditionally filled by women and hear their own views about the lives they led, their own suggestions about what was needed, if anything, to make things better. For a long time the public spotlight had focused on other women, other kinds of jobs. Although the women's movement was in fact extremely varied, in certain feminist circles anything that smacked of "women's work" had been either angrily derided or haughtily ignored. In the center of attention during the late 1960s and early 70s, stood—and marched—college-educated professionals and young single women who fervently believed in the primacy of work-and-achievement (meaning work and achievement outside the home and outside the usual female realm) and who were urging other women to hurry and rip the domestic curtains from their eyes as well.

Then, as the 1970s proceeded, the focus widened somewhat, concentrating more and more on those women, both in professional and nonprofessional jobs, who were now courageously crossing the employment borders to formerly male-only terrain. The outlook was clear. The winds were strong. Every day in every way, to judge by the popular media, things were getting better and better for American women workers. At least for those with the right consciousness. And yet . . . in the Labor Department statistics I was poring over, a decidedly different story was beginning to unfold. Decidedly less joyous. Decidedly more tricky. Yes, yes, to be sure more women were working outside the home, but that was a trend that had started far before the rebirth of the women's movement, ever since the Civil War in fact, with the most pronounced increase beginning after the end of the Great Depression, after 1940, a breathtaking upward pattern that had first included (in addition to the young single women already there) older married women, and then mothers of school-age children, and then more and more mothers of preschool children in numbers and proportions still growing to this very day. However: far from getting better and better every day in every way, the relative economic position of women had been declining in recent years. And declining. Steadily declining in comparison to men in a number of ways.

There was, for example, the little matter of unemployment. In the no-nonsense officialese of the Women's Bureau's *1975 Handbook on Women Workers*:

> Concern about unemployment among women has heightened. . . . This concern is a reflection of the marked increase in the size of the female labor force coupled with a worsening in the unemployment rate for women as compared with that of men. . . . In 1947 women accounted for 28 percent of the civilian labor force and 27 percent of the unemployed. In 1973 they accounted for 39 percent of the civilian labor force and 48 percent of the unemployed. In 1947 the unemployment rate for women (3.7) was less than that for men (4.0) but in 1973 the rate for women was much higher . . . 6.0 compared with 4.1 percent. In 1974 the comparative unemployment rates for women and men were 6.7 and 4.8 respectively.

As in past years, black women suffered roughly twice the jobless rate of white women, teenage females more than double the rate for older women, and black teenage females had the bleak distinction of possessing the highest rate of unemployment of any group (including black teenage males) in the nation. In the first quarter of 1975, unemployment of white teenage females stood or rather slumped at a depressive 18.1 percent. For black teenage females the rate, the rejection, was—and this is not a typo—43 percent. A year later, while everyone was noting the great economic recovery, the rate for black teenagers had barely moved.

Moreover, while the overall disparity in unemployment between men and women had been widening, the income gap had been worsening too. In 1956 when the feminine mystique was presumably holding sway (among the middle-class women who could afford it) the median earnings of women working full-time and year-round came to 63 percent of men's earnings. By 1970, the fiftieth anniversary of the winning of the vote, women's earnings had tumbled to 59 percent of men's. By 1974 (a full thirteen years after the signing of the federal equal-pay act, twelve years after the establishment of the Equal Employment Opportunities Commission) women's portion was down to 57 percent.

Meanwhile, as usual, the ones to be hit the hardest where it hurts the most were the ones already in the greatest economic need. As the income gap between men and women widened, the already oceanic divide between female-headed and husband-wife families spread even further. In 1950 the median income of families headed by women had been 56 percent of those with a husband as sole earner. By 1974 the income of the female-headed family had plummeted to 47 percent of the modest bundle the male earner was taking home and would have been far lower still in comparison to the higher earnings of the huge and growing numbers of families with both husband and wife in the labor force.

Although the percentage of female-headed families living below what some government economists or bulldozer defined as "the poverty level" had decreased somewhat (to a still horrendous one out of every three), the actual members of these families had been rising substantially along with the general skyrocketing of the divorced population. (Which many were saying was a wonderful sign of our increased liberation.) A third more children were living below this official poverty level in 1974 than had been in 1960. The majority were in families headed by women.

Now how could all this be true? Surely women have been making authentic progress. Tremendous progress. Hardly a month has gone by in recent years without another breakthrough announced in the press: The first woman to install a telephone line, celebrate communion in an Episcopal church, conduct Mozart in Carnegie Hall, direct traffic at Hollywood and Vine, found a bank, patrol a crime-ridden ghetto, wheel and deal with other vice presidents of General Electric, demolish Bobby Riggs on the tennis courts, become a state governor (without having been the wife of a former governor), a rabbi, ambassador to Ghana, television anchorwoman, managing editor of a big-city newspaper, sportscaster, chief justice of a state supreme court, commercial pilot, commissioned officer of a Navy warship, West Point cadet, Air Force cadet, Coast Guard cadet, Princeton valedictorian, Alaskan pipeline worker, and the list (which I have partly appropriated from the congratulatory "Women of the Year" issue of *Time* magazine at the end of 1975) could surely go on and on.

There is, however, one small problem with such a list, as impressive as it may sound, as impressive as in many ways it truly is. Or rather there are (at least) three problems. Very often when you check back through history you will discover that what has been labeled a "first" is really not one at all. Very often when it *is* unprecedented, you find that the numbers following after turn out to be disappointingly small. And third, even when there is a substantial dent made in a formerly "male" occupation, the odds are enormous that you are still talking about only a tiny fraction of the female workforce (usually, although not always, the more privileged) and that within that occupation the highest levels continue to be reserved for males.

For example in reading Edith Abbott's remarkable book, *Women in Industry* (first published in 1909 and recently reprinted, but too expensively, by Arno Press) I was amazed to learn that out of 303 separate occupations listed in the Census in 1900, women were recorded as employed in all but nine. Among the occupations that passive, dependent American sex objects were then pursuing were: farmers, lumbermen, engineers, policemen (yes), firemen, detectives, telegraph and telephone linesmen (yes), architects, physicians and surgeons, barbers, bartenders, bootblacks, hunters, trappers, bankers (yes), brokers, journalists, lawyers, chemists, accountants, teamsters, steamfitters, plasterers, roofers, undertakers, auctioneers, brickmakers, tilemakers, steelworkers, marble and stonecutters, fishermen and oystermen, gunsmiths, locksmiths, coal miners, gold miners, silver miners, blacksmiths, printers, lithographers, publishers of books and newspapers (yes), federal, state and country government officials, manufacturers, mining officials and for that matter every other occupation of the time except, for some unexplained reason, helpers to roofers and slaters, helpers to boilermakers and brassworkers, fire department foremen and, patriotically of course, our then all-male U.S. Army, Navy and Marines.

Well, quite obviously the overwhelming majority of American women in 1900 were not in the above positions (and we, or rather

I, do not really know the exact level of any of these stated jobs). Just as the overwhelming majority of American women today are not TV anchorwomen or chief justices of state supreme courts. (Neither, to be sure, are men. Marina Whitman of the Council of Economic Advisors has calculated that in 1970 there were more male janitors—1.1 million—than male doctors, dentists, lawyers, judges, and physical and social scientists put together.) As encouragement; as simple information on what changes are truly taking place; as what now some quaintly call "models" for young girls choosing careers; as pressure to see that their numbers increase—there are undoubtedly many fine reasons to keep calling attention to the exceptions in the female labor force—so long as the overwhelming majority still working in the traditional areas is not lost sight of. So long as the deep and enduring nature of this pattern is not underestimated, and that the hard questions, the old reporter's who-what-where-when and, most especially, why questions, continue being explored.

In 1900 the most common occupation for an American woman was unpaid labor in the home. As is still true today.

In 1900, while a fraction of women were filling all those untraditional jobs, most women in the paid labor force were in occupations disproportionately filled by women. Still true today.

In 1900 there was one occupation that accounted for nearly a third of the female labor force. Domestic service. Today there is one occupation that accounts for over a third. Clerical work.

In 1900 most members of the female labor force could be found in agricultural, manufacturing, or domestic service jobs. Today nearly two-thirds can be found in clerical, service or sales jobs.

In fact a number of different scholars have now determined that the rate of occupational segregation by sex is exactly as great today as it was at the turn of the century, if not a little greater.*

*Francine Blau Weisskoff, "Women's Place in the Labor Market," *American Economic Review* 62 (May 1972); Barbara Bergmann and Irma Adelman, "The 1973 Report of the President's Council of Economic Advisors; The Economic Role of Women," *American Economic Review* 63 (September 1973); Valerie Kincade Oppenheimer, *The Female Labor Force in the United States: Demographic Factors Governing its Growth and Changing Composition,* Population Monograph Series No. 5, Institute of International Studies, University of California, 1970; Edward

Only the jobs, not the proportions, seem to have really changed very much.

Throughout all the years between 1900 and 1960, Valerie Kincade Oppenheimer estimates that well over half of all women were in occupations in which at least two-thirds of the work force were female. Equally true right now.

And that somewhere between 30 and 48 percent were consistently employed in occupations in which *80 percent or more* were female. Exactly the case right now.

Moreover, the more detailed your analysis of a particular occupation becomes—by specific type of work performed; by industry; by firm; by department within the firm; by level of advancement achieved—the higher the rate of occupational segregation becomes.

For example, as Oppenheimer points out, assemblers in the higher paid automotive industry are usually male while in the lower paid electronics industry, they are predominately female. Or, to use an example I learned about concretely for this book, in the department store where I sold women's coats, take the position of sales clerk. In 1973 women were officially listed in Labor Department statistics as comprising 41.4 percent of those in the general occupational category of sales. And that would seem to have made it a most sexually integrated field, since the proportion corresponded very closely to the 39 percent that women then comprised of the labor force as a whole. However among salespeople working in retail trade only, women constituted a disproportionately high 69 percent of the work force. Among those selling in department stores and apparel shops, women were over 85 percent. Among those in the particular coat department where I may-I-help-you'd, women were 100 percent (not counting Ed, our erratic male manager). However several flights up in the higher paying furniture department, women were zero percent of the sales force. This is what economists call the internal labor market; the job structure within a company, which is typically as segregated by sex as is the labor market as a whole.

Now, of course, as everyone knows, all of this didn't just get

Gross, "*Plus Ça Change . . .* The Sexual Structure of Occupations Over Time," *Social Problems* 16 (Fall 1968).

started yesterday, nor for that matter in 1900. In 1776 and 1492 and 1812 and throughout recorded history and a week ago last Tuesday, there was and has always been two separate and distinct labor markets, although we like to think of it as just one: a mainly male one; a mainly female one; plus a small integrated pool in which certain oddball groups, writers for example, are allowed to swim, or, more commonly in this instance, sink.*

On an individual basis there have always been exceptions. Models. Tokens. On a regional basis there have always been variations, some too absurd to try to fathom. (For example, Oppenheimer reports a National Manpower Council finding that in the Midwest "cornhuskers are traditionally women, while trimmers are almost always men. In the Far West cornhuskers are men and trimmers are women.") On a national basis there have always been temporary shifts during periods of emergency. Come war times and boom times, when there are not enough male hands available, and you will invariably find women being allowed into the male market—usually to be shoved out later when it's all over. Come depressions and recessions, when there are not enough male jobs available, and you will find men to a lesser degree entering the female market.

Over time, naturally, as the nature of our work economy changed, so did the nature of the major male and female markets.

* Among other seemingly well-integrated occupations in 1975 (integrated at least in terms of the overall figures, with women being represented in roughly equal proportions to their then 39.6 percent of the labor force as a whole) were: psychologists (42.6 percent of whom were female); editors and reporters (44.6 percent); painters and sculptors (46.6); secondary school teachers (49.2); college and university teachers (31.1); real estate agents (40.1); personnel and labor relations (36.5); bill collectors (52.1); insurance adjustors (48.0); bakers (40.7); busdrivers (37.7); bartenders (35.2); ticket and station agents (39.0). The busdriver category however gives the show away. Most female busdrivers drove school buses. There's definite progress in some of these figures—for example substantial gains in the numbers of women bartenders (although often in the smallest, least unionized places) but far less progress than meets the eye. And far more segregation within the occupation (both in terms of where you are working and how far up the ladder you climb) than the overall figures show.

"Women's work" itself has been transformed as the nation moved from:

—an agricultural economy, in which the strenuous labor of women (child rearing, animal care, food gathering, baking, churning, cooking, canning, weaving, sewing, producing vast amounts of household goods for barter and sale) was of dire necessity to the economic survival of the family . . . to

—a manufacturing economy, in which, contrary to the usual conception, young women and not men were the first to enter in significant numbers, pioneering in the early textile mills while "men's work" was considered more valuable and irreplaceable in the fields . . . to

—our present predominantly service economy, in which once again women are the pioneers, holding sixty percent of all jobs in the service sector while men now retain the largest share in the manufacturing sector. Indeed, as Bruno Bettelheim has noted, in modern times the concept of women's-place-is-in-the-home has always been a concept that only a certain degree of affluence has ever made possible.

Over time also, as technology progressed, we have seen some occupations formerly on male turf (clerical work is the largest example) broken up into smaller parts and then gallantly handed over (along with the new machines and half the wages previously paid to men) to women. We have also seen, as male-dominated unions gained power, certain of the more lucrative jobs formerly open to women (printing, for example) being yanked away. The permutations are endless. They are also fascinating. But after you get through reading about all the historical changes, after you stop tracing all the twists and turns women's work has taken over the years, after you finish paying the necessary homage to all the exceptions and variations and tokens and models, this is what you always find: the vast majority of American women getting up in the morning, getting dressed, maybe grabbing a bite, and then going off to work at jobs (either within or without the home) where women form the bulk of the labor force; where pay is usually nil or low (in comparison to what men of the same or lower educational levels are making); where unionization is usually nil or weak; and where equal-pay-for-equal-work laws are of little or no meaning since if women are competing with anyone for these jobs they are competing with other women.

For of course, as with black children in school, the issue is not simply that most women are in a separate labor market. So are most men, but they're not complaining. The real issue is that the labor market women are mainly in is unequal in a myriad of bread and butter ways. Power and privilege ways. The current strategy to encourage women to prepare for and look for work outside the typical areas makes great sense if only for this reason. And the strategy is not wholly failing. It is important not to overstate this. Women have made definite relative gains in a variety of untraditional occupations in the past ten years and the numbers will surely continue to increase. But what the strategy has missed is this:

By far the most overwhelming increases have taken place in precisely the jobs where women have been working all along. Indeed it is Valerie Oppenheimer's contention, after a detailed study of the growth and changing composition of women in the job market, that the major *reason* for the extraordinary rise in the numbers of married women working outside the home has been that the *demand* for workers in the traditional female occupations has also soared.

Other factors have played a part to be sure. Smaller families, the need for increasing the family income, the growth of single-mother homes, women's interest in outside activities, among others. But none of these factors, in Oppenheimer's analysis, begins to approach the overriding influence of the great demand in the 1940s, 1950s, 1960s and (with the exception of teachers) in the early 1970s for workers in the predominantly female markets.

According to an analysis by Stuart H. Garfinkle in the November 1975 *Monthly Labor Review*, an official publication of the United States Department of Labor:

> Between 1962 and 1974 the number of employed women increased by 10 million or 45 percent, and their proportion of the work force increased from 34 to 39 percent. The largest employment gains for women occurred in those occupations in which women have been more likely to be employed. The largest gain, 4.8 million, occurred in clerical occupations in which women accounted for al-

most 70 percent of all employees in 1962. By 1974 women held almost 4 out of 5 jobs in this category and—undoubtedly—the rapid rate of growth of women's employment in this occupation helped to account for a substantial portion of the overall increase in the number of women in the work force . . . At the detailed occupational level . . . women cashiers increased from 82 percent to 88 percent of all such workers, women bank tellers from 72 to 92 percent, women payroll clerks from 62 to 77 percent . . .

In other words, while our attention has been focused on women entering the male side of the labor market, the most pronounced changes have been taking place on the female side. While it has become commonplace to discuss how the lines between so-called blue collar and white collar work have been fading (with more and more machines moving into the office), it has been barely observed that the most dramatic distinctions continue between what can most descriptively be termed pink collar work and work in the male and integrated markets. And these distinctions are far greater than I had ever expected before beginning this pursuit.

In addition to the female-concentrated jobs already mentioned here are some of the pinkest of pink collar occupations today:

	Percent female in 1975	Percent female in 1962
Registered nurses	97.0	98.5
Elementary school teachers	85.4	86.5
Typists	96.6	94.8
Telephone operators	93.3	96.3
Secretaries	99.1	98.5
Hairdressers	90.5	88.1
Waiters and waitresses	91.1	88.1
Nursing aides	85.8	75.2
Sewers and stitchers	95.8	94.1
Private household workers	97.4	97.3

And of course Homemakers, 99.9 percent, then and now.

Since seven out of eight women in the labor force today do not have college degrees, I decided to concentrate in this book on those jobs most typical for noncollege women. What did these occupations have in common? Why did the women enter them? The main theory put forth in recent years has been the socialization, or what I have come to think of as, the pink blanket theory. The little girl is born. Is cuddled and coddled. Is given a doll to cuddle, and then as she gets older, a bigger doll. Then one day while brother is busy playing with his doctor's kit, she is handed a nurse's kit. Ergo she becomes a nurse. If you want to change the situation buy her a doctor's kit instead. Well, you'd better be sure to give her fifty thousand dollars, too. There are exceptions and models and tokens but occupational choice in this country is still largely a class matter as well as a matter of gender. Most brothers of nurses do not become doctors. And those 1.1 million janitors—it's clear they were not socialized for that role since mother was doing most of the cleaning at home. No, other factors besides socialization obviously apply.

I finally settled on five traditional female occupations: beautician, saleswoman, waitress, clerical worker, and the largest one of them all, homemaker. How did the women in these jobs actually feel about their work? What were their lives like? What was it like to be performing the work from *their* point of view? In this country we are so used to emphasizing the new and the novel that we often end up knowing less about what is in front of our noses. Why *did* these women choose these occupations? Did they wish they had chosen something else? At a time when job satisfaction and "humanizing the workplace" are supposedly public issues, what were their own suggestions about making their worklives better, more humane. What were their unions like, those who had them? Did those without them feel that unions were the way to improve their situation? What were their employers like, what was the "internal labor market" like, the chances for advancement? In the work vs. family debate, what position did these women take? How did those who were mothers manage the day-by-day conflicts in playing both roles? Were the homemakers as isolated and miserable as everyone was saying—or as happy and fulfilled as they were touted as being years ago? Every question I thought of seemed to lead to another question.

Thanks to the deep interest of Robert Schrank and Susan Berresford in these issues, I had the good fortune to receive a grant from the Ford Foundation for the first year of this effort. But I had neither the resources, nor the background, nor for that matter, the inclination for anything approaching a formal "study" with statistical tabulations and control groups and all the rest. It had to be something smaller, more personal, with no pretensions to social—or anti-social—"science."

As it turned out my method of approach in each of the five occupations was somewhat different. In the case of the hairdressers, the workers of my then neighborhood beauty shop in California gave me permission to hang around over the course of one summer. In the case of the New York department store, I decided to try it out myself when I saw Christmas jobs being advertised in the newspaper. Although that experience turned out to be one of the richest, and I probably learned things I could have learned in no other way, I had felt deeply uncomfortable about not having come immediately clean with my fellow workers about why I was there, and so I didn't again use the I-Was-There approach. In any event, had I tried taking a job as a waitress myself, the outcome would have been largely a Perils of Pauline story, or so I realized as I began to appreciate how difficult and confusing that job can be. Instead, a friend introduced me to an experienced New York waitress who introduced me to others, and I also introduced myself to waitresses at different kinds of places. A number agreed to meet with me after work. (And, a number of others, I might add, particularly older women, were afraid to say a word. "Of course they won't talk," one told me. "They're afraid of losing their jobs.")

For the office section, a former clerical worker introduced me to friends still working at a large Chicago insurance company, a place I was particularly interested in since it prided itself on its sophisticated personnel policies, including a recently inaugurated job-enrichment program. How did the women workers respond to this program? Were their jobs really getting better or was it just

23

the company that was getting enriched? In the case of the home-makers, I had a made-to-order framework from which to begin when I learned that the Wisconsin Governor's Commission on the Status of Women was going to be holding a series of confer-ences where homemakers would be discussing their attitudes to-ward their work.

In addition, over the course of these—can it now really be—three years, I have talked, joked, commiserated with, attended meetings with, had dinner, lunches and drinks with many many additional women besides those mentioned in these pages (almost all, by the way, pseudonymously).* They have included nurses, receptionists, keypunch operators, legal secretaries, domestic workers, medical technologists, teachers, dental assistants, sew-ers, telephone operators, supermarket cashiers, among others in female-dominated jobs. I can't tell you how many there were be-cause I never kept count. Maybe there were 123. Maybe 180. Maybe 206. It doesn't really matter, does it? They're women, not data.

One of the women I talked with was someone I had known as a child. When we were both about nine or ten we had once toured our neighborhood (Kew Gardens, New York) selling packages of flower seeds, my own first pink collar job. We had grown up, gone off in totally different directions. She had married early. I had married late. She had raised two human beings. I had edited a small magazine and three books. We were reunited at the sec-ond-wedding reception of another childhood friend after not see-ing each other for almost twenty years. She looked wonderful. Now forty, now divorced, she had a job corresponding with the customers of a suburban importing company near where she and her two daughters lived. She liked the job very much but the pay was depressingly low. We talked. We reminisced. Remember that maniac who opened the door the time we were selling the seeds? Remember how we had run? God, how many things had changed since then. Sometimes she tried to explain the differences to her daughters, but they could never understand. For instance, once

*If both the first and last name are given it's real; if only the first, it's not.

when her oldest was about seven she mentioned that when she was that age people didn't have television sets in their homes. "But mommy, what did you do instead?" the little girl asked. Well, sometimes we listened to the radio. "But mommy," the child persisted, "what did you do with your eyes?"

Getting to know more about the lives and jobs of singular women in traditional occupations is what I have lately been doing with my eyes. On a small scale, on a human scale, I set out to ask who, what, where, when, and why.

2

Beautician

Once in a while in the midst of a tint or a set or a bleach, a customer would trot out that old only-my-hairdresser-knows line, and then whoever heard would usually laugh in return. But aside from those moments, the woman who worked in that shop almost never referred to themselves as hairdressers, and so I won't either in these notes.

They stuck to the plainer term beautician. Or, sometimes, simpler yet, beauty operator. Maybe that's because not one of them was in a high enough income bracket to give a hang about job titles yet, first things first. No question, it was also because they were women; men in the same line of work no matter what they earn seem always to be called hairdressers, don't they? if not the newer, fancier term hairstylist. Imagine calling the famed Mr. Kenneth or Vidal Sassoon a beautician.

Then, too, men—although they only account for one out of every ten persons in this occupation—seem somehow to mysteriously land the majority of the hairdressing jobs in most of the so-called high-status shops. Meaning, of course, places where customers pay and workers can make the most money. Just like the typical division of opportunity between waiters and waitresses (where the ten percent male, ninety percent female ratio also applies by the way). Waiters at the best restaurant and the best hotel in the city. Waitresses at Howard Johnson's and the Corner Coffee Shop and the diner a mile out on the highway.

But the trappings of a high-priced beauty salon in any case were the last thing the owner of that particular shop, where I recently spent a good part of a couple of months, was trying to set before you. He had the exact opposite enticement in mind. As the sign on the window, in bold black letters, visible from ten feet away, announced at once.

BEAUTY ON A BUDGET *** NO APPOINTMENTS NECESSARY

And then in smaller letters for those interested enough to come closer:

Shampoo and Set .... $ 2.95
Touchups .... from $ 4.50
Frostings .... from $12.50
Permanents .... from $ 6.95

Such prices in most areas of the country today are apparently remarkably low. They were far lower, at least, than the prices of the other beauty shops in that same community, where I happened to be living at the time. Located about fifteen miles from San Francisco, the town is built on a wide and steep hill—with the beauty shop in the middle of a shopping center at the foot—and as is the common case the higher up the hill you climb generally the higher the prices of the homes and the incomes of the residents become. In terms of income I gather the range is roughly from people who average about $8,000 a year to those making more than five times that. But at a time when everyone is trying to cut expenses, to save wherever they can, the shop draws women from the entire community, from the bottom to the top of the hill.

At the Shop

It looks tiny from the outside, surprisingly spacious when you enter. Opening the door you find yourself in a softly lighted rectangular room, everything pink and lilac and gold and white. Ultrafeminine in the pre-feminist sense of the word. Dainty. Hand-lettered signs on the wall urge you to buy special hair spray and conditioners and custom brushes. And: *Did You Know We Specialize in Complete Wig Care?* And: *Fancy Hairdo's from $1.00 Extra.* And: *Not Responsible for Stolen Possessions.*

There were five women working here the first time I stopped by, all of them in their twenties. Suzy who manages the shop was the one I saw immediately, since she was sitting up front ready to greet me and any woman who walked in and since she was so (how else would a sallow native Easterner like myself perceive it?) California looking. Tall and tan and blonde and slim, like all the old stereotypes, like all those Sun 'n' Surf ads. And *happy*, that was the thing. Suzy was trained to look always happy I was to discover, to smile always with delight when a customer appeared whatever she might be really feeling. When she welcomed you with that rusty old standbye, "What Can We Do For You Today?" she *welcomed* you. "It's part of my job," she later told me, "a very important part, to make the women who come in here feel good," and she was unquestionably proud of her ability to do so. The only time I ever saw her let down, saw the glistening smile fade a bit, was after the thing that was to happen with Jackie, but even then she never actually stopped smiling, never was unpleasant, just a little restrained in her usually radiant greetings to her customers as they came and went, came and went.

Then, on the left side of the room, on that first day I was there, standing behind a row of gold-framed mirrors and pink dressing chairs where their customers sat—their "ladies" they called them—were Avis and Marianne and Jackie, the shop's three full-time all-purpose beauticians.

Marianne, at the middle table, was the most animated of the three, talking and laughing with her customer, her lady, and also the most eyecatching, for not only was she the only black woman in this all-white shop and strikingly—at least six feet—tall, but she also bore a vivid resemblance to Angela Davis, who turned out indeed to be one of her heroines.

In direct physical contrast on either side of Marianne, both barely reaching as high as her shoulder and both as blonde as September corn, were Avis and Jackie. Jackie, on Marianne's left, was extremely heavy in those days, maybe forty or more pounds overweight, but in a country in love with thinness, she seemed to carry that weight with the hauteur of a *Vogue* model. In turn, Avis, on Marianne's right, appeared skinny and fragile and shy.

Finally in the back of the room where the sinks were, her hands full of suds as she finished a shampoo, stood or, rather, bent a small woman with short, fluffy, heavily sprayed auburn hair. That was Linda, at 29 the oldest worker in the room.

So those were the five of them, Suzy, Marianne, Avis, Jackie, and Linda. But in addition there should be one other person mentioned in this rapid survey, even though he wasn't in the shop that first day I was there. He is the owner of the place—the owner of a number of other shops as well—and while he calls Suzy constantly to check on his investment, he comes by only once a week to look things over personally. In deference to the women who still work there and need their jobs I can't tell you his real name, nor the real names of the workers, but it won't hurt I think to pass on the flavor of the nickname his five young workers devised for him. It will give you a quick insight into the state of employer-employee relations at the time I was there. Bumblebrain.

Talking with Suzy

One sizzling morning in July I walked into the shop and asked Suzy if I might spend some time there for the next couple of months, watching what happens during the day and getting to know the women who worked there.

By this time we knew each other slightly. I had been in a couple of times strictly as a customer (haircut by Jackie, shampoo by Linda) and Suzy and I had talked a bit. I knew she was recently divorced ("I'll never get married again") and that she was a beautician herself before getting this job as manager ("But I'm still a beautician, too"). She knew I lived close by, was from New York, was married and just getting started on a book about working women.

"So it occurred to me, why don't I get started here?" I said to her a little hesitantly. "But then I thought—your boss. He'd never agree to it, would he?"

"But why does he have to know?" she replied with a grin, and then I saw that she couldn't be more delighted. "It really would be something to read about what happens in a beauty parlor, what beauticians have to go through, good and bad. It's never been done, and I'd like people to know."

So that's how we began. Suzy said she would talk to the other women to see if they were willing to join in, too, and I said I'd drop by the following day to find out. They all were, and so off and on during the rest of the summer we talked in the shop and in our homes, never knowing how different things would be by the time I left California in late September.

At the Shop

Nine thirty on a Friday morning, usually one of the busiest days in the week in this and any beauty shop, but since it's summer there's a lull. Customers are away on vacations and business is slow. I sit under a turned-off plastic bubble hair dryer and flip through *The American Hairdresser.*

There is a sleepy quality in the shop today and the music on the radio lulls everyone further. "On a Clear Day You Can See Forever." Jackie yawns. Standing next to her, Marianne mimics the yawn, two notes lower. Then Avis yawns. They laugh.

Eleven A.M. Business picking up. Five customers now. One, who must be over seventy, has just asked Suzy to find her someone who knows how to set with pincurls not those newfangled rollers. Another, an auburn-haired woman in a flame-red cotton pant suit, has come in with a photograph showing a haircut she wants duplicated—"exactly."

Avis gets the woman with the photograph. She is a child psychologist, she says, and appears to be in her late fifties. The picture she gives Avis is of a very young woman with a shag cut, extremely short. Avis props it by the mirror, and takes out her scissors.

Now Jackie is brushing out a set. Through the mirror she can see the face of her customer watching her own reflection intently. Jackie brushes the woman's hair upward and teases it a little. The woman admonishes her to stop. "Please don't do that, it makes my hair break off." Jackie says nothing, shrugs slightly, and then quickly finishes brushing the hair into place, polishing it off with one, two, three whiffs from a can of hair spray. "That's it," she says, removing the yellow plastic cape from the woman's shoulder. But the woman continues sitting, continues staring at her reflection in the mirror.

"Could I have a comb please?" Jackie hands it to her without looking and then strolls to the shampoo area in the back of the room where Linda is rinsing out a black tint, her rubber gloves covered with dark oozy dye.

Jackie plops her ample body on a nearby chair. "Is everyone in a funk today or just me?" she asks the world of beauty at large.

"Part of the problem is that godawful funeral music you keep playing," answers a voice from the bottom of the sink—Linda's tint. "Can't you put on something more lively?"

"Well, we tried to," Jackie says, "but the man who owns this place says this is the only kind of music our customers like and he won't let us play anything else. I took a poll of all the ladies in here one day—I asked them if this is the kind of music they wanted to hear and they said no, every damn one of them, but you know how pigheaded bosses can be."

The customer is now sitting upright as Linda wraps a towel around her wet head. "How often does your boss come around to check?" she asks.

"Not very often," Jackie says and then, after glancing at the front desk and seeing that Suzy is out on her lunch break, she walks over to the radio and changes the station, her first rebellion of the day. Stevie Wonder replaces Lawrence Welk.

Meanwhile Avis' shag has left and she gets the woman who wants the pincurls. Avis is very quiet as she works, very serious and methodical, a scientist in a laboratory. On the other hand, Marianne standing next to her is effervescent. Marianne's current customer has short wispy gray hair, hair that is obviously starting to vanish, but she nevertheless wants it cut. "Well," Marianne tells her, "today is your lucky day. It just so happens I give fantastic haircuts."

Another comb-out for Jackie, usually the fastest operator in the shop. Three women sit under plastic hairdryers reading (1) *McCall's,* (2) *Good Housekeeping,* and (3) *Modern Screen.* I sit and watch Jackie at her craft.

A simple style, short and straight. Brown bangs. Peter Pan, 1948. The woman is pleased. Jackie adds the finishing whiffs of spray, a few more touches with a comb. The woman, who lives on top of the hill, is talking about her husband, the anniversary present he just gave her—a diamond pin—and the trip to Carmel they'll be taking together this weekend. Jackie listens, smiles, but there is something cold and blank in her eyes. The woman gets up. "I love it!" she exclaims, patting her head and then offhandedly, as if it were an intimate secret between them, she slips a half dollar into the hip pocket of Jackie's yellow smock. "See you next week, dear."

"See, didn't I tell you I give fantastic haircuts?" Marianne is saying to her balding customer who smiles and obviously agrees.

Now Suzy is back from her half-hour lunch. Immediately goes to the radio and switches it back to the original station. Frank Sinatra replaces Mick Jagger. "You understand I have no choice," she says to Jackie, knowing instinctively who had changed the music.

No new customers now. Avis retires with a cheese and tomato sandwich she has brought from home to a tiny room behind the shampoo area where the workers can eat their lunch or smoke or talk together when there's no work to be done. I sit with her while she eats until Suzy interrupts to tell her there's a call. It's from her seven-year-old son, home alone with a cold. "Just stay inside and don't forget to take your Ritalin later," Avis tells him and then hangs up.

With Avis

"A housewife. That's what I dreamed about being when I was little. I didn't think about working at all."

Today is Tuesday, Avis' day off, and we are sitting together in her living room sipping coffee. The house itself, which Avis rents for $136 a month, is tiny and tattered on the outside, but the room where we sit is pleasant to be in, the furniture old and brown and comfortable, a bright multicolored rug in the middle of the floor.

"Harvey and I made that from scraps," she tells me with pride—pride in the rug not in the man whom she lived with for three years then sent on his way six months ago.

While we sit and talk we can hear sounds from the kitchen: Avis' son Johnny playing catch the plastic bone with their black and white dog.

Avis may never have thought about having to take a job when she was little but by the time she was fifteen you could find her every night serving cocktails at a neighborhood bar, precisely as her mother had done when she was the same age too. Hating school, Avis simply cut classes until she was sixteen and could officially drop out. Two months later her dream came true. Marriage. To John, an older man of seventeen who was working at the local gas station.

Although she is now twenty-five Avis doesn't look much older than seventeen herself this morning with no makeup on yet and her long yellow hair flowing. She pours some more coffee.

In those early-marriage days, she says, "We didn't have a fantastic income but we got along, and that made us feel good." Until she got pregnant the following year. And Johnny, Jr., was born. And Johnny Senior lost his job. And then began worries about money and fights about his staying out late. "The old story."

After three years of marriage they broke up. At which point Avis decided to be a beautician.

"Why? I guess I didn't know what else to do. I couldn't stand the thought of babysitting, couldn't type, hated the thought of staying home all the time. I was on the county then—on welfare—and I'd have done almost anything to get off."

Her "dole" was $148 a month. "Out of which I had to pay for everything for the baby and me, our rent and our food and then for babysitters and tuition to beauty school and all the extras they make you buy—uniforms and brushes and supplies and your transportation back and forth and, as I already said, for babysitters. Finally the school let me go on a special program they call 'Workway.' That means you don't have to pay tuition, but you do have to do extra work for the owner, like cleaning up the place, and you have to stay there longer. But even so you still had all those other things you had to pay for. In my own case if it hadn't been for one girlfriend who watched Johnny for practically nothing, I wouldn't have made it.''

She finally found a child-care center in the neighborhood, ''but that was such a hassle getting him there in the morning and rushing to pick him up at night, that it wasn't worth it.'' It was also during that time that Johnny began having problems. ''They told me he was going wild there, hitting the other kids and even the director. I took him out. I didn't trust the place.''

So there were difficulties at home—with her son, with money—but how did she like the school itself?

''I surprised myself. I really enjoyed it. I loved styling hair and trying new things out. Once I even won a trophy in a contest they had. It was only third place but it meant a lot to me. I was really feeling pretty good.''

''And then?''

She lights a cigarette. ''And then I met Harvey.''

After seeing each other for two weeks Harvey moved in with her. A week after that he quit his job.

''You see, he said the reason he quit his job was that he wanted to find something better. But the way it worked out I started supporting him—out of that same $148. And I didn't go for that. So we would fight and he would say he was looking for a job and then finally when I got out of the beauty school and he still wasn't working, just staying home all the time watching television, I said, the hell with you, I'm going to stay home too unless you go out and work.''

Harvey found a job. And then she did too, at a beauty shop in a department store. She stayed there six months. By which time Harvey had put in a total of three weeks of work.

''It wasn't only Harvey. The girls were all snotty and the boss was always switching my days around, and then she would swear at me because I wasn't building a clientele, which is pretty hard to do if nobody knows when you are going to be there. And Harvey still wasn't working. So finally I quit and then for the next two years he would be in and out of a job and I would be on and off the county and meantime I'd do a little babysitting or sell some Avon cosmetics, and then, well, it just got to be too much. All we did was fight. Everytime I got a check he would snatch it. So then, well I'm the type of person who has to know she's going to be secure, so just before I told him to leave I went out and got the job I have now, and then I told him o-u-t."

That was seven months ago and since then, she says, she's felt a million times better. The dog has now come in from the kitchen and Avis is caressing him on her lap.

"I like it at the shop, I really do. I like it especially when I'm busy. I hate to just sit around. And I really like the girls, they're not snotty like at the department store, and we have pretty good times together. Sometimes we'll go out at night some of us and do different things. And Suzy's about the best boss anyone could ask for, she runs everything nice and smooth—that's until Bumble-brain comes in and gums up the works."

One difficulty I'm having, I tell Avis, is in understanding the way she gets paid. I know it's part salary, part commission and part tips. But I can't seem to get it straight.

"Okay. We get paid an hourly rate. I get $1.85 and so does Jackie. The others get $1.75. That figures out to $74 or $75 a week. Then if we double that amount—if our customers bring in more than, say, $150 in business, then we start to get a commission of 25 percent of what they bring over that, see? And then if we triple our salary, if our customers go over $225, we get a commission of 50 percent on everything on top of that. Okay?"

We are laughing now because I'm obviously so confused. "But what does that mean for you in actual dollars?"

"A few times I tripled and in a good season—not in the summer like now when everyone's away—I can usually double. On the average I guess I take home about $300 a month, figuring my commissions in. And then on top of that figure about $100 a month in tips. So that's $400 a month. And now at last my ex-husband has started to chip in with child support, so that's another $75." The dog jumps off her lap and runs to Johnny who has come in to collect him.

"And how does that work out?" I ask.

"It works out fine. My only problem is . . ." And she points a long red fingernail at her son who is standing close by now listening intently. "He's destructive, he tears everything up. I don't know how much you know about hyperactive children, but I can tell you they're a handful." A flatness in her voice. "Look, ha-ha, he's rubbing his butt, he got a spanking last night that wouldn't quit, didn't you?"

A little boy's big brown wary eyes.

"Tell her," Avis says, "tell Louise about the bruises Mama put on your leg last night. Yeah, I'll give you some more if you don't behave tonight."

Pause. Then, "Okay, *okay* Mom," and Johnny and dog return to the kitchen. Avis and I return to the original subject.

"So money isn't a problem now?"

"No, I don't worry about money that much. The rent and gas bills are paid and we don't have much besides that. I hardly buy any clothes and we don't eat anything fancy, that's for sure, but I don't worry about it. Which is funny because when I was married or living with Harvey I was always thinking about how I *had* to have something. But now I feel different. Maybe that's because I'm happier now."

I ask her if she'd ever marry again.

"Not for a long while anyway. I figure it this way. I was married to John and then I got together with Harvey, and both times when it was over I ended up in the same nowhere position. I don't want to do that again, and that's why I don't date much now, I mostly stay home. I get hung up on people and I'm afraid of that. I just want to stay free and clear and do my work."

"But is that because you really want to work or because you feel you can't depend on a man to support you and Johnny—or both?"

"Well, I don't know. Maybe it's true I've become very sus— All I know is I'm not going to go and work and support any man."

"But suppose you didn't have to contribute a dime. He was perfectly willing to take on the whole load, then would you want to stay home and let him?"

A search for matches, then she lights another cigarette. "Well, I doubt it, because I'm very— I don't trust men anymore. It's really hard for me to trust anyone. I don't know why. I haven't really had so many bad experiences, but anyway it would take me

36

a long, long time before I believed in anyone again. And also as far as work and men and everything goes, I'm changing my mind about myself. I used to be the domestic type, but now staying home and cleaning sounds like a real drag. I enjoy working."

She puts a pillow in her lap where the dog had been and looks at it thoughtfully. "And as for the future I'm not going to worry about it. I like doing hair and if I'm going to stay in a job that's what I'll probably do. If I wanted to make more money I should probably be in another field, but I'm not going to let money rule me. Too many people, they outdo themselves, they outspend themselves, they have to have the best of everything. Me, I've got a couch to sit in, a bed to sleep on, a stove to cook on, a refrigerator, a car that's rickety and falling apart, but it takes me where I want to go. The only real problem I have now is with Johnny. I love him and all, but I get tired of cleaning after his messes. But I don't let things pressure me. I don't dwell on things that aren't possible or can't happen because there's really no sense in it, and if you just look at the way things are, and take it for what it is, and make the best of it, then, you know, you can be happy."

The Education of a Beautician
This is the school that three of the five beauticians attended. The man who runs it has a long gray beard, gentle green eyes and a soft hypnotic voice that can talk nonstop for hours. And so I listen.

"My school is completely private, but it is regulated by the California Board of Cosmetology, which sets standards we have to meet.

"Here are some of the requirements for entry if you want to come here. You have to be at least sixteen. You have to have a minimum of a tenth-grade education. And to get a degree you have to complete 1,600 hours of training with us. (That's a state requirement, by the way. Some states require less. In New York it's only 1,000 hours. Some require more. The highest is the State of Washington with 2,000. You also have to pass a lengthy state board to get your certificate).

"If you attend our school on a strict five-day, forty-hour-week basis, those 1,600 hours will average out to about nine months. But many students stretch it out to a year or more.

"Different schools charge different amounts for the nine-month period, but around here it's generally between $300 and $500. As a student you have to pay this (unless you are in a special Workway program or the welfare department is paying us for you), but remember you also collect tips here from the customers you work on. The customers pay us for the work you do, just like at regular beauty shops, but we charge much less, say $1.50 for a wash and set.

"Why are women attracted to this field? One good thing is that you can learn to be a beautician in only nine months. For stenography it takes about a year and a half. Nursing takes three years.

"But overall, since you want to write about this occupation, you should know that this is a dwindling business. Young women don't come like they used to. They used to come for a wash and set once a week, a permanent two or three times a year. Now only the older women seem to be going regularly.

"And it's also a lot harder to recruit students these days. For one thing, homosexual men aren't as interested as they used to be, since they have more acceptance now in other fields. For another, a lot of women think the work is menial. Washing and brushing another woman's hair is like a state of servitude to them. It's related to the whole attitude toward service work in our society."

At the Shop

When I told Suzy what the director of the beauty school had said she said he was dead wrong.

"The business isn't dying," she said, "it's just changing. Okay, it's true most of our regular customers who come every week are older women. But younger women are paying more attention to hair health and hair styling now than they did before. They come too but not as often. And now that styles are beginning to get short and curly again they'll be coming more often, you'll see."

"Perhaps," I said, "but don't you think the woman's move-

38

ment has something to do with it, too? Maybe women are spending less time worrying about how they look because they're spending more time worrying about how they live."

"But that's not the way it works," Suzy said, eyeing me closely. As usual she looked like an advertisement for California living, all in crisp yellow that day and I, as I remember, was all in rumpled tan.

"You can't tell me it's bad for a woman to care about her appearance," she continued. "I do, and I think I'm as liberated as anybody, and you know I think everybody does, no matter what they say. Don't you?"

"Well yes, but—"

"And you also can't tell me"—she was smiling, but totally serious—"that just because a woman cares about her appearance that's all she cares about. The women who come here do a lot with their lives. And we're certainly not hurting them, we're making them feel better, so that can't be bad. And also a lot of these women, you wouldn't believe it, they come to us like men go to bartenders, because they are so lonely. They talk to us about the most private things, their divorces, their children, their abortions, all their problems. So what we do here is a lot more than people think."

With Linda

She lives on the lower floor of a two-family house ten blocks from the shop. Moved here with her husband and six-year-old daughter a month ago. Is relieved that she can now walk to work. Before she had to walk six blocks *and* take two buses "and that nearly drove me crazy."

She is delighted with her bright new apartment. Only problem is the rapid transit station that was recently built a block away. The trains weren't running when she first saw the apartment, and she hadn't realized the roar they would make, as they pass by every ten minutes during the day, every twenty minutes in the evening until midnight.

Before Linda first went to beauty school, she had been a waitress ("too hectic"), a car hop ("they make you work outside even when it thunders") and a warehouse packer ("faster, faster, is all they care about"). And a mother. She quit working when she became pregnant, but the father of the child walked out on her long before she gave birth, and so she had to go on welfare until she decided what to do. She chose beauty school when she heard that she was eligible for a welfare department Work Incentive Program that would pay her expenses. And then she found she enjoyed the school "pretty much."

"I didn't like the written work that much, but I did like the working with hair, and I liked the permanent waves and experimenting with different colors. There's a lot you have to know besides just washing and setting hair. You have to learn how to give a facial, how to give a manicure, scalp treatments, perms, hair coloring—it takes a lot of time and concentration."

Since getting out of school Linda has worked in a series of shops, sending her daughter to various babysitters. She has also gotten married. And now, she says, she is waiting for the day she can quit.

"I don't really like working now. I'd rather be at home watching my own daughter. But we need the money, we've had some problems paying some bills from the time my husband was sick, so I'll just have to keep on working till we get everything straightened out."

As with Avis, we are meeting together on Linda's day off which as it happens is also her day for doing the heavy housework and the weekly shopping. Later we will drive to the supermarket together and talk on the way, but right now Linda says she feels like sitting and taking a break.

I ask, what about her job particularly bothers her?

"My work it's hard because of the job, but also because of having to get my husband and my daughter up and out. I get up at six fifteen usually and then I get my husband off to work—I make his breakfast and fix his lunch—he's a welder—and then after he goes I get myself dressed and then when I'm ready, usually about eight, I'll wake my daughter and give her a bath and feed her and help her get dressed if she needs help and then I'll straighten the house a little and then we'll be off—we'll walk up the street to the babysitter if, like now, she's not going to school and then I'll walk

40

the ten blocks to the shop. By the time I get there I feel like going back to bed."

She used to do only shampooing at the shop, but now she has had a promotion. She shampoos half the week and the rest of the time she joins Avis and Jackie and Marianne "on the floor" as an operator. She likes that better, she says, but still wishes she could stay home. I ask her how she likes the atmosphere of work in a beauty shop.

"It all depends on the girls," she says. "Some are snotty, some don't talk to each other, it all depends. I'm quiet myself and most of the other girls in the shop are outgoing. But I'm quiet. Because I'm married and I'm settled down, I have what I want and I'm not trying to look for something else. But some of the other girls are single. They can run around and do anything they want. They don't have any responsibilities. I'm married and I have a daughter. I had my fun."

"You and Avis and Marianne are the three in the shop who have children?" I ask rhetorically.

"Yes, and for some of us it's difficult. Most of the girls they have cars, and they can go wherever they feel like. I can't. I have a daughter and she's at that age where she needs attention, and if I'm not there to give it to her she's not going to get it. My husband really doesn't care about kids. And my husband also takes the car, so I'm not able to work late like some of the other girls."

"But he comes home early, around four o'clock you told me. He could pick you up?"

Her voice is dry, emotionless. "Yeah, he could but he doesn't like to be inconvenienced."

"Does he ever help around the house?"

"No, and I wouldn't want him to. I'd rather do my own cooking and my own housekeeping. I don't believe in women's lib. And I don't believe in all that crap—making a husband do half the work." She stands up and gets ready to go to the supermarket.

"But why not," I persist foolishly, "since you both are working at outside jobs?"

"Because I was raised that way!" She sounds furious, exasperated, frustrated, all three. "My mother taught me it was the

responsibility of the woman to clean the house and cook and clean the clothes and everything. *And my mother is that way and I'm going to stay the way my mother is.* Because I don't believe in all that garbage and my husband thinks it's a lot of garbage too."

Now I finally perceive how anxious this subject makes her. I can almost see the scowling faces of her mother and husband in the room with us, and I beg off, change the subject, angry with myself for causing this bad moment.

I ask her what else bothers her at work.

"I'd rather be paid more than I'm getting," she says, sitting down again. She is calmer already. "It doesn't seem like we make that much money," she goes on. "The way they pay you with that commission stuff, it's a lot of phooey. For a professional person like us we should be paid a lot more. I don't see how they expect us to survive, with all those prices for food and everything."

I ask her about fringe benefits.

"You get nothing. No extras. If you want medical insurance they take it out of your wages. But if you let them take twenty dollars or more a month out of your little bitty one dollar seventy-five an hour then you wouldn't have nothing left. You don't get paid if you're sick either, even if you have to go home from the job. And you get one big paid week's vacation after a year. If you last that long."

Finally, as we now both get ready to go, I bring up the question of unions.

"There is one around here," she tells me as we walk out the door. "But it's lousy, it doesn't help. I wouldn't belong to it. As I said, it's rotten all around. If I had my way now I'd be staying home taking care of my daughter."

A Union for Beauticians

I am dialing the number of a person who I have been told is the head of the local union for beauticians and now after two rings the phone is answered by "L. C. Woods speaking," which indeed is the name I have been given, but the voice is distinctly that of a man. Since officials of unions are generally 99.9 percent pure male I don't know why I'd expected differently in this case, but for some reason I had. In any case L. C. Woods sounds pleasant enough, very willing to help in any way he can, he says, and so we make an appointment to meet right after closing time at the shop where he works.

Driving over that evening I think that, if the head of the local for beauticians couldn't be a woman, at least he is a worker and not the usual pie card, and so he should have some interesting things to say.

The first surprise comes when I pull up in front of the address he gave me. It is not, as I again had somehow assumed, an elegant beauty salon staffed with high-priced male hairdressers, such as the union official I was about to meet. It is not even a beauty shop. It is an old-fashioned three-chair barber shop, complete with everything but the old red white and blue pole. And L. C. Woods is not a beautician, he is a barber. And, third surprise of the night, he owns the place.

Among the 3,000 facts about this occupation that I had not yet learned is that the only union representing beauticians in the area—is officially called the Journeymen Barbers, Hairdressers, Cosmetologists and Proprietor's International Union of America. Note barbers come first. And note *proprietors.* I am genuinely taken aback.

"Isn't it rather unusual for the employers and the workers to be part of the same union?" I ask L. C., who turns out to be a sandy-haired man in his mid-thirties, dapper and just as affable as on the phone. We are sitting in a vestibule in the rear of his shop.

"Yes, probably," he agrees. "But you have to remember that many owners of beauty shops and barber shops are workers, too. Like myself. And also that a lot of these proprietors have only one or two people working for them, if that."

"How many or rather what proportion of your membership is composed of owners—over half?"

"Oh yes, easily," he says, smiling pleasantly.

"And what percentage of the membership is male?"

"Well, to be frank it's mostly all male. Maybe ninety-seven percent. Probably less than three percent of the women who work in beauty shops around here are organized."

"And why is that?"

We are sitting on old swivel chairs and he gives his a swing to

43

the right. "You have to understand," he says, "that women very seldom come to our meetings, they don't get involved. They're more interested in staying home with their families."

"They usually have no choice," I say.

"Okay. Whatever." Now he swings to the left. "But the second thing, let's face it, is that work for women doesn't have the same meaning it does for men. Usually, that is. So many of them just go in for a year or two before they get pregnant and leave. And many others today, more and more of them, they just work part-time, for extra money and to get out of the house. It's not the same thing for them. That's why they fought the pension and quit us."

"Quit?"

"Well, we did have a lot more women in the union four or five years ago, but then they wouldn't go along with the pension the men wanted. Said they weren't going to be working until they were 65 and so they weren't going to let us take the monthly deductions for the pension. So they quit."

"And the men let them walk out without finding a way to compromise?"

"Well, it wasn't my doing. I personally would like to see more women get involved, but they don't come to meetings like I said."

I ask Mr. Woods how the wages of beauticians in the union compared to those of the barbers.

"Barbers probably make 30 percent more on the average," he answers, obviously finding nothing strange about that.

"Even though," I ask, "the work beauticians do is often vastly more complicated than the work barbers do? How does your union justify that kind of disparity?"

A swing to the right, a swing to the left, safe at second base. "We don't try to justify it, but we do have different contracts for barbers and beauticians, and the barbers, yes, are guaranteed more. But they are men after all, they have families to support, and they also usually work more hours than beauticians—six days instead of five or five and a half for beauticians. And they're also not against pensions like women."

"And the owners in your union set those guarantees?"

"No, we all do."

"Are most of the officers in the union proprietors like your-self?"

"Not all, but yes, probably a good proportion are."

At the Shop

"You know, in many ways this is really the best time in my life."

It is another quiet summer day and Suzy and I are sitting at a dressing table close to the receptionist desk. She is combing a blonde wig as we talk and every few minutes she has to jump up to answer a phone or greet a customer or check a bill.

"The pay is lousy," she continues, "the security is lousy, the benefits are lousy, the union is lousy—but it's nice here, isn't it? It's a happy place. That's why I like to work in beauty shops. It's not like working in a dentist's office or a hospital. And we've also got something good between the girls here, and that means a lot. How you get along. I guess that's true in every organization but here it's especially important because you're in such close contact all the time."

One day, Suzy says, she would like to own her own shop, but for now, just coming out of her second marriage, she doesn't want anything or anyone to tie her down. She is enjoying being single, she says, and she is enjoying her work. As manager she is responsible for everything from opening the shop to mixing tints to supervising the workers to handling any problems that arise with the customers to keeping the books. The shop grosses over $1,000 a week. Suzy grosses $135.

She has a definite philosophy about how to supervise:

"I'm never pushy with the girls but they know we have to get things done. I think you have to treat your help the way you'd like to be treated yourself. And I think we have a good relationship. My boss thinks it's too good. He doesn't like me to socialize at all with them, but I can't be like that. And as much as possible I encourage you to use your own methods, your own way of doing things. I don't like to be told what to do, so I won't order anyone either. But ask me nice and I'll do anything you say if I know you're being fair. And that's the way I try to be."

Her only problem at the job, she says, is Bumblebrain himself. Adhering to his demands. "He sees everything in terms of money, nothing in terms of people." In a half an hour, for example, because it is so quiet at the shop today, she is going to have to tell Marianne and Jackie to go home. Another precise moneysaving system devised by B. "You see," Suzy explains, "the weekly payroll must never come to more than forty-two percent of the gross receipts. When it looks like it's going to I have to tell some of the girls to go home. They lose their hourly wages then but they understand. It averages out over the year."

So in a little while though it's only three in the afternoon, Marianne and Jackie call it a day, and it's true they don't seem at all surprised. "Really girl," Marianne tells me when I look concerned, "you should see how they treat us at other shops—a lot of places you don't get any money at all while you hang around waiting for a lady to fall from the sky. You just work for commissions, period." Jackie on the other hand says nothing as she leaves, a remote don't-bother-me-I'm-busy look in her eyes. "Hey Jackie," Suzy says, "give us a smile." No answer.

With Jackie

We've had food and wine, and cheese and wine, and wine and wine, and the hour is late, tomorrow another workday, but now Jackie lights a joint and asks me to join her. "After all you say you want to know what my life is like. Well, this is what my life is like every night and a lot of mornings and afternoons, too."

Yes, I do want to know about your life, Jackie. Fact is I have probably felt closest to you of all the women in the shop in the six-odd weeks I have been coming around now. I'm not sure why. Each of you has traits I admire. Suzy's superb understanding of how to treat the women she supervises. Avis' honesty. Linda's love for her little girl. Marianne's drive and wit. So why do I feel closest to you? Perhaps it's your obvious sense of outrage, your anger at being treated as less than you know you are, the same anger that turned me and so many of my friends into feminists, that makes me feel glad for you but also a little tender and sad, for I have a hunch it has to bring you pain and problems as well as pride.

This is what I'm thinking, not what I'm saying. In my wine soggy state, all I say is yes, thank you, as she passes me the cigarette perched between the prongs of a black bobby pin. (You see, we can't get away from hair.) We talk some more. Jackie is twenty-two, single, lives with a roommate her own age. Has fought the cycle of her particular feminine heritage. A grandmother who married and had a baby at sixteen. A mother who married and had a baby at sixteen. A sister who married and had a baby at sixteen.

When she was growing up Jackie always felt she was different from the other girls in her neighborhood, always *wanted* to be different, felt she had far to go. Thought of singing when she was little. Then of writing. Thought of being a nurse. A dental assistant. The dreams narrow down as she gets older. A beautician.

"How did I get interested in hair? I really don't know. I guess I just fell into it. I knew some women who lived near me who got into the beauty business at a pretty young age, so I started getting hairpieces, and playing around with them, and thinking about doing it for a living. I guess when I saw these women, they were twenty-six or twenty-eight, and the way they came across, with every hair in place, well, I thought it was kind of a glamorous thing to be."

I can see why she had originally wanted to be a singer. She has a beautiful voice, deep and husky, and now with the hour and the smoking it is deeper, huskier.

"And my dad said he'd pay for it, for beauty school, after I got out of high school, so I registered. And I enjoyed it. It was difficult in the beginning—we had to know a lot of stuff—but it was also fun. Of course a lot of the time they made you work on mannequins, you'd have to give them phony facials and manicures, and that was stupid. But I liked working with real people, because then you could talk to them—if they weren't deaf or didn't have their heads under the dryer. You have to understand that people who come to beauty schools to get their hair done are usually pretty old."

The bobby pin is passed back and forth again.

"And then some of them had lice. You wouldn't know it though until it was too late. You'd be washing her hair and all of a

47

sudden you'd see the things running and then you'd have to sterilize everything you had touched. One of the rules in California is that you can't send anyone out of the shop with a wet head, so you'd also have to let her sit under the dryer until she was dry and you just knew the eggs were hatching under there. So then when she left you'd have to take the dryer apart and sterilize it, and the chair where she sat, the combs you used and everything."

It is not funny, it is sad, those poor women, but we've got the hashish giggles, we can't help laughing, and then suddenly Jackie is deadly serious again.

"And then sometimes you'd get the ladies with the growths in their heads, and they are not going to hurt you of course, but it's a shock if you don't understand what it means. As I say, a lot of these ladies were very old and I really felt like a nursemaid to some of them. And—I know this doesn't make me sound very nice—I resented that part of it. I didn't want to have to do anything except what I was being trained for and now I don't want to have to do anything except what I'm being hired for. I don't want to have to sweep the floor, I don't want to have to clean the toilet, I don't want to have to pick those ladies up and out of the chair. I know that maybe that's not being a good Samaritan, but I'm not there to be a good Samaritan, I'm there to do my work and that's all I get paid for, and I don't get paid very much."

Jackie's resentment, Jackie's pride.

"I was taught to do the competition hairdos, the fancy sets and good coloring jobs, and I used to love haircuts. Shampoos don't really bother me and I don't mind washing tint off or taking permanent wave rods out—it's just time consuming. But when I do those things some of the ladies are so rude I get so I have to walk away to cool down. I really thought I was a patient person before, but now if my attitude is gruff toward a lot of the women, which I guess it is, it's because I really resent those other things I have to do, that I should be paid a lot more for the knowledge I have and if I were paid more and they let me spend more time with each woman, then it would really be different. Then I could get into hair again. Because I can do it. I can really do good work if I take my time, but I get into this bitter attitude. I feel, hell, I'm going to do half the work since I'm getting half the money. Okay, Suzy

48

and the other girls are real nice and they're my friends and that's what makes it bearable. And some of the ladies are nice too. But some of the others, some of those rich bitches from the top of the hill, they come down and you do them and then they give you a big half a dollar. They think their shit is cleaner than yours. Well, I could spit on them.''

At the Shop

Days pass, summer ends. I make a reservation for a flight to New York the end of September. At the shop business starts picking up. Jackie learns she has to have a tonsillectomy in the near future—she has no sick leave, no medical insurance, will have to call on her parents for help. Suzy has met a new man, is talking starry-eyed about love and babies.

"But Suzy," I say, "you swore you'd let nothing tie you down for at least two years. And you said you never wanted children."

"Yes," she says, sweetly, calmly, Suzily, "but then I never knew I'd meet a man like Bob. To tell you the truth my previous two husbands didn't really want kids so I knew the load would have fallen on me. With Bob it's something different, he wants children and he'd make a great father."

September 8. The first Saturday after Labor Day. The shop is now swamped with customers. Women waiting to be shampooed, to be set, to be colored, to be cut, to be dried, women waiting. Suzy leaves the receptionist desk and joins Linda in the shampoo area. "No time to talk, no time to even go to the bathroom," Avis tells me when I catch her alone for a second. "But you know," she says, "this is the way I really like it. I guess you think I'm crazy."

When the day is finally over Jackie has done a total of 22 heads, as they put it; Avis has done 19; Marianne comes in third with 17. ("My problem," Marianne tells me, "is that I get too involved with my ladies. If you want to make money you have to get them in and out fast. But then I don't think you do such a good job.")

Suzy turns the lights off and they all file out, exhausted but enjoying that it-feels-so-good-when-you-can-stop feeling. And also the fact that today their commissions will amount to a lot more than they have in a long time. Te celebrate, Jackie and Avis stop off for a combination pizza and beer at Pete's, across from the shop. (Avis' cousin is staying with Johnny tonight.) Suzy hurries home to get ready for her date with Bob. Linda and Marianne return to their second jobs as wives and mothers.

With Marianne

Of the five women who work in the shop, Marianne is the only one who always wanted to be a beautician, who dreamed of it as a very young girl. When Avis and Linda were eleven and twelve they saw themselves as future mothers, period. Jackie was practicing Peggy Lee songs in front of the mirror. Suzy was thinking about being a teacher. But Marianne behind the closed doors of her bedroom was already experimenting with hair, with her best friend's hair to be specific.

"I was making it shorter, making it straighter, making it frizzier, making it purple—I did everything I could think of to that poor child."

To be now the only black woman in an all-white shop is like a trip back into childhood for Marianne, who grew up in the only black family on an all-white block in San Francisco. "I learned then," she says, "that the only way to handle yourself is to know you are as good if not better than anyone else."

But there are difficult moments at the shop. If a customer comes in cold, not knowing anyone, the system is to give her to whichever beautician is available, on a rotation basis. She is told to sit and wait at a certain table. Sometimes when one sees Marianne coming, and realizes she has been assigned to this strange black woman, she'll jump up and take a seat at the next table, fast. Marianne has a way of handling this, she says.

"I'll walk up to them and then very quietly ask: 'You're not prejudiced are you? You're not going to deprive yourself of the best haircut or hairset of your life, are you?' I laugh with them and most of the time it works."

If they stay, there are often routine questions Marianne has to answer.

"They'll see a picture of my husband Curtis propped by my mirror and for some reason they're usually astonished that I'm

50

married. Then the next thing that will pop out of their mouth, nine times out of ten, will be, *'Oh, and does he have a job?'*

Unlike Jackie, however, she doesn't then want to spit on them. "You see, Jackie comes in and puts down this and that, but I try to turn it into my advantage. Like a woman comes in the shop high and mighty, Jackie won't even speak to her. Me, I get higher and mightier. I tell her, Mrs. Riches, you are now going to get the best haircut you have ever gotten in your life. I bullshit her because you see it's all a game. If I can get her mind in the right attitude about me, then I've got it made. She'll really believe what I do is good. But if I don't tell her beforehand, she'll never know what to think."

"So it's all a game?"

"Yes—except that I really care about the game. I really do think I give great haircuts. And I want everyone to think so, too. If a woman walks out and she doesn't like what I've done, then I really feel bad. Because you see that's my good name she's going to be spreading bad tales about."

Marianne is now twenty-six, has had a number of jobs before this one. The one she remembers best was her first, and the story she relates is about as typical a story of a beautician's first job as you could find.

"Here's what he'd do, see. He gave you a guarantee of $60 a week and for that you had to clean the toilets and take his laundry out and sweep up at night in addition to taking care of the customers. Something like now, but much much more because the only one doing it was the newest flunky, which then was me. He'd keep you busy with that and then let you do some shampooing and setting, but if you ever got close to the amount you needed to make commission over that original $60, he'd stop you fast, by sending you out for some more laundry or something. And another thing, he'd never ever let you do the glory work. And the glory work you have to understand is the comb-out. That's what you get the praise for, even though a comb-out is only as good as the set was, but the customer doesn't know that. So I'd do the set and he'd do the comb-out and he'd get the praise. I was the youngest, and it was taken for granted that this was the way things were."

51

That was eight years and many jobs ago. But after all this time Marianne still enjoys doing hair as well as being a mother to Curtis, Jr., her chubby six-month-old baby, who at this moment is sitting on my lap gurgling. His father, Curtis, Sr., won't be home until midnight, several hours from now when his shift is finished at the sugar-packing factory where he works. When he arrives Marianne will have his meal waiting, the apartment just the way he likes it, which happens to be "just so," the baby in the crib. Unlike Linda, she doesn't make a virtue of having to do everything herself. She says, very simply, "probably the trouble is Linda and I would just feel too guilty if we weren't good housekeepers the way our mothers were, and our husbands would make sure we did if we didn't. It's just less hassle doing it myself." And, again, unlike Linda, she'd rather work than stay home, although she is unhappy about having to leave Curtis, Jr., with people she sometimes can't trust. She just hired a new baby-sitter after finding out the last one was nodding off on Budweiser in the middle of the day.

"And what do you want for the future?"

"Oh, another kid, I think. And a new apartment. And, oh yes, my old dream, the dream of a lot of us—my own shop."

"You have a name for it?"

"Yes, I'll call it Madame Marianne, and finally I'll have others to work for me and do all the shit jobs."

"And?"

"And then this time I'll be the one who gets the glory work."

At the Shop

California, there I leave. In only ten days now. Busy with cartons and finishing an article and pre-moving tensions and saying good-byes, I haven't been to the shop in almost two weeks. Last time I was there it was decided that we'd try to select a night when we all could get together before I left. Now I come to set the date and the place.

I open the door. Frank Sinatra is still plugging that small hotel with the wishing well. Hasn't it gone out of business by now? Suzy gives me the Suzy welcome, but this is the time I notice something amiss, a power failure in her smile.

"Everything's fine," she says automatically when I ask, "except . . ." and then she slowly swirls her eyes in a semi-circle around the room.

I follow the direction of her eyes. Linda is in the back rinsing out a bleach. Avis is in the middle of a complicated upsweep replete with myriad ringlets and waves, a $2.00 extra comb-out if there ever was one. There are also, I notice, two new beauticians whom I've never seen before. And Jackie isn't around. Neither is Marianne.

"Jackie go off to have her tonsils out?" I ask Suzy.

"Tomorrow—but that's not why she's not here." She is speaking very softly. Her eyes still roaming back and forth among the customers in the room. "She was fired last week and yesterday Marianne quit and . . ." I try to interrupt, but she is in a hurry now. "And I'm going to quit, too. I have to get out of this business, there's no security here."

I ask her to slow down, to tell me what happened and she does, in bits and pieces, still watching the customers and still smiling tautly all the time. As she talks I can't help thinking how very recently we sat here together while she told me this was the best time in her life, this was work she so much enjoyed. Later that night I call Jackie, who's getting ready to go to the hospital the next day, and I also speak to Marianne who starts a new job next week. From the three of them I hear the following story.

It seems Bumblebrain had been going through one of his periodic tight-ship periods. Get the ladies out fast, get the workers on point, stop all that shmoozing around when the place isn't busy. Jackie was never one of his favorites. His favorites are invariably the most pretty and, next in line, the most passive, and Jackie is neither striking like Suzy and Marianne, nor frail and appealing like Avis, nor compliant like Linda. She talks back, complains, grumbles, is fat, often looks a mess. He's never liked her, but her work, her output at least, getting those ladies in and out, has been the fastest in the shop so he's had to keep still.

Now what happened was that about two weeks ago Bumblebrain's wife was scheduled to come in for a frosting, her first time in this one of her husband's growing chain of beauty shops. Her appointment was on a Monday, Suzy's day off, when another receptionist-manager from one of the other shops regularly came in to fill in. Call the other receptionist Robin. Robin is Bumblebrain's second-in-command. Robin comes in on that Monday and warns Jackie and Avis and Linda (Marianne is also off) that Mrs. B. is on her way and they'd better look busy. Better clean the place up, wash those plastic bubble dryers, shine the gold frames around the mirror, look like they're working even though, as usual on a Monday, there are practically no customers around.

Jackie says bullshit. "I wasn't hired to be a janitor." Robin starts to flare up, but right then Mrs. B. appears. Much nervousness. Avis is elected to do the frosting, although she's never done one before. Robin is to mix the bleach and oversee the whole project. Jackie is to please look busy and also to tell Avis and Robin what to do, because neither of them is as knowledgeable as Jackie about frostings. Jackie advises. Robin disagrees with the advice. Avis gets confused but listens to the one in charge, Robin. The die, as it were, or was, is cast. Ninety minutes later Mrs. B. rushes out of the shop looking like a giraffe in heat.

Robin of course blames Jackie. Jackie of course blames Robin and saunters off home to tell the story to her roommate. They laugh and smoke till four A.M. Next morning, still feeling as high as a $3. extra beehive bouffant, Jackie returns to the scene of the frosting to find B. himself waiting, in a rage.

"I want to talk to you, Jackie."

"Hey, don't blame me, I didn't put a hand on your wife."

"Yeah, I understand you didn't put a hand on anything, you wouldn't touch nothing, just sat around while everyone else was working."

"Right. Because there were no customers for me. I'm not your maid. I'm here to set hair. Period. Don't blame me for what happened to your wife."

After he left everyone agreed it had been a triumph for Jackie. She had remained cool and strong while Bumblebrain was flustered and confused. "What a jerk he is. Great going, Jackie." Two hours later he called Suzy, told her to fire that broad immediately. Suzy protested, reminded him Jackie was about to go into the hospital, needed money, couldn't look for another job now, was a good worker, hadn't actually done one thing wrong.

"Who's the boss, here, Suzy? I want her out by the end of the day."

No severance.

No notice.

No union, no grievance procedure.

No unemployment compensation if B. had had his way—he was going to say he had fired her for insubordination, but Jackie found out about that (through Suzy) and sent word that she would sit and scream and yell and pee if necessary in front of all his shops every day of the week until she was paid.

So she got the minimum unemployment: $40 a week. And prepared for her tonsillectomy.

And meanwhile the tight ship got tighter. "After the blowup with Jackie the good atmosphere we were all trying to create blew up, too," Suzy told me. Marianne decided that if Bumblebrain could do it like that to Jackie he could do it like that to her, and so when she heard from a friend about another job in the area she grabbed it and quit. (B. was outraged that she had the audacity to leave without giving notice.) Suzy, still waiting to see what will happen with Bob, has applied for a job selling cosmetics. Linda and Avis, both needing the money and having no other place to go, are staying on for the time being. "But the morale," Avis said, "the thing that made it fun, is completely gone."

Postmortem

Jackie couldn't get here tonight. She had that familiar hospital experience. The operation was a success but the patient is still reeling from the medication. A week after the surgery she is in bed in her parents' home (she gave up her apartment when she lost the job) fighting a fever and an infection.

Linda couldn't make it either. Her husband didn't want her to leave him alone with the child. Or so she said and I certainly don't disbelieve her—it sounds exactly like the man she told me about—but I can't forget the look in her eyes that day we talked about the woman's movement and I have a sad hunch she didn't want to confront that subject again.

So it's just the four of us. Suzy, Avis, Marianne, myself. We are sitting in Avis' living room around a table that stands on top of the multicolored rug which she and Harvey made. Munching peanuts, olives, crackers with sesame seeds. From the kitchen we can hear sounds of Johnny playing Green Beret with the dog until Avis calls out to him to get the hell to sleep.

Marianne is festive tonight, all in pale green and full of stories about her new job. She likes it, she says, her new boss seems willing to treat her with respect, and she is hopeful the money will be good once she builds up a clientele. But she misses her old co-workers, her friends.

Suzy, who's the last to arrive, apologizes for being late. I have never seen her look so tired.

It might be nice to think that since Jackie and Marianne left, and Suzy and Avis stopped caring as much, that business at the shop has started to dwindle and that Bumblebrain is now regretting his tactics. In fact there's been no difference in volume. Only in terms of spirit. Only.

The prices at the shop are so cheap, comparatively speaking, that customers keep coming even if their favorite beautician is gone, even if the pleasant atmosphere they used to find has turned tense and grim. Which, Suzy assures me, it has. Faithful customers who want to search for Marianne—and a few have—will find when they locate her that they must now pay almost twice as much for a set or a cut at the new shop where she works. So the odds are, most will drift back to the old shop and this is the difference, Suzy says, between working in a budget shop and a more expensive salon, and also the reason why Bumblebrain is so unconcerned with how he treats his workers.

"A shop can have a relaxing atmosphere, which my boss didn't want to create," Suzy says now, sitting at the head of the table. "All he cared about was getting the most work done, the most dollars, and he knows there are so many unemployed beauticians around that he doesn't have to worry. And that the customers will come back because of the prices, no matter what. That's why he doesn't care about the way he pushes us."

"But it wasn't just the pushing that was so bad," Marianne says, sticking a toothpick into a black olive, her first bite of food since lunch. "It was the *way* it was done and who was doing it. When Suzy was there you didn't mind it. She had a way of managing the shop that made everybody feel good. And you always knew she didn't push you any harder than she had to or than she pushed herself. Whereas with Bumblebrain in, well I'd slow down everytime he started running things, I'd finish that cigarette first if he said to go and get that lady with the wet head. I'd insist on taking my lunch if it was busy and I'd go on strike till I got it. But with Suzy, if she was in charge and the shop was really busy and we had to get them out, I wouldn't mind missing lunch."

Avis nods. "Yeah, because when Suzy pushed I knew she really hated to have to do it. And because she ran the place the way she did, and we all got along, we did things to help each other. I'd clean someone's brushes if she were busy and she'd do the same for someone else. I didn't mind doing it for her and she didn't mind doing it for me because there was no *real* pressure. Maybe pressure from the ladies pouring in the door, but not from Suzy. It's all in the way it's handled. If Bumblebrain told us to stay one minute overtime none of us would be happy to do it. We know he's got two dollar signs for eyes. But with Suzy it's something different. The difference is the personal touch."

I ask how they feel about the commission system of payment. Is that a good way of getting paid or would you prefer having a larger salary you knew you could count on?

Marianne answers first. "I don't mind the commission. I don't mind it if I see I can make it without killing myself. And if there was no commission, and I could see that I was doing three times as much work as the girl standing next to me and then we both made the same salary, well then my mouth is going to stick out quick."

Avis leans back in her chair. "Well, I agree if one girl works her fanny off and is really serious about it, then she should be paid more for her troubles than someone who isn't. On the other hand, to make commissions you really have to push your ladies to buy or use things they often don't need. And I find it awful to have to tell lies so that I can make some more money. To talk someone into something that's just a big line of b.s. Like hair coloring for instance. A lot of people don't look good with their hair colored, but you're supposed to sell them this product which will really make them look worse. What it means is you have to be a liar and a bullshitter if you want to survive and this is the part of the business I can't take.''

Suzy agrees. "It's true. If you want to make money you have to sell, and B. is always after all of us to sell.''

"Well, I won't lie to them," Avis says. "I just won't do it. If a lady asks me for something and I know she doesn't need it, I'll tell her the truth, because in the long run she's going to trust me that way and she's going to buy something when I finally tell her she should. And if I think I can save them money, I'm going to, because I'm not money hungry. I make enough to just get along and I believe in being honest.''

"But I'm not like you, Avis," Marianne says, taking another handful of peanuts, "I want to do more than just get along. I'm not a greedy person but you can always find something to push without really lying.''

"But," says Avis, leaning forward now, "you know how often Bumblebrain pushed us to sell some new product which we would all laugh about because we knew it wasn't going to do anyone any good. Most of the time we'd die before we'd use any of that crap on ourselves.''

I take a handful of peanuts myself, and ask, "Doesn't that whole commission system put you exactly into this bind, where you have to either lie a little or earn much less?''

"But don't you see," says Marianne, "that in this line of business there's no one who is going to keep you if you *don't* sell his products, even if he's paying you a set salary. Because if you don't sell it, believe me, that other girl over there will. That's the whole thing we talked about before. There are so many others in this field they'll fire you as fast as they can say hello if you don't do what they want. Look what happened to Jackie. I could afford to take a chance and try this new job because if anything goes wrong Curtis will still bring home enough money to pay the rent. So I'm a little freer than others. That's not true with any of the others at the shop. Linda's husband is in debt. And the rest of the women are on their own.''

"And there's no union to protect you." Me.

"No," agrees Suzy, "just a union to bleed you if you let them. I was part of that union, five years ago before the pension fight.

58

They wanted us to pay five dollars a month for the pension in addition to the regular five-a-month dues. Now that might not sound much to some people, but when you're making as little as most beauticians it's a lot. And for what? Most of us can't keep working in this business until we're sixty-five so we could collect the pension. It's too hard a life. On your feet all day, running around all the time, you can't do it when you're old. That's why most of us find something else later. Or only do it part-time. I was seventeen when I got into this business. What did I know then about where I would be when I was sixty-five?''

"And who wants to go to a union meeting where your boss is sitting next to you?" Marianne.

Avis: "Yeah, can you imagine fighting side by side with the big B.?''

"But if there *was* a really good strong union," says Marianne, "that fought for our rights, then I'd be the first in line."

"The trouble," says Avis, "is that most women don't have the time to do it themselves. We're beat at the end of the day, and then we have to take care of the house and the food and the kids. It's hard enough just getting through the day, without going to meetings, too."

"But it would be easier, wouldn't it," I ask, "if those who had husbands could get them to share the family obligations? Of course, if you have a husband like Linda's, forget it; I understand he wouldn't even let her come here tonight."

"The truth about Linda," Suzy says, "is that she probably disliked working at the shop more than any of us, even when things were good. She was kind of shy with the rest of us, felt tired all the time, and she also really wanted to be at home with her daughter. I don't know if she told you about her situation. The sad thing is that because of their money problems, she'll probably be working at the shop longer than any of us."

I ask whether they would go into this work again if they were starting over again. Marianne and Avis say they would. Suzy says she would go to college, become a teacher. And then I ask whether they'd want their daughters to become beauticians.

Suzy: "No. I'd want her to be doing something where she gets more respect. People won't tell us this, they think we don't know what they're feeling, but a lot of them think we're cheap, think we're lower class. Now I know that's not true. But I wouldn't want my daughter to have to go through that.''

Avis says if she had a daughter she'd let her do anything she wanted. "It would be up to her. I wouldn't mind either way.''

And Marianne: "Well, it's funny. For me I think it's great. I dig doing hair, I really enjoy it, I'm going to keep going. But for my daughter . . . if I ever have one . . . I hope she wouldn't. You know, I hope she'd find something where she'd have less of a hassle.''

3

Sales Worker

Fifty women and men are standing in line in the basement of one of Manhattan's most popular discount department stores. Filling out forms, fidgeting, waiting for their turn. Yesterday and today there were help-wanted ads for Christmas jobs here and at other stores in the *Times* and *Daily News. Earn extra cash . . . Be in the center of things for Christmas . . . Come meet the nicest people . . . Apply now.*

The line moves slowly, or feels that way at least. "Two hours now I've been waiting," says a tiny woman with delicate features in a high soprano voice. "You'd think they'd have the courtesy to provide us some chairs."

"Why should they?" a basso profundo behind her rejoins. "You don't get to sit when you're on the job." And then, flirtatiously; "Maybe you can't take it."

The soprano, half an octave lower now: "Buzz off, honey."

In front of the line, a door marked PERSONNEL. Every three or so minutes it flashes open, an applicant departs (did she or he get it?) and the next is ushered in. Meantime, for those still waiting there is an arithmetic test to complete in addition to the ritual (name-address-age-education-experience-references) application form. A two page test. Add up a column of figures, then another a little longer. Subtract the following. Now multiply and divide. What's seven percent of $5,794.89?

Nervous or simply restless, many on the line go over and over and over their answers. Including me. I am here to learn firsthand, if I can, what it is like to work at a large store such as this, and although I ostensibly mastered simple arithmetic a thousand years ago, now for some reason I find myself hesitating too, checking and rechecking as the line inches up. Perhaps I'm really concerned about all the blank spaces I left in the application form under "experience." In any case, I'm working on $5,794.89 for the third time when a young man comes out of the office and nods, "You next."

Inside, a thin blonde woman sits behind a desk overflowing with applications and arithmetic tests. She indicates a chair by her side. Glances quickly at me, my filled out papers (too rapidly to evaluate the answers *or* the blank spaces), looks up and asks what I'd prefer, sales or cashiering.

"Sales."

"Any special department?"

"Yes, coats. Or suits. Dresses. Something like that."

Then she gets to the questions about my previous selling experience (I have none, I admit, as the application shows; I would like to find out what it's like). She consults a chart on her desk. Makes a large check in one of the boxes. "I think coats and suits will be okay."

"And the pay?" I ask, relieved that it was all this easy.

"Two fifteen an hour."

Which is even lower than the low wages I had supposed. No wonder it was so easy. "Any commission above that?"

"No, two dollars and fifteen cents straight for the Christmas help. Of course you also get ten percent off on most of our merchandise."

She smiles a take it or leave it smile. I ask her when I can begin. She says in two weeks and that being that I leave the office to be immediately replaced by the next person on the still growing line of applicants hoping for the opportunity to earn $86 a week

62

before taxes, about $70 after, in one of the most expensive cities in the world. Did someone say people don't want to work anymore?

True, many on the line appear to be students on Christmas vacations. But there are also many—particularly among the women—who are in their forties, fifties and even sixties. Are they here because they enjoy this kind of work, even though it pays so little? Or because it is the only work they can find? Or are they mainly here, as the help-wanted ads suggested, to "earn extra cash for Christmas" and "be in the center of things"—a few weeks of diversion with pay for the housewife and then happily back to life as usual. In two weeks I should start to find out.

Birth of a Saleswoman

Standing in line again, two weeks later, fifty or more of us as before.

"Do you know what department you're going to?" the woman on my right asks. She is a short plump woman with fluffy red hair. Late fifties, or so.

"Coats and suits," I say.

"Oh, then you'll be with Peggy," she says, tapping the back of the large black woman standing in front of her. "I'm Lillian," she continues. "Dresses."

Then my new co-worker, Peggy, turns around and introduces herself, too. Seems she and Lillian met earlier in the lunchroom where we all had to go first to pick up our "Kit for Employees." (Contents of kit: One large blue and white badge reading TRAINEE, one employee discount card, one locker room key, one brochure about the store, one plastic see-through case for I don't know what.) Unlike me, Peggy and Lillian are both old hands at department store selling, but Peggy turns out to be the one with the particular information we are all avid for now: she worked in *this* store once before, only six months ago in fact.

So how is it? we both ask, what's it like?

"Well, you know, like everywhere else it all depends on which department you're in," Peggy answers, keeping her voice low. "Naturally it's how your manager and the other people you work with treat you, and that's different all over the store."

"Which manager is—" Lillian starts to ask but she is interrupted by a voice from the front of the line: "PLEASE FOLLOW ME UP THE STAIRS INTO THE MAIN FLOOR AND THEN UP THE ESCALATOR TO THE TOP OF THE STORE WHERE THE TRAINING ROOM IS."

The voice is that of the blonde woman from Personnel and we follow her now. Out of the dim basement into the bright main floor, a typical department store main floor—*cosmetics, blouses, jewelry, perfume, scarves, gloves.* Up the escalator passing the second floor—*books and records, small appliances, men's wear;* the third floor—*robes and lingerie, women's and junior sportswear;* the fourth—*coats and suits* (Peggy's and my new home) and *dresses* (where Lillian will be) and *shoes;* and then the fifth—*toys, infants' and children's wear, nursery furniture, sporting goods;* and the sixth—*vacuum cleaners, major appliances, fishing equipment, silverware and dishes;* and the seventh—*luggage, stereo sets and television, tools, furniture, carpeting, hardware;* and finally up a flight of stairs into the attic, the main stock area for the store. At the end of a long corridor full of cartons of all sizes is the training room, a tiny room with a blackboard, a desk, wooden chairs lined up in rows.

The woman from personnel is sitting behind the desk when we arrive waiting for us to be seated too. Peggy, Lillian and I find three chairs together.

The woman rises, a thick looseleaf manual in her hand. Tells us her name (Andrea), her title (assistant to the manager of personnel) and apologizes for the long wait we had downstairs.

"But it's a crazy day as you can all see. We have over 150 people starting today alone, 350 in all for the Christmas season. So it's quite hectic to say the least. But what I have to say now shouldn't take that long."

Sits down again, placing the manual on the desk in front of her. Flips slowly through the pages, stopping at certain places to inform us of company regulations. About:

Time: "Naturally it's important not to forget to punch in or out. If you want to get paid, that is. The company gives you a ten-minute leeway for lateness in the morning, anything above that you're docked. The usual system. Since it's the Christmas rush,

64

you'll all be working some nights and most Saturdays. Your manager will let you know by the preceding Thursday what your schedule the next week will be."

Breaks: "You get a half hour each day, usually divided fifteen in the morning and afternoon, but some take it all at once."

Lunch: "You get an hour each day, although by state law the company doesn't have to give you more than 45 minutes when you work an eight-hour day. Only thing we require is you don't take lunch between twelve and two, since that's the busiest time of our day."

Dress: "Women are allowed to wear pants if they're selling, so long as it's not dungarees or anything that doesn't look proper. We don't ask you to wear only dark colors or only dresses like some stores. Try to look decent, is all we ask."

Shoplifting: "It happens all the time, you wouldn't believe how often. If you catch someone, you get an award, fifteen or twenty dollars. But don't ever try to apprehend a shoplifter yourself. The secret is: Be alert. If you see someone suspicious, call the security officer on the phone in your department right away, describe the suspect and let the officer take it from there. You'll get the award if the person is caught. And another thing. I know this sounds like a terrible thing to say. I know it sounds insulting. But I have to. *Don't shoplift yourself.* That may seem like a crazy idea to you, why should a person who comes to work want to do that, but you'd be surprised how many try. And that's very dumb of them. There are security cops and one-way mirrors all over. And if you're caught we don't only fire you, we prosecute. So if you're going to steal something, go to a bank and take a million, not a little item here. Another thing. If you catch a fellow employee in your department stealing, you'll get an award of twenty-five dollars or more if you report it."

Lockers: "You must check your coats and other street clothes in your locker before punching in. Women must check their handbags, too. Take your wallet out and anything else you'll be needing during the day and put it in that plastic case we gave you in the employee kit." (So that's what the see-through case is for: to make sure we're not stealing anything.)

With that, Andrea closes the manual. "Unless you have any

65

questions, that's all for now. Those of you who will be cashiers, keep your seats, you'll be getting special training this week. The rest of you line up and proceed downstairs back into the basement where someone from your department will come to pick you up."

Coats

Back in the basement Peggy and I stand together, waiting to start work. Very soon our names are called and we're introduced to a middle-aged woman named Alice, who has come to escort us to coats and suits. Short gray hair, stern expression.

On the escalator, Alice gives us a bit of advice. "It's a nice department, coats, but one thing, you really have to *worrrrkk*."

"Oh, is that what we're here for—to work?" I joke to break the tension.

Bad joke, bad start.

Alice stares straight ahead, silently, as the escalator carries us up.

Peggy fills in the gap. "Are you the department manager, Alice?"

"No."

"Assistant manager?"

"No, Peggy, but I have quite a bit of authority here, as you'll both be seeing."

Peggy mentions she only asked because she's hoping there'll be a permanent spot for her after Christmas, does Alice think that's possible?

"Well maybe, it's very hard to tell." Continued ice cubes and silence the rest of the way up.

Arrive safely at coats. Meet Ed, our manager, early forties, curly brown hair, Bugs Bunny smile. Seems surprised to be getting two full-timers, only expected one. Also seems preoccupied (it's the noon rush hour by now) but amiable enough in a distracted sort of way.

"Well, I guess I should show you girls around." (Yes, sisters, I know he should call us women, but this is *not* the time to argue.) Peggy and I follow him to the middle of the department, a huge department really, taking up at least half the entire fourth floor.

66

"See over there," Ed says, pointing a Glen Plaid arm in the direction of some racks near the wall twenty feet away. "Those are our bike jackets, and next to them are our car coats." He moves his arm a fraction to the right. "And those, see there in the corner, those are our half-sizes." Moving across the floor now, with us following, he points to " . . . our fake-fur three-quarters and fake-fur full-lengths, on those racks, see, next to the rabbits, and on that circular rack we have our real fur jackets, some lambs, raccoons, we even have mink." We are moving in a circle. "Then, there are our leathers, the imitations and real leather coats over there, next to the imitation and real leather jackets. We have a sale on today on suede jackets, see the sign. $39.99?" We are about half way around the circle, and now Ed is pointing to the "camel coats"—camel-colored not camel hair—to coats with fake fur collars and coats with real fur collars, to plain cloth coats at regular lengths, at midi lengths, at lengths for the petite, to raincoats with no lining, with detachable linings, with sewed-in linings, to coats on clearance and jackets on *final* clearance, to ski jackets and bike jackets—and then finally we are back where we came in. The circle is complete.

"Starting to get the pattern?" Ed asks, obviously impatient to get the whole thing over with.

Starting to get nothing but confused, I wait for Peggy to answer first, since she is the more experienced. "Mmm hmm," she says.

"Mmm," I say, wondering if she could possibly have meant it.

"Good," Ed says, "now let me show you the stockroom." Still in a rush, he leads us to a small room off the floor, with coats and jackets lined up on a long single rack facing one wall, an old wooden desk and chair facing the other. "I suppose you know," he says, "that all of our sales people at this store must also do stock work, so you're going to have to do it, too. What you see here, today, are mainly layaways, that's one of the biggest kinds of business we do at this store. People who don't have all the money and pay us in installments. Come on out, I'll show you how to do the form."

Out of the stock room and over to the cashier booth—a kind of circular cage near the front of the department. Peggy and I are introduced to two cashiers standing inside the booth, both about nineteen or twenty. One works full-time, the other 12 to 4. We also meet two other saleswomen in the department, again one full- and one part-time and they are in their late fifties. So we come in many categories here, I'm learning. Sales and cashiers. Full-time and part-time. Permanent and Christmas.

Ed shows us how to write out a layaway form, which looks simple enough, and our training period is pronounced over. Took, figuring generously, about eleven minutes.

"Now why don't you go and help the customers?" Ed says. Can he be serious? I think. There are about a dozen customers roaming around, all of whom must know the department better than I. Peggy goes to one side of the floor and I to the other.

I approach a woman in a black and white checked coat. "May I help you?"

"No, thank you."

On to the next. "May I help you?"

"Just looking."

A woman in green. "May I help you find something?"

"Not right now, thanks."

A woman of ample proportions. "May I help you?"

"Yes, miss, do you have any cashmere coats in black, size eighteen?"

Look vacantly around the room. Racks and racks and racks and racks of mysterious garments. "Black cashmere? Well, let's see. Over there are our fur-trimmed coats I believe and. . ."

"Not fur-trimmed. Cashmere. Plain black cashmere."

"Right, but next to the fur-trimmed I think are the plain coats. Shall we walk over?"

We do. The coats I saw turn out to be midi lengths, but next to *them* are the real untrimmed regular lengths. Relieved at finding them, I start to look through the rack.

"You don't call those cashmere, do you, miss? Cardboard would be more like it."

"Something the matter over here?" says a voice behind me. It is Alice, our escalator escort.

I turn to her. "Black cashmere. Size eighteen."

"Cashmere? Are you kidding? Someone told you we had black

68

cashmere? Here? Sorry for wasting your time, madam," she says and stalks away.

Next: "May I help you?"

"No, just looking."

"May I help you?" A stunning black woman in a brown wool suit.

"Yes, I'm looking for a plain camel colored coat, size six or eight."

Scan the floor again, then remember. In front, near the cashier's booth. Walk decisively over. Finger through the racks, find three for her to try on. The last looks wonderful, and at $48 is a good buy. She takes it, looking immensely pleased. I'm a bit surprised to find I'm feeling pleased myself.

Lunch

At 3:30 Ed says go to lunch. He's apologetic; usually we are to eat earlier, but today, because of all the training (sic) and confusion we're behind schedule. After punching out, I wander outside the store, find a coffee shop across the street. As I enter a woman waves to me from the counter. It is Lillian, the redheaded woman in dresses I met earlier, sitting with another woman also on her first day. I take the stool next to them, order a hamburger and coffee.

Lillian wants to know how I like it so far and I tell her, I don't know, it seems okay, but it's probably too soon to tell.

"How about the people?" she goes on, very curious. "The manager and the people in your department, they're nice? You like them?"

I tell her I don't like them or not like them yet. "I've hardly said a word to any of them really, except for Peggy, the woman you introduced me to, and except for the woman who came to pick us up—we sort of brushed each other the wrong way on the escalator."

"Oh, that's too bad," Lillian says, but she's obviously bubbling over with her own news. Good news. "In my department they're very friendly. All the women—there are four I've met so far, seem very sweet. Including my manager. She's a woman about my age. She's very sweet and friendly, too."

"So it looks good for you?" says the woman sitting on the other side of Lillian. She is an attractive blonde, heavily made up, with an accent hard to figure out. Her name is Marlene. Robes and lingerie.

"And you?" Lillian asks Marlene.

"Me, not so bad, I don't know yet. They keep me busy so far taking nightgowns out of boxes and putting labels on them. That's all I do so far."

"You want to work here after Christmas?" Lillian asks.

"Yes. If it works out. I go crazy at home all alone since my boy went away to college. What about you?"

Lillian nods. "I'm hoping they'll let me stay." She looks questioningly at me.

"No, I'm just here for Christmas," I say, feeling uneasy about not telling her more about myself yet.

Lillian looks at me closely. "I bet you'd rather work in an office, wouldn't you? I know I would. But at my age they almost never hire you. They want younger girls." She takes a sip of her coffee. "Or if they do give you a chance, the few places that do, they make you take a typing test, and that I could never never pass. I don't know why, I can type fine, really. But if there's a test my fingers start to freeze."

"Why do you think office work is so much better than selling?" I ask.

"Well, for one thing, the hours. You don't have to work nights or Saturdays. And the pay is better usually, and the conditions in general, and the way people act toward you."

"And you can *sit*," Marlene says and we all laugh and groan for a minute about our feet. Then Marlene goes on: "But really I don't want to sit all day. I think I like selling better—if they would let me sell. Not just put labels on nightgowns."

Coats

In the brief amount of time left in the day after I return from lunch at 4:30, our department is very quiet, and Peggy and I are given our first stock assignment. We are to put all raincoats with price tags reading $16.66 on a special rack marked $16.66 SPE-CIAL. The raincoats are in different places on different racks and

70

it takes us almost an hour to get them together, a very pleasant hour it turns out since we are able to talk with each other while we work. We talk about the east versus the west—I mention I recently relocated from California and Peggy tells me she once lived in Texas. We talk about children—Peggy has five, ranging from a son of twenty-three to twin girls of five. We talk about this and that, and the hour goes quickly. Then with all the $16.66 raincoats in one place, it's time to help a few customers, take our allotted break, help still a few more, and then finally it's 6:30, time to punch out. Our feet burn, but we made it.

Employee Quarters

If you work in this store you must enter and leave through the Employee Entrance on a side street next to the trucking zone. You will push open a heavy green door and then walk down a flight of stairs (dousing your cigarette, because you can't smoke inside except in prescribed areas) until you reach the basement, which also serves as a general stock area. Cartons and cartons of merchandise all around. A uniformed guard will check to see that you have your employee badge, and then you may proceed to the locker room—there's one for each sex. Luck in the morning, if you happen to be fighting the time clock, is having no one blocking your way in the tiny locker room aisles, so you can get your coat and handbag tucked away fast. Luck is also not having to share your locker with more than one other person. During the Christmas rush some had as many as five. Finally, if you happen to own a navy blue jacket, as I do, luck is never having to share your locker with a white angora sweater, as I do.

Leaving the locker room, you walk down a long narrow corridor. Announcements on the wall of new union stewards, of salespeople who have won awards for catching shoplifters, of scholarships being given to children of employees, of a special employee discount day coming up during which you can get twenty percent off instead of the usual ten. In the middle of the corridor you will find, on one side, the time clock; on the other the employee lunchroom. Lunchroom, not cafeteria. A small square room with six or seven rectangular tables and matching benches, plus a half dozen coin machines for coffee, cigarettes, potato chips, soda, cookies. On the wall more announcements: one reminding you of that scholarship program for children, another of the $25 award you can get for reporting a dishonest fellow worker.

In addition to coming here to eat the sandwiches that you, like most employees, will probably bring from home, it is here in the lunchroom that you will usually take your breaks. It is here that you will begin to meet people from other departments. And to hear the latest rumors making the rounds.

Such as (during the first week I was there):

They've overhired for Christmas.

Business is slow and everyone's worried.

They're going to be laying off like crazy.

A nurse is coming and all the Christmas help is going to have to take urine tests. (This was already a regular practice among the permanent employees, to spot drug users.)

The last two rumors prove not to be true.

Coats

During the first few days I've been here, business has indeed been slow. Now that Peggy and I are over the initial excitement of starting a new job, and learning the stock, and making sales, the pace of the working day has slowed down to the true pace of the work. Only during the noon and five-to-six rush periods are there really many customers. And then there's no time to think about time. During the rest of the day, when there can be hours with only two or three customers on the floor, and four or five salespeople to help them, our favorite question to each other is "What time is it? What time is it?" Neither of us is wearing a watch, but as we pass each other on the floor, Peggy and I ask it again and again.

The hours drag for us, and also for the young cashiers, so they tell us, when business is slow, but not, it would seem from their attitudes, for Alice and the two other permanent saleswomen, all of whom have been working here for close to ten years: Nor does time seem to drag for Ed. They have all learned to pace themselves apparently, and when there are few customers around they seem sufficiently preoccupied with other matters—filling out inventory forms, going through the stock, or, what seems to be their biggest preoccupation of late, "supervising" Peggy and me.

That may be the most aggravating aspect of the slow business for us. It gives the higher-ups too much time to breathe down the necks of the lower-downs. "Break it up, break it up," Ed and Alice will say to Peggy and me when they see us talking for a minute, treating us like children in school, although there are no customers around for us to help. Whenever possible they find stock work for us to do at those times. That work seems to fall into four general categories: (1) mindless work for one person alone (like recovering all the empty hangers), which allows you to think your own thoughts as you do it; (2) mindless work done with somebody else (like putting all those $16.66 raincoats together with Peggy), which gives you a chance to talk to each other; (3) work for one person alone which requires your concentration (like taking a count for inventory); or (4) work for two or more people together which requires concentration. If you asked me which of these categories of work I prefer, I guess I'd have to say different kinds at different times. There are times I like to talk with Peggy, times I prefer to think my own thoughts, times I like to work by myself, times I like to work as a team. Spread it around I would say if anyone was listening. But back to reality. Right now the immediate issue is how to avoid the eagle eyes of Ed and Alice when business is slow. Super-vision indeed.

An incident with Alice the other day: I was filling out a layaway form. Sonya the cashier, was watching, as was the customer, as was Peggy, who happened to be standing near the cashier booth too. With so many eyes upon me as I wrote the simple information down I felt absurdly self-conscious and I must have been writing slowly. In any case, all of a sudden I felt someone grab the pencil from my hand.

"Here. I'll show you how to do that!" It was Alice, who had come over to join the circle of observers.

Without thinking. I grabbed the pencil back. "It's okay, Alice, I know how."

Incredibly, she had then stormed away, and started hollering at the top of her lungs to the empty department. "Well, the hell with her! That's the last time I'll try to help."

"You shouldn't have done that," Peggy said to me later, worried that I was headed for problems. "Let her say and do what she wants and keep your thoughts to yourself, if you're smart."

73

"But I didn't think. I just got angry when the pencil was grabbed away like that."

"Well, you better learn to control your anger, if you want to stay here long. Take my advice, I know what I'm talking about."

Lunch

Someone from small appliances has a plan to cheat the time clock. All you have to do, he says, is hang around the basement fifteen minutes after you're officially off and *then* punch out. "After a week you'll accumulate over an hour, at time and a half. In a month it will add up to practically a day's extra pay. They're too busy now to check."

Robes and Lingerie

"I've been wanting to have lunch with you and Lillian again, but my manager never tells me when I can go until the second before," said Marlene, emptying a box of pink and white corsets.

Dresses

"I still like it here except for two things. Number one, all the stock work they give you—I'm taking dresses out of the dressing room all day long. Number two, the travel and the hours. You know, it takes me an hour and a half to get here from where I live in the Bronx—I have to take a bus and a subway each way. So when I have to work here until the nine-thirty closing, like last night, I don't get home until after eleven. And then this morning I had to get up at six to get my husband's and son's breakfast and get here by nine. I'm not complaining, but at my age you don't have the energy you used to," said Lillian, hanging up an armful of dresses.

Coats

"May I help you?"

"May I help you find something?"

Our department is still pretty slow, but for some reason Ed is in rare spirits this afternoon. Had lunch with a regional manager or someone like that. Maybe had a drink or two or simply a pat on the back; in any case he's full of Bugs Bunny smiles, cracking awful jokes. His usual nervousness is gone.

And his mood seems to sweep the whole department. Sonya is laughing about something in the cashier booth. Peggy and I feel free to talk between May-I-help-you's. Even Alice, my nemesis, is smiling. "How's everything going with you, dear," she says to me at one point. *What did she say?*

I think about that. About the usual chain of pressure from the top, now the unusual chain of relaxation. Generally, whenever Peggy and I see Ed or Alice watching us, we freeze a little. Alice hardly freezes when Ed is around, but she is noticeably more at ease when he is away. Ed, for his part, gets obviously tense whenever the floor manager comes around to check the way our department looks, which he does at least twice a day. The floor manager no doubt has his own problems with the store manager. But today something went differently. Business is still slow yet the nervous watchful atmosphere is gone. The day ends with a lot of mutual kidding by everyone, including the increasingly friendly Alice. Have I misjudged her? It's amazing. Are we all feeling so good simply because someone treated Ed like a human being at lunch?

Punching Out

A huge man in a brown suit blocks my way in front of the time clock.

"Something the matter?" I ask.

The huge man raises one enormous and bushy brown eyebrow. "I haven't seen you before. Which department you in?"

"Coats and suits—" I say, wondering if he's a security cop. "You?"

The enormous eyebrow descends. "Jewelry," he says and smiles. "Stick with me, I'll get you diamonds."

Coats

Today is my first Saturday at work. Ed introduces me to Pam, a student who will be working in our department for the next six weeks as part of her college's—a local fashion institute—work-study program. After she graduates six months from now she'll probably get a job as an assistant buyer or as an executive trainee at a department store, this one or another. She is twenty-one, blonde and bright and extremely eager. She finds "the world of

75

merchandising *very* exciting." She will be Ed's right arm while she is here, learning what it is like to run a department. Ed will tell her what is to be done today and then she will tell Peggy and me.

A job for me. Pam explains what Ed wants. "Today you are to learn how to stylize and colorize."

"Stylize and colorize?"

"Yes, those are the words. Haven't you heard them before? It's in all the books."

We walk over to a rack of jackets. Pam says, "Okay, here's what's involved. All the fur-trimmed jackets should be together on this rack here. And all the untrimmed on that one over there."

So that's stylizing. "Sounds simple enough," I say.

"Well, there's more involved," Pam says, and adds that within those categories the solids must be together and the plaids together. And within *those* categories each style of jacket and color within that style must be together. Finally, the jackets on the rack should not be spaced too tightly nor too loosely. Admittedly, that can present a problem if you have only one rack for your fur-trims and you have a whole load of solids and just a few plaids, but you have to find a way.

I mean Pam has to find a way and I have to execute it. I mean Ed has found a way and has told Pam who tells me. Trouble is, sometimes the way Ed has found doesn't lead to the desired results. As an example he wants all the fur-trimmed plaids on this rack, but some of them are bike jackets not pant coats, and those are to be separated, too. It's a problem of typology, really. A sociologist's problem you might say—too many types, not enough racks.

Pam tries to follow Ed's directions and tells me to do the same. But certain irreconcilable conflicts continue to arise. Certain fur-trimmed plaid bike jackets remain too close to certain untrimmed solid pant coats. But life is a compromise and we have to live on—averting Ed's eyes.

Lunch

One good thing about working on Saturday: you get to go out the same time as normal workers—between noon and two—since there is not the usual weekday rush of customers on their own lunch breaks. A second bonus today is that Peggy and I are allowed to go out at the same time, something we haven't been able to do before.

We plop our homemade sandwiches on one of the tables in the lunchroom and put twenty cents apiece in the coffee machine. We sit down at the table and talk.

Peggy says, "You don't know what it's like having a mess of children to shop for at Christmas." She takes a bite of egg salad with tomato on rye. "But I'll tell you something. If it weren't for those older kids of mine I wouldn't be here right now."

Then she tells me how she and her husband and older son and daughter rotate work shifts to take care of the younger children in the family.

When Peggy was sixteen she landed her first regular job selling pots and pans at Gertz's department store in Jamaica, Queens. She was very proud. Hardly any black women sold in those days. A year later, marriage and an apartment in Harlem. A year later, her second regular job, a nine-pound baby boy. A year after that, a baby girl.

"Now *that* was hard," Peggy says, "those early years. There were no washing machines then, at least not for me, and you had to scrub with those washing boards, remember them? Over the sink for hours. My husband was away in the service, the Merchant Marine, and there were no older kids to help out."

But she did have an aunt who lived in the neighborhood and also a sister-in-law (her own parents died when she was small) and with their help she was able to continue to work off and on, off and on, as the children got older, as others were born. Now with her husband working at odd jobs when he can, and the oldest children in their early twenties, the family is like a factory in a way; all through the day, different members leave the apartment to work on different shifts. That first boy, now twenty-two, leaves at eight in the evening to play the piano at a bar on 135th Street. That first girl, now twenty-one, leaves at five in the morning to answer phones from people seeking reservations on Eastern Airlines. Peggy, now forty, leaves whenever the store tells her she must. In between they all make sure someone is home to

77

watch over the children who are still small. "So compared to the way it used to be," Peggy says, "it's now a breeze."

Peggy has eyes like giant Greek olives. In the six days I have known her I have never heard her complain. Now she moves those olives to the left and to the right. She looks directly at me. " 'Course when something goes wrong, I'm always the one who has to take over. I'm the one who is the mother, nobody else."

Then she talks about what happened the last time she worked at this store, over six months ago. She was working in robes and lingerie, where Marlene is now. Like Marlene, she found the manager very tough, eyeing her every minute, constantly finding something to disparage. Still, Peggy wanted to stay on the job. It was hard to find anything else. And so after she had been there a month, as is the required policy, she joined the Retail Clerks Union which represents this particular store, paying an initiation fee of $35, plus six dollars for the first month. Shortly after that, one of her five-year-old twins became ill with an undefined rash, a raging fever. Alarmed, Peggy took the girl to the doctor. Who recommended another doctor. Who also didn't know what was wrong. Just keep her in bed, he said, it will probably pass. "Well, even though my son was home I was too worried to leave her." So Peggy stayed out of work for three days.

On the fourth morning the child's fever was back to normal, and that afternoon Peggy went back to the store. The manager was furious. How could Peggy have done that? Staying out that long when it was such a busy week. What a filthy trick, waiting until she was in the union so that it would be difficult to have her fired. "She wanted to get rid of me, but she knew I would fight, so instead she just kept making things worse for me, complaining all the time, giving me all the Saturdays and nights she could, picking, picking, until finally she won. I couldn't take it anymore. I went down to personnel and said, transfer me or I'll have to leave. They were nice, but they had nothing else. They said go home, we'll call you as soon as something turns up. Well, you know what happened then. I heard nothing for six months, then they finally called me about a job for Christmas rush. And in between, business was so bad at other stores I couldn't find any other work anywhere else."

Coats

"May I help you?"

Time on this Saturday afternoon is passing much faster than usual. Partly that's because of the noon lunch I think—the more even split in the day. Partly it's because of Ed's attitude—not as euphoric as the other day, but still more relaxed than usual. And also it's because business has finally started to pick up. We're not as busy as we might be, but the pace we do have is probably ideal. Customers all the time. But not so many you can't give them your attention.

"May I help you?" A woman in her sixties with a brutal scar on the left side of her face, the corner of her lip curved permanently upward in a horrid smirking grimace.

She says she is looking for a raincoat, "not too expensive." I show her one I like particularly, in pale blue, and another style in green, both on the $16.66 rack.

"Which do you like better?" she asks me after trying each on slowly, turning around and around before a full-length mirror. She is a perfect size 12 and they each fit her well.

I tell her, the blue one.

"But the collar is so pointy," she says.

"Well then the green one is also nice."

"But I like the blue one more," she says.

I nod.

"You really think the blue one is pretty?" she asks.

"Yes I do."

"But the green one looks good too."

I agree.

"I really do like the blue," she says.

I repeat I do, too.

"Except for the pointy collar."

I suggest she try on some others if she's still unsure.

"You think the collar is too pointy?"

I tell her no, I happen to like it, but of course she's the one who has to be satisfied.

"But don't you like the green one, too?" she says.

We continue like that, going in circles like an old Abbott and Costello joke, the green or the blue or the blue or the green, and

79

PINK COLLAR WORKERS

after a while I suggest I leave to give her time to think it over but she says, no, no, please stay, and then it begins to dawn on me that perhaps she is not really here to buy a raincoat, that something else may be happening, she is here to find someone to talk to her, to look at her mutilated face, to touch her as she tries the coats on and on again.

"Louise, could you come here right away."

It is Ed, standing by the cashier's booth. He has been watching me, he says, and I have been spending too much time with that woman. "Far too much. There are other customers around to take care of, too, and besides we never waste our time on the cheap raincoats." He pauses and points a finger to the side of his forehead. "And besides, she looks a little dingy to me. You have to watch it. They come here all the time."

I walk back to the woman to tell her I'll be around if she needs me, but by then she is already talking to Peggy, asking which she likes better, the blue or the green. Later Peggy tells me she bought neither one.

Punching Out

"Thank God tomorrow is Sunday," says Lillian to Peggy and me as the three of us walk out into the street. Tonight if Lillian's lucky—if she makes the right train and bus connections—she'll be home by eight o'clock.

"Do you still want to work here after Christmas?" she says to Peggy. "I'm not so sure myself anymore, I'm getting a little tired."

" 'Course, I do," says Peggy. "For me it's a one-fare job."

Feet

Soothing Refresher for Tired Feet—Just add a packet of this special formula to warm water to soak away foot discomfort reads the blurb on the box of Dr. Scholl's product I use without results on Sunday afternoon.

In the evening my husband and I visit some friends for dinner. Across the table is a young doctor, an internist. I ask him, "What does it do to people to have to spend most of their working day, year after year, on their feet?"

"I'm not sure it does anything," the doctor says, cutting a

80

piece of chicken. "Aside from some corns and calluses maybe. A few varicose veins. Depends on the kind of feet you have, and of course you should be wearing the right kind of shoes. Maybe support hose, too. But for most people it's really only dangerous when you can't move around, when you have to stand still and the blood has no chance to move."

Like Sonya and the other cashiers have to do behind those little booths.

Later at home, I think about categories of work I never paid attention to before. Standing jobs and sitting jobs. Standing still jobs and walking around jobs. One-fare jobs and triple-fare jobs.

Coats

Fairly active Monday morning. First, Ed tells Peggy and me to dust off the top of the coatracks. "So this is our responsibility, too," I say to Peggy, thinking of Jackie at the beauty shop in California, how angry she used to get when asked to clean up as part of her work.

Peggy, however, is unconcerned as she wipes off the top of a display holder across from me. "Well, they do have some other people to clean the bathrooms, but they don't do the racks in the department. I used to mind, but, hell, what's the difference?"

Customers. We're actually busy for a change. The reason, aside from the fact that Christmas is drawing closer, is that we have a one-day special on rabbit coats today, twenty percent off. As in other department stores, these advertised specials are now standard practice every week, bait to bring in the shopper who might not come otherwise and now might be tempted to buy other products as well.

A young woman walks over to Ed, obviously upset. Bought one of the identical rabbits here four days ago for twenty dollars more than she would have had to pay today. "When you work as a bank teller twenty dollars is a lot of money. Why couldn't they have let me know?" Ed shakes his head. He's sorry, he says, putting his hand to his mouth to stifle a yawn, but he never knows when specials are coming either. "It's always a surprise, that's why you have to watch the ads."

"But how could I have known there would be a sale when I bought it four days ago?"

Another shake of the head. "What can I tell you?" and Ed wanders away.

"Will you help me, Miss?" A plump young woman, early twenties. "I was here last week and tried on a mink jacket, do you still have it?"

"Think so, let's go look," I say. It is the joke of the department in a way, our most famous item, a mink in a store like this. But Sonya, the cashier, doesn't find the joke funny; she is in love with the jacket, likes to fondle its soft fur, looks mournful anytime she sees a customer trying it on. As the woman is doing now.

"I'm coo coo about it," the young woman says, eyeing her reflection in the mirror. "Shouldn't. I really shouldn't. Spend the money, on my puny salary. I'd have to put it on layaway. But it's so *gorgeous,* what do you think?"

What do I think? I think it looks awful on her. I think she is short and squat and the jacket makes her look shorter, squattier. I think she could do a thousand things better with $250. I think we should all read Veblen again. I think I have no business telling her or anyone else what they should do with their money. But in any case she does not wait for my profound counsel.

"Never mind, I'll take it."

"We do have some other fur jackets you might want to try on before deciding. They're not mink, but they're quite nice, and not as bulky as this one, also they're less money."

"No, I told you, I'll take it. I can give you a $30 deposit, is that okay?"

We walk over to the cashier's booth, where I get a layaway form from Sonya. Who gives me a sad little smile. "I hate you for selling it," she says softly.

"Oh, Sonya, you weren't really planning to buy it, were you?" I know that she is only working here to save money for college.

"No. I guess not. I never could have afforded it, even on layaway. But it was a nice dream while it lasted."

Lunch

Rumor of the day: the layoffs are starting to come.

Source: the young man from small appliances with the break-the-time-clock scheme.

Immediate denial: from a very thin elderly woman sitting next to him.

Small Appliances introduces us. "You are now going to meet the oldest employee in the store," he says to me.

"Not the oldest," she interrupts, "the *first*."

Her name is Margie, and she is a cashier in books and records.

"Margie works in a class department," Small Appliances says. "They got a much better type of customer than we do. I wish I could work there."

"How long have you worked here?" I ask Margie.

"Fourteen years. No, going on fifteen now. I came here a year after my husband died, when the branch was just opening."

Small Appliances asks her how she was able to last so long. She gives him a sympathetic smile. "I haven't just lasted, young man, I've *enjoyed* it." Then she looks at me. "You may not believe this but I'm here in the store before I'm supposed to every morning, probably before you get up. I come in and dust everything off in my department, make sure it all looks perfect when the people start to parade in."

"How much they pay you for that?" Small Appliances asks.

"They don't pay me, young man. They don't ask me to do it. At nine I go back downstairs and punch in at the regular time."

Small Appliances looks incredulous. "Yeah, I know what you're thinking. My friends say I'm crazy, too. They say, what is it at the store with you, Margie? Is it your second home or something? And I tell them, no, it isn't my second home. Not at all. It's my first home. There's this empty apartment where I go to sleep at night. But this is where I live. This is my first home. They've been very kind to me here."

I want to ask her more but the huge man from jewelry has just walked in and sat down next to me. The eyebrow is up again: that same you-and-me-baby gaze. What is there to say?

"How's business?"

"Pretty good with the watches, not so hot with the diamonds. Why don't you come over and see?"

Coats

Alice is back in Mood Number One. On the prey. At one point, while I'm waiting on a customer, she rushes over, exclaiming loudly: "Never, never, *never* let anyone put their own coat on our racks!" Then marches away. A few moments later I hear her calling my name while I'm showing a leather jacket to a pale soft-spoken young woman, very shy. What in God's name have I done wrong now? I think as I walk over to where Alice is standing. "That woman you're waiting on," she says in a whisper, "she's a shoplifter. The security officer told me to get you away from her."

She walks with me over to the other side of the department, suddenly Alice the Sweet again, offering me motherly advice about wearing more comfortable shoes. "I see you're limping a little, you ought to try something like this," and she points to her own rubber soled oxfords.

"Don't *your* feet ever get tired, after all the standing?" I ask.

"No, well, maybe a few bunions. I'm tired at night, but nothing serious. You get used to it after ten years. If you didn't you'd have been gone long ago."

Alice has been working full-time at this store since her youngest child (she has two) entered high school ten years ago. Now both children are married. She is a grandmother. During the ten years she has worked here she has seen a legion of part-time students and young cashiers and Christmas temps *and* managers come and go. Like Margie, she is still in the same job in the same department as when she started. Twenty-one-year-old Pam is already in a better position. "You've got to understand she needs to feel she is important," Peggy once said to me after Alice barked at us to hurry up with some rack changes we were making. The assumption was that this was her only way. Is helping to apprehend a shoplifter another?

I turn around to look at the leather section. The security officer and the young woman are gone.

Now Pam comes over and says Ed wants me to, yes, stylize two racks. "The leather jackets should be where the regular jackets are, and vice versa." Apparently the floor manager was here earlier criticizing Ed for the way the section was set up. Pam and I make the change together, but the results are even worse than before. Not enough rack space for the jackets, too much empty space on the other rack. Our stylizing is a mess. Ed comes over to check. "That's awful, change it back to the way it was before," he snaps, looking harried and confused.

Robes and Lingerie

"I no care what happens tomorrow; we have lunch, right?" Marlene says as I pass by her department on my way home. Both of us are scheduled to come in at noon. Our lunch breaks should come at four. "Right," I say, "whatever happens," not knowing that what will happen is that it will be my last day at work.

Coats

When I arrive at noon the department is the busiest I've ever seen.

"May I help you?"

"No, just looking."

See Peggy. "May I help you find something?"

"Yeah, a chair."

Show a size 18 all the fake furs. Nothing right.

Show a bald young man looking for a present for his wife three leather jackets. Buys the last.

Help an elderly woman go through the raincoats, hoping Ed or Alice won't get started again about wasting time on people looking at the cheaper goods. No sale.

Help a woman in a purple hat find a rabbit coat that fits her. They are on special again, twenty percent off. Success with a size 8. She'll take it, on layaway.

Walk over to the cashier's booth to write it up. Twenty percent off $125 is $25. That leaves $100 plus seven percent sales tax, $107. Minus the woman's $25 deposit. The phone on the top of the cashier booth rings. It is for Ed, from personnel. The balance is therefore $82. I give the layaway form to Sonya, who, as is the practice, checks the addition on her register. Next to me, Ed is on the phone, saying, "Can't we wait until two o'clock? She's in the middle of a layaway now, and after that she's going to be busy with customers for a while." The addition checks out; Sonya returns the form to me for the customer to sign. I turn to Ed for an explanation but he simply hangs up the phone and walks away.

It's 1:45 now. The woman signs the form. More customers, more sales, more no-sales. At two Peggy goes to lunch. A few seconds later Ed leaves too, without saying a word. At 2:30 Pam tells me to go to the luggage department. I've been transferred. No good-bye's, no explanations. Like that.

Luggage and Personnel

You get there, if you want to get there, by going to the seventh floor, walking past the stereo sets and electric organs and plastic lamps. It is there, but you have to look for it, in an isolated narrow row. Luggage. Deader than coats. Nobody there when I arrive but one salesman, a handsome black man, surprised that an extra is coming. Except for the lunch rush, he tells me, there's been very little business, and all of it handled by four full-time men in the department. No other women except a student on the register, five to nine. I say good-bye to the handsome man. "I think I'll go to personnel to find out what happened."

"We overhired for Christmas, but we're trying not to lay anyone off," Andrea tells me when I ask why I was transferred. "We had a part-time woman with no place to work so we sent her to coats, and put you in luggage where they didn't have any extra help. It's a nice department, you'll see when you work there awhile."

But I decide it's time to leave. I want to be able to tell Peggy and Lillian and Marlene and Sonya and Margie exactly why I've been working here. I am increasingly fond of them and increasingly unfond of this bogus role I'm playing. Increasingly guilty about being evasive. (What will you do after Christmas? Peggy or Lillian will ask; "I'll tell you later," says the spy who comes in from the coats.) So now feeling like an absurd imitation of Rod Steiger leaving the sheriff's office forever, I take off my store badge and put it on Andrea's desk. "I'm going to tell you something that may surprise you," I say. "I've been working here because I'm writing a book about women in certain occupations, including saleswomen, and I wanted to understand as much as I could about their day by day life. I figured the best way to do that would be by doing the work myself."

"Well, that makes sense," Andrea says slowly, looking mildly interested, not wholly convinced.

"But now," I continue, "since you've transferred me to luggage where I'm not really needed, I think I can learn the rest of what I want to know from the outside, particularly if you'd let me come back and interview you."

"You know something," Andrea says, after we have agreed to meet in a few days and she has put the badge away in her desk drawer, "this has to be the weirdest reason for quitting anyone has ever given me."

Marlene

We meet at the coffee shop where we had lunch that first day of work. She says she is glad I am going to write about what happened but doubts anyone will want to read about it. "People want to hear about Jackie Onassis and Elizabeth Taylor. Who cares about an ordinary woman like me?" I tell her more than before—I think. Not enough, but more than before. She looks dubious. We both order hamburgers and coffee. "Still it's good that you do it anyway," she says.

We talk about robes and lingerie. How does she like selling now?

"What you mean selling?" she asks between mouthfuls in that musical accent of hers, an accent with traces from Spain I learn, the country she lived in until she was twenty. "This is not selling, this is showing."

"What's the difference?"

"Selling is when it matters how you and your customers get to know each other, how you help her find what's best, how you understand what she needs. Here you no sell. Lady comes in, asks for something, you go find it, she buys or she no buys, that's it, you never see her no more. That's not selling. That's showing. But most of the time, you don't do that even. You're putting labels on corsets, or emptying boxes. They care more for that than anything else.

"And never a thank you, not once a please or a thank you, just do this, do that, hurry up, and always keeping me guessing about when I could go out."

Not quite as bad in our department, I think, but almost.

"Other stores are better maybe," Marlene says. (She has a friend who worked in Bloomingdale's.) "There in some departments you get a little commission, not much, one-half percent or something, but then the women all really try hard to sell."

"I've heard some complain they have to compete with each other to make a couple of dollars," I say. "They're under pressure to grab each customer and sell them, while at least here we never felt forced to talk anyone into buying anything. Maybe that's the opposite side of the coin."

Marlene nods. "It's true. Those women probably don't make much money either.

"Still, I would rather work at a place like Bloomingdale's or Saks Fifth Avenue if I could. You feel like you're somebody. Everything looks so pretty. Maybe some day I go there."

She looked for this job for three months. Other stores, including Bloomingdale's, turned her down because of her English. They suggested she take some courses, then try again. "My husband wants me to do that, too. He doesn't need for me to work, we aren't going hungry, but he knows how I go crazy in the house alone. He jokes, I want to be liberated woman; and he's right."

"You believe in the woman's movement."

"I'm all for it. That's what I like about this country most. Remember I come from Spain where a man has two women: one the wife he marries and has children with and keeps locked in the house; the other, the mistress he sleeps with and disgraces."

Personnel

Today is payday, and her little office is jammed. People asking questions about deductions, about the amount of their checks in general. I could come back another day, I say to Andrea, but, no, she says, sit down, it won't be long.

My first question, when the office finally clears out, has to do with the ages of the women who work there. I mention the pattern I've noticed; young women in their late teens and early twenties mainly working part-time as cashiers or in sales; and then the women in their forties or older, working full-time for many years in the same spot. Andrea agrees that that is the general pattern, not only here but at other department stores as well. "Does that mean there is a trend toward recruiting mainly part-time now?" Andrea says yes. Aside from the special situation at Christmas they have reached the point where there are now more part-timers than full-timers. "We are developing four shifts," she says: nine thirty to two thirty; eleven to three; three to seven; and five to nine. "The early shifts are mainly young mothers with school kids. The three to seven are high school and college students coming after school. And the five to nine are mostly students again and people who moonlight. We still hire full-time, when someone good comes along, but we're doing very little recruiting of women there."

"Is that because the company saves money on part-timers?"

"Yes, that's certainly one of the factors. You can cover yourself during your rush hours and have less people around when it's quieter. Also there can be some savings on fringe benefits a company has to pay. If you work here a month you have to join the union, and that means, if you're full-time you're immediately eligible for health insurance. But if you're part-time you have to wait six months, by which time many of our part-timers are gone. Also we only have to provide health insurance if you're not covered elsewhere, and almost all of our part-timers are covered by someone else in their family."

I ask about the wage scale, and she says, "This is the way it works. If you get a job with us you make $2.15 an hour for the first month. Then after thirty days, if your manager gives you a good evaluation, and if there's an opening in your department and you want to stay, you get raised ten cents an hour and you have to join the union. Then after six months, if everything's still okay, you get another ten cents an hour."

I shake my head, wonder how people in New York can manage on this.

Andrea agrees. "I certainly couldn't live on it, even with my husband's wages." Then she quickly becomes her company's spokesperson again: "But of course the kind of work they do is nothing they should be paid much for. There's no responsibility, the jobs are not difficult or challenging. What's the big deal in folding a pair of pajamas and putting them away in a drawer?" I think of Marlene going crazy folding those pajamas and start to say perhaps people should get paid more precisely to the degree they're not *allowed* to do the more challenging work, but now

89

there is a young black man, about twenty, standing by Andrea's desk, waiting to be noticed.

"Yes, John," Andrea says. He is a Christmas full-time, toys.

"I'm wondering when I can join the union," he says. "I want to stay for good if I can."

"Well, we'll have to wait until January 15 to see what our needs are going to be, John, and also to see what your manager says about your work. So until then, why don't you just keep doing what you're doing?"

The subject closed, he leaves the room and I remark that even at these absurdly low wages they obviously have no problem getting workers and that that is perhaps the chief difficulty.

"Oh, yes, well you saw what happened when we put in the Christmas help-wanted ads, the place was flooded for days. Many were happy to get anything we could give them; they didn't even ask about the salary, some of them."

I mention that there seemed to be a great deal more black women on the line that first day I came to apply—perhaps 80 percent were black—than those with me—about 40 percent—when I returned to start work. And most of the black women were hired as cashiers.

"Oh, yes," Andrea agrees readily. "That's one of the first things I notice when people come to apply. We have a kind of quota system here, all stores do."

Since there is a massive equal employment opportunity sign outside her office door, I'm rather surprised she is admitting this so easily.

"How does the quota system work?"

"Well, the rule of thumb in most places is that your sales help should be as much like your clientele as possible. In other words if this were the suburbs and your help was all black and your customers all white, well most of them might just walk out. So there, our help is mostly white. Here, our customers are more mixed so our help can be pretty mixed too. But I try to see that it's equally divided; you know, that there aren't all blacks in one department or floor, that it's pretty much spread out through the store."

"And what about the male-female differences?" I ask. "The fact that the men are in the big commission departments, and not the women."

"We're trying to equalize that, too." she says. "But certain departments—the heavy stock departments, for example, like major appliances, are mostly requested by men, and certain jobs, like cashiers, tend to be female. Even though I try to spread things out. See, men don't ask for cashier jobs, and I try to put people in places they want to be. And women almost always ask for soft goods, for sportswear or dresses nine out of ten times, so I don't have too much chance to do what I'd like, do I?"

"And managers?" I ask.

"Probably about sixty percent men, forty percent women. But remember we're a young company, we're still changing, and the tendency now is to push women into the better jobs. But even here there are problems. We recruit from outside for these kinds of jobs, because our managers usually have to have college degrees and most of our sales help don't have that much education."

Meaning Terry or Peggy or Lillian or Marlene could never be managers.

I think about Ed. "How much does a department manager make?"

"Oh, maybe, at the beginning about $175 or $180 a week, after a while say $200 a week."

So even the King of Coats is barely topping $10,000 a year.

"I'm just amazed by these salaries."

"It's true," Andrea says. "Retail salaries are notoriously low, even in management jobs. Only on the top, where they make $125,000 a year or more, does it seem to pay anything."

"And one final thing," I ask. "Why isn't it possible to have chairs for the workers? Particularly for the cashiers. But also for the sales help. Couldn't there be chairs so the employees would be able to rest their feet when business is slow?"

"I can't answer that," Andrea says. "I don't know why. I guess it's just always been that way."

Diamonds

Q: May I ask you a personal question?

A: What could be too personal? I'm kind, sweet and romantic. Too bad you're not.

Q: How much do you earn?

A: A little over $10,000 a year.

Q: That's more than most managers here.

A: Damn right it is. And that's because I've *earned* it. I've been here nine years now and I've built myself up to a point where I'm very valuable to this store. I'm the only one here who really understands fine gems, who can make appraisals. I went to school to learn it, and now I'm an expert.

Q: Does your salary include commission?

A: Used to, but last year they cut them out. In my department, I mean. In furniture, major appliances, carpets, they still have them. TV and men's wear, too. Also there may be some spiffs in other departments I don't know about.

Q: What's a spiff?

A: A spiff is an extra commission a manufacturer gives you for selling his particular product. Like, say Westinghouse is trying to push a particular refrigerator; they may say, okay, all salespeople will get so much money directly from us for every refrigerator they sell. This is in addition to the commission the store gives you.

Q: That could make you push products you didn't think were any good.

A: Sure it does. That's why I'm glad they cut them out in our department. But I do miss the incentive of the regular commission.

Q: How do you feel about your work?

A: I like to sell. I have an interest in jewelry. I like it when I'm busy; if it's slow I get nervous.

Q: Are there women in your department?

A: A few part-timers, one full-time. The three people on the top, including me, are men.

Q: How do you get along with the women?

A: Okay. You want me to be honest? The more women in my department the more work for me. They all act like they're helpless. Will you get that for me? Can you reach that box over there? Can you fix the strap on this watch? It's funny, here they can't reach the third shelf, but at home they won't let you lift a finger, they take over the whole show.

Q: Your wife won't let you lift a finger?

A: No, I thought I told you I wasn't married. I live with my mother.

Q: Do these women in your department earn the same amount as you?

A: No, nothing near it. But that's because they're not *producing* what I am, they don't have the knowledge, they haven't studied the merchandise. If they want to earn more, they should learn more. Hey that rhymes, put it in your book. But I'm not kidding. Look, I'm forty, it took me years to get where I am and I'm not making that much. If you want to avoid getting underpaid, you have to know something. You don't walk in with no skills and expect not to be considered cheap labor. You've got to have a specialty, like furniture, and get to know everything about it, not just come in knowing nothing.

Q: But they usually don't let women work in the furniture department in the first place, or in any of those departments with commissions or spiffs or whatever.

A: Okay, maybe that's true. I think there's a lot of prejudice around and when a woman works as hard as I do she should be paid the same. I know a woman here who fought for years for a selling job in major appliances and the men who worked in the department wouldn't let her in. Now, these guys happen to be my friends, but I don't think that's right. She's a good saleswoman, she supports a kid, she needs the dough. I think what they did is rotten. So you see I'm not a male chauvinist pig if that's what you've been thinking.

A: You're not?

Q: No, I believe in being fair. It's not fair they don't let women in some of the money-making departments. But it's also not fair that some of the women play helpless and make me do all the work. I wouldn't mind so much if they were young and blonde and buxom, but these are all grandmothers mostly, either that or they're part-time students and couldn't care less.

Lillian
She quit her job in dresses a week after I left. Mainly it was the hours. "I couldn't keep them up, especially when the store started staying open until ten for the last-minute Christmas shoppers.

I just didn't feel safe coming home that late." We are having lunch a block from the store. "But I don't want you to think I'm complaining. If you're not skilled you have to do something. And remember, we were just Christmas temporaries—the lowest of the low."

It was as if she had been listening to diamonds.

In the early years, when Lillian was single and working full-time, she found the work fun. "Or that's how I remember it. I was selling at Wanamaker's in Philadelphia, selling expensive wastebaskets. I mean *expensive*. This was right at the beginning of the year, World War Two, and we were young and proud of what we were doing, just working but proud of that. And at night the girls I worked with, we were all friends, we would go out together, to the movies sometimes, or to get a bite, or sometimes on dates."

Then came marriage. And after the children were born continuing to work part-time. "Not that I wanted to, but there was always a money problem, so I would look for jobs in stores during the hours my husband could stay home and baby-sit. It wasn't like it was before when I was single and had nothing else to worry about, I can tell you that. And, then, too, when you work part-time or temporary, they treat you differently, they don't take you as seriously I think; it's different, you run in and run out, you don't feel as much a part of things."

Standing behind the cashier booth in coats, twenty-three-year-old Sonya had once said something in a similar vein about temporary work. "It's all right," she had said, "but only for a little while. It's a means to an end. It's getting me through college. Only if I thought I would have to be a cashier for the rest of my life, then I would feel very very sad." This was the fifth store Sonya had worked in since starting college. Next year she hoped to graduate and start work as a speech therapist.

Thirty years older than Sonya, Lillian has also found the temporary and part-time job a means to an economic end throughout the years she raised her children. But the impact for her after all this time is obviously quite different. For Sonya such jobs have been a helpful part of a plan to move ahead. For Lillian, working on and off throughout the years, depending on her family situation, has meant she has never built up seniority in any one place, has never developed the specialty Diamonds prescribed, has never advanced at all. Now, with the Christmas job over, she will start from scratch again, looking for another opening at another store. At her age and with the job market tight, she doesn't know where she will begin.

The Union

He is reading the labor leader's bible, the *Wall Street Journal,* when I enter his office on the morning before New Year's Eve. His name is Sydney Heller, president of Local 888 of the Retail Clerk's International Association, which represents the store where I worked.

I ask how the store did over the Christmas rush. "We're still waiting to find out. It looked bad for a while, but I hear it may be a lot better than everyone expected. Which is naturally better for us, and the demands we can make."

Speaking of demands, why are wages so low in a union store?

"Well," he says, "you have to remember retailing was one of the last industries to be organized in this country. Most department stores, four out of five, aren't organized today. What success we had in department store organizing was mainly in the 1930s, that was when Macy's, Gimbels, Bloomingdale's were organized. After that the other non-union employers realized they were vulnerable and they gave the workers a little more, just enough to keep them from being angry and just enough hardline stuff to make them worry about losing their jobs if they tried to organize. The only place in retailing where we were really successful was supermarkets. Almost all supermarkets in New York are organized today and because of that we're able to get better and better contracts for our members there."

He folds the *Journal* carefully. "But in an area like department stores, where the industry is mostly unorganized, you are not in a position to get as much. You can't knock your employer out of business by demanding he pay far higher wages than the guy across the street, who can then undersell him. If we put him out of business our members are out of business too. Now of course you can't tell that to your membership. From their point of view,

95

there's no excuse for the low wages and of course I understand, what with prices up and everything, but there's not that much that can be done.''

I ask why they have been so much more successful with super-markets than department stores? He lights a cigarette, looks out the window at a superb view of Manhattan skyscrapers.

"Let me try to put this to you straight. I'm a working man my-self, you know. Started out as a grocery clerk, that's where I come from. Grew up working like a horse. And we all worked a lot harder than you do in department stores, that happens to be the truth, and maybe that's why we were faster to organize, we knew who we were—we were workers. Now department store employees, they think they're different a lot of the time. They think they're more genteel, more like white-collar workers. They get up in the morning, get dressed very neatly, come to work and say hello to Mrs. So and So, hello to Miss Fancy, handle the pret-ty merchandise. If they work at Lord and Taylor they go home and tell their friends, look at me, I sold a dress to so and so today and they look down their noses at the women who work at Macy's, who look down at the women at Alexander's, and so on. They've got everything, right? Except wages. They're better than those low-down grocery clerks, right? Except their paychecks aren't better a lot of the time, they're often worse. I can get you $131 a week after two years at one of my supermarkets. And that's because in one place we have power and in the other we don't.''

I mention that for some reason they seem to have a lot more power in the departments men work in, although less than twenty percent of department store workers are men. He says that that is partly because the men had earlier set precedents in the specialty stores where they had first started selling in those areas—furni-ture stores, men's wear stores, radio and TV and appliance stores. "Those stores are highly unionized, we had luck there, and the men came in to the department stores wanting the same remuneration if not better, usually based on commission. Why have we not had the same luck with women's specialty stores? They seem to have a different attitude, like I told you before. They think unions are low class and they're high class.''

I let that go, and ask his opinion about the trend toward more part-time workers. He says he is disturbed about its future effect on opportunities for full-time workers but doesn't know what to do about it yet. "The trend has been growing for about a decade, and it's still growing. In department stores business comes and goes in cycles, as you saw. So one day someone said, 'Why the hell do we have to pay people for eight hours? Get the numbers in when we need them and that's all.' Now I don't like it, but there's not much I can do. It hurts us a lot of ways. Fewer full-time jobs for our people. A bigger problem in organizing, since a part-timer is just not committed to the work in the same way usually as the full-timer. And the turnover is not to be believed. A part-time job can turn over ten or more times in a year. So we're worried about it. There may come a time when we'll try to make a contractual agreement about the allowable ratio of part-time to full-time employees."

What is the turnover among full-time workers?

"It's also high, but nothing like the part-time. Maybe fifty percent in the first year, but after that it goes down steadily as people stay longer."

"They get used to the low wages?"

"Look, I'm the first one to want higher salaries. But you have to be realistic. We're talking mainly about unskilled jobs, and you have to take a look at the labor market as a whole and say, if someone spends the entire day folding pajamas, what is that labor worth?"

Where have I heard that exact line before? "It's worth a lot more than they're paying now."

"Sure, but how do you get it?"

Women Organizing Women

"This is what we did," said Eleanor Tilson, who is the administrator of the health and security plan of another union representing sales help, the United Department Store Workers. "We got out the payrolls of all the workers at the two major stores we represent—Bloomingdale's and Gimbels—and we tallied up how many men and how many women were making over $10,000 a year. Needless to say, those who were were almost exclusively men.

"Then we pressured our male executives to pay attention to

97

these statistics. Since the overwhelming majority of department store salesworkers are female and since 80 percent of salesworkers are *not* now unionized we asked them, is it possible, is it perhaps a little bit likely, that the male leaders have simply not known how to speak to the real needs of women workers? Is it possible that they haven't even understood those needs? That if women had been doing the organizing themselves, had been planning the drives and talking to the women, that the results might have been very different?"

The pressure by the women had several effects. The men reluctantly agreed to let the theme of their next conference for stewards be entitled, "Women in the workforce." And out of *that* conference came another decision to hold a series of classes near the different branch stores where the members worked.

"To begin with," Tilson said, "this was the first time these women ever got together to discuss their problems on the job openly; problems similar to the ones you observed at the store where you worked. Transportation, supervision, low pay, and so on. But the women also began to discuss some of the fears they had about moving ahead, about taking a crack at the high commission jobs. Over the years the men in our union had said the reason there were so few women in those spots was that the women didn't really want to be there. Well, we talked about that in our classes, and it turned out the women *did* have some fears about taking on those jobs. But there were solid reasons for their fears. They were worried, yes, about being too competitive, about alienating men if they were too aggressive, but they were also afraid the jobs weren't really open to them, that the men in the departments didn't want them there, and they were right. Many hadn't even been told about the tremendous difference in earnings these jobs can provide. So what has come out of the classes? I hesitate to call it consciousness raising, but that's what it is. And we have to change the consciousness of the employers, too. We've started to do that, to put pressure on them to promote women—it's in our contracts now—and thanks to the new attitudes of women we've seen more and more apply when something does open up. If you go to Bloomingdale's, you'll see the first women salesperson now in the furniture department, and that's a direct result of our efforts. So it's a very slow process, but some things are starting to happen. Come to our class and you'll see."

Peggy

It is early in February, about one P.M. on a Tuesday. I dial her number, and one of her five-year-old twins answers, then another young voice, male, comes on the phone. His mother is dozing in front of the television, the boy tells me, no, she's up, here she comes now. Peggy's voice in the background. Scolding the twins. "You know you're supposed to be taking your naps—into the bedroom now, fast." Then she picks up the phone.

The last time we talked was after Christmas. Peggy had just left coats. She was feeling discouraged. Ed had said nothing about offering her permanent work. She was also angry about the way she had been treated in general. "You know, I was never one to talk back. You remember how I was always telling you to be careful, but it seems to me it really got worse after you left. Everyone wanting to order me around, everyone wanting the authority—Ed, Alice, even Pam after a while."

That was over a month ago and I ask whether she's looking for another job now. She says she's tried to, but can't seem to get out of the house very often. "Something's always happening with one of the children, getting sick or needing something. If you're lucky enough to get a job, then you can get away from it for a while, I can get the others to help out, but if you're home you're stuck in the middle. I look at the ads, of course. Nothing so far. Not one blessed thing. Maybe Ed will call me one of these days."

"You'd go back to coats?"

"Sure I'd go back. In a flash."

A Store and a Home

Hicksville, Long Island: The last of the union-sponsored classes for the Gimbels' women in the area is being held. It is April now. About thirty women have attended the series, the majority over forty—as are the majority of full-time workers in the store—but there are also four or five women in their early twenties.

One of the young women rises. "All I know," she says, "is when *I'm* fifty or sixty I don't want to be standing around some nickel and dime department drooling about how beautiful my grandchildren are. If I'm still working at Gimbels, I want to be where I can make some real money."

"She's really a doll, isn't she?" says one of the grandmothers.

"She only talks like that because she's so young and inexperienced."

"The money part isn't that important to me, either," agrees another woman who works in the men's wear department of her store. "My husband, thank God, makes a good living and I enjoy what I'm doing, so why should I complain? Even though I happen to know the men in my department are making commissions and I'm not."

Shouts from some of the women when they hear this. "Do you think you can sell as well as a man?" one of them asks.

"Well, to be modest, I think I could run my whole department. But I'm just not ready to make a big issue over money now."

"But that's not where it's at," Eleanor Tilson says. "We have to support each other as women. You may feel you don't need the money, but not to protest and fight for it is to allow the same situation to continue for women who *do* need it. Women who are in this room. Women whose husbands aren't as fortunate as yours. Or who don't have husbands and have to support themselves and maybe also their children."

"Okay, I can see that. I agree."

After the discussion is over there is coffee and cake and the women gather around and talk about how much they've enjoyed the sessions. Then one of the younger women approaches Eleanor. The store where she works is going to be laying off some of the full-time workers, she says. Since she's one of the newest there, she fears the layoff will include her. "They've already offered me a part-time job instead, but I need the full-time wages." Eleanor suggests she check with her steward to find out if it's a false rumor—"it often is"—but admits that if layoffs are really coming there's not much that can be done. "We're starting to really fight for the advancement of our women, and we're going to keep that fight going. But if the store is in trouble, then we're in trouble, too. And seniority is one of our oldest principles when it comes to layoffs. You wouldn't want us to give that up, would you?"

"So the part-time trend is hitting your store, too?" I ask another woman who works at the same branch.

"Yes, they're trying to get a three-platoon system going as much as possible. Which is good for the young mothers and students who only want to work for a few hours, but not for those of us who need a whole day."

Driving back to Manhattan that night, Eleanor says, "If it's true the store is laying off, then we're in trouble, but I haven't heard about it."

I remark how many of the older women said they wanted to keep on working a full day, even though they didn't really need the money.

"Well, I think that's only half true. If you had pushed them a little harder, I'd think you'd find they all need the money, although some are still ashamed to admit it. For instance one of the women who spoke tonight told me later she was only working to help her youngest son go to college. Only! But it's also true they want to keep working for other reasons too. I've been amazed myself. We hold pre-retirement classes for our oldest workers and time and time again we hear them say they don't want to retire, they would miss their friends at the store, they're afraid of being home all alone with nothing to do. Remember a lot of our members are widows."

All of which made me think of Margie, the oldest worker at our store, who had said, "This is my first home, not my second." I had last seen her a couple of weeks ago when I had dropped by the store. I had stopped at the jewelry counter, but Diamonds was nowhere to be seen. Then I had gone up the escalator to coats, intending to say hello. There were only two customers in the department when I got there—and only two workers: Ed, talking to one of the customers, and, all alone behind the cashier booth, that old nemesis of mine, that old tiger, the woman with all the authority, Alice. Whether she was there because of a drastic

101

cutback in staff or because of a rash of colds among the part-time help, I didn't stop to find out. For some reason, I couldn't bear to talk to her.

Instead, I went back down to the second floor to see Margie in books and records. She was ringing up a couple of albums for a redheaded boy in dungarees and she was full of her usual cheer. "These look very good," she said to him and then she smiled as she saw me coming. "Hi, what you been doing? I've missed seeing you around," she said.

I told her about the book I was trying to write and she said, "Good, make sure you tell your readers how much I have enjoyed meeting them at the store and helping them. Tell them to come back and see me."

I told her I certainly would, but she should also know that I was going to write about all the problems I had observed, about the generally awful supervision, the absurdly low wages, the unequal opportunities for men and women, particularly for black women, the senseless rule about having to stand all day (which later I would learn was illegal). Margie gave what seemed at the moment an odd answer: "Good, do that, it's important to say that. But you know you also should try working here again sometime. It's hard at first, like you say, but you'll find you'll get used to it after a while—it'll become a home to you, too."

Then we said goodbye—she had to wait on another customer. And I went home and called Peggy to try to arrange a reunion with Lillian and Marlene that we had talked about before. It was now over three months since all three had left the store and not one had yet found another job.

4

Waitress

Ingrid was an accomplished waitress and after fourteen years on the job she had the biceps to prove it. Otherwise slender, skinny really, she could carry five food-laden plates on one outstretched arm, three on the other, take on an entire dining room alone if she had to. She was equally adept at jammed, hectic, fast turnover lunches ("Five minutes, miss, and I *gotta* be back at the office"), gracious leisurely dinners ("May we see the wine list, please?"), banquets and parties. Introduced to me by a mutual friend, she was my initial guide to the world of waitressing, my mentor as I talked with her and others in the occupation.

She was in her thirties, lived alone in a rent-controlled apartment in Manhattan's east fifties. Two rooms on the top floor of a fifth-floor walkup. On the walls were bright prints and tapestries collected from the trips (California, New Orleans, her native Germany) she saved for and took almost every summer. On her desk, papers and books for the courses she was now taking at college as well. Sometimes she would study before going to bed, sometimes first thing in the morning. Then at ten minutes to eleven she'd stop; lock the double lock on her front door; start down the stairs; step into the city block of all city blocks she had ironically found to live on: a block full of restaurants.

From one end to another of Ingrid's block, counting both sides of the narrow side street, were eleven different food establishments . . . offering four different national cuisines: French (five of them); Italian (three); Spanish (one); Chinese (one); and American Fast Food (a burger snack bar on the corner). Ingrid would walk up her street, passing them all. Had she wanted a job on the block where she lived, the snack bar would have been her only bet. All the others had a waiters-only policy.

She would turn left at the corner. Fact was, so I had learned, in Ingrid's immediate area, the heart of Manhattan's most expensive restaurant district, there were only a relative handful of "tablecloth restaurants" that hired women for anything but hat-checking. At the same time further uptown and downtown, farther west and east, throughout the other boroughs and for that matter, in most of the less expensive restaurants and coffee shops and diners everywhere in the nation, the overwhelming majority of those serving food were women. Indeed only one out of ten in the occupation were male. But as the U.S. Department of Labor points out in its *Occupational Outlook Handbook* (1972–73 edition), without pausing to comment on the flagrant discrimination implied: "Jobs for waiters tended to be concentrated in those restaurants, hotel dining rooms, private clubs and other establishments where meal service was formal." And wages and tips the highest.

Ingrid would keep walking. Sex discrimination was not an issue that concerned her. At least when we first met. She never thought about it. She had her own job. True, it wasn't at a restaurant quite so high priced and elegant as those on her block, it was in the moderate category, but it did a smash business, at least at lunch, and in economic times like these Ingrid believed that was what mattered most. She had been there eight years, was reasonably content. When she wasn't tired out. When Tony left her alone. Furthermore she was going to college now, didn't expect to be in the business that much longer. Although naturally you never knew.

She would continue down the avenue—the fact that her job was within walking distance was another important factor to remember—"Imagine all the carfare and time I save"—and as she went along she would frequently meet up with one of the other waitresses or bartenders on their way in, too. Except for Tony and the kitchen crew who all got started much earlier, everyone on the lunch shift was due in at eleven.

She would enter a building painted red and brown. How to describe it further? Inside the decor was supposed to convey the mood of a romantic English inn. Deep reds, raw woods, electric candles softly glowing. A long mahogany bar. Beams. A lunch menu that could hardly have been more varied: from hamburgers to chicken curry, corned beef to escargot, filet of sole to beef and kidney pie, a hundred items for Ingrid and the other waitresses to remember. A seating capacity that was large, over 180 easily; yet during lunch there were almost always people sitting at the bar, waiting for tables; the place was that popular. At dinner, however, at least during the last two years, it was often half empty.

But probably the most important feature about the restaurant, from Ingrid's and the other waitresses' point of view, was the fact that it was built on two levels. The bar was on the main floor, the kitchen on the floor below, and there were dining areas on both. That meant that as a waitress you were doomed either way. If you worked on the main level you had to descend the stairs to the kitchen and then climb back up with your heavy and unwieldy food orders—as much as you could collect on each trip—down and up throughout the course of the meal. Working downstairs near the kitchen was somewhat less strenuous, but you still had to go upstairs to the bar for your drinks and to get the customers' change (one of the bartenders handled the cash) and to use the credit card machine . . . and then back down again. There were nineteen steps on that flight of stairs. Ingrid, who worked on the upstairs level, estimated she went down and up, down and up them a minimum of sixty times during an ordinary lunch.

The first time was immediately upon arriving at the restaurant.

Next to the kitchen was a tiny cubicle where the waitresses changed into their uniforms. Once I had asked Ingrid: what of all things about your job would you most like to see altered? More fringe benefits? Higher tips? A lobotomy for Tony? Ingrid had answered immediately: "A hole in the wall of my own." Instead of a locker, let alone a locker room, each waitress was lucky to find a vacant hook on which to hang her clothes, and this fact rankled Ingrid, slow to anger about everything else, constantly. "Did you ever complain to Tony?" I asked. "Oh, you know, a lot of good that would do." Since the cubicle was too small for more than two waitresses to change at once, Ingrid would wait on line for her turn. Then she would step in cautiously, being careful not to trip on the cans of floor wax and boxes of Brillo pads that were stacked on the floor—the cubicle doubled as a storage space for cleaning supplies. She would hurry out of her clothes.

The current uniform was simple: any white top, short black skirt of your own, plus a black standard waiter's apron with the all-around slit pocket for your tips. This was the fourth uniform Tony had devised for them in the eight years since Ingrid arrived, and was definitely her favorite. The worst had been a leatherette mini outfit which literally dripped with sweat by the time you were finished serving, was still damp when you were ready to put it back on the next day. After wearing it for a month Ingrid and another waitress had had a close call with pleurisy.

Then Tony had decided on tight red nylon dresses that barely covered your behind when new, were so cheap they shrunk two sizes after the first wash. Luckily they had only lasted about two months before starting to shred and fall apart. His next inspiration: The Sweet but Sexy Milkmaid, featuring a skirt with a cummerbund so tight it constricted you while serving and a blouse with long flowing white sleeves that invariably found their way into the chicken curry and beef gravy. In desperation at that point, Tony had conceived of the bring-your-own white and black combination, his finest idea, Ingrid believed.

She would change, place her street clothes on a hook, fully expecting that with all the traffic running in and out, they'd be lying on the floor next to the floor wax and Brillo pads by the time she returned.

Once in uniform, it was time to set up the tables. Red cotton tablecloths for dinner, but now for lunch red plastic. Red cotton
napkins for dinner but now red paper. For each table setting: silverware, a glass, a butter dish. For each table as a whole an ash-
tray, salt and pepper, and at lunch, sugar and a bottle of ketchup.
If all the other waitresses were in on time—there were eight on
duty for lunch—you could be through setting up in twenty minutes flat.

That would leave another fifteen minutes or so to grab a bite to
eat—coffee and a roll usually, something you could take yourself
without disturbing the cooks who were still preparing the day's
specials. Later, after the lunch crowd left, you'd have something
more substantial. The fringe benefits of your job.

Ingrid would take her snack over to a table in the back where
some of the other workers were sitting and eating. Usually at this
point Tony was away at his own midtown apartment, shaving and
changing for his maitre d' role, and this was a time you could relax. Gab and gather energy for the impending onslaught. A fairly
typical conversation (based on several I heard):

Arnie (younger bartender, a student): How'd you make out
yesterday, Joe?

Joey (older bartender, former construction worker): So good
you wouldn't believe it. Hit it in the fourth.

Arnie: Damn! I knew I should have bet something, too. Say (to
a waitress with long blonde hair, about twenty), you're new here,
aren't you? What's your name?

Lisa: Lisa.

Frank (busboy): Hey, Ingrid, you promised you'd help get my
wife a birthday present.

Arnie: Leeeeesa. Leeesssah. Always liked that name. Nice to
make your acquaintance, I'm Arnie.

Ingrid: Give me five dollars, I'll pick her up some sexy cologne
tonight.

Lisa: Nice meeting you too, Arnie.

Ella (waitress): How late you work last night, Maureen?

Arnie: I hope you'll like it here.

Maureen (waitress): Took the tablecloths off at eleven. Lousy
night.

107

Joey: Anyone know what kind of a mood Tony's in today?
Frank: I only talked to him a minute. Not so hot, man, if you ask me.
Lisa: Thanks, Arnie, I'm sure I will.

Not counting Tony, this was generally the friendliest, most cooperative group of workers Ingrid had ever encountered. Counting Tony there were fifteen on duty for lunch, including, in pecking order: one owner-maitre d'; one head cook; two bartenders; one shortorder cook; the eight waitresses; one busboy; one dishwasher.

And in typical restaurant fashion, the jobs were segregated not only by sex but also by race and by age. Any kind of discrimination you happen to be interested in, you could find.

All the employees were male, except the waitresses.

All those dealing directly with the public—bartenders, waitresses, Tony—were white. "Tony hire a black waitress? You have to be kidding."

All the waitresses were fairly young (Ingrid was the second oldest); the large majority were in their early twenties.

The two workers lowest on the totem pole—the busboy (busperson?) and the dishwasher—were nonwhite. (Frank, the busboy, by the way, didn't actually bus tables; the waitresses cleared as well as set up their own, carrying the dirty dishes and glasses to a table near the stairway. Frank would then carry the dishes in trays down to the kitchen.)

With the exception of the shortorder cook, who had started out as a dishwasher and was then trained and promoted by Tony, job advancement was unheard of. Everyone remained at the same level on which she or he had entered. And, as usual, the lower the job level, the higher the turnover (whether by firing or quitting). So although the head bartender and the cooks were all there eight years ago when Ingrid began, there had been a constant stream of new busboys and dishwashers, and that had also been true of about half the waitresses. As is becoming the case in more and more offices and stores and other kinds of businesses, Tony had learned to cut costs by relying on a very small hard core of workers on whom he could always depend—then hiring and firing the rest, depending upon the latest fluctuations in business or merely on his whim. These waitresses were never officially labeled "temporary help," but for all practical purposes that's the way it ended up.

Ingrid divided the waitresses at Tony's into three categories:

1. "Life-long professional waitresses, a number of them first-generation Irish or like me from another country or from the middle west."

2. "College students or temporary middle-class dropout types."

3. "Would-be actresses or models here between possible engagements if they ever get them."

But of course there were overlaps. There was Ingrid, who had decided to go to college *after* years of waitressing. Or, more commonly, there were students and aspiring actresses and, what seemed the largest new trend, ex-office workers who, for one reason or another, continued to work as waitresses far longer than they had ever expected. In any case, the supply of candidates for the job seemed endless. Hardly a day would pass without one or two dropping by to ask Tony about openings. That was the main way you looked for work, not through the paper or an agency, but just by walking up and down the street, stopping and inquiring at those places that looked good to you or about which friends in the business had told you. Tony would look the applicants up and down, ask a few questions. About once a week, or so it seemed to Ingrid, he'd say fine, get yourself a white top, black skirt, be here at six Saturday night. Then half the time when the woman would return, there would be no station for her. Ingrid would watch, mouth open, while Tony told the waitress, who was carrying her new white and black outfit, that she must have made a mistake, he had never hired her.

After all these years, Ingrid could still not get used to him. If he had been simply all-tyrant, all-bully, it might have been easier, but he could also be incredibly kind, almost like a father. One day he would be telling Frank, the busboy, to get his fat dumb ass out of there, the next day he would be giving him a couple of his hardly worn expensive suits. Or he would be snapping at Ingrid for being as slow as the new girls (The new girls! There was no worse insult for a waitress as fine as Ingrid) but then when it turned out she had the flu, he'd sent Frank over to her apartment with hot soup and stew. Or another time when she was having bad headaches, he had referred her to his own doctor, a Park Avenue specialist whom she could never have afforded, and then paid the bill. But then, typically, a week later, after she had told him she had made other plans for Sunday night: "Either come in or forget about working here."

He didn't mean it, most of the time. When he would tell one of the waitresses (not Ingrid; he was more careful with her) to "move it, you dumb bitch," he would often be kidding and joking with her an hour later. He was abusive despite himself, Ingrid felt. He had this violent temper that he couldn't control. Partly she sympathized with him. Partly she was fond of him, charmed by him, appreciative of the special treatment she knew she received. But basically, she said, she despised him. "Because he knows he can afford to be a bastard except when he *feels* like being nice. And that's because if two of us leave today, he knows he can always find five tomorrow."

But, again, aside from Tony, Ingrid had never worked in a place where the workers got along so well. Even the cooks, so notoriously temperamental and coercive in other places, and Ingrid had known her share of those, were generally easy to work with here. Ingrid had several theories to explain the unusually good relations.

One had to do with the nature of restaurant work in general, the busyness of their place in particular. All the workers had to interact constantly to get their individual jobs done. Each relied on the other to give a good performance, and so it helped to be nice to each other. "The waitresses have to be nice to the bartenders because we need our drinks fast. The bartender has to be nice to us, because if our customers complain and it's his fault, Tony may blame him, too. The bartender cannot serve his own customers if the busboy ignores his pleas for more ice. The busboy relies on the dishwasher for fresh supplies for the waitresses. The waitress cannot serve her customers efficiently if the cook is slow or forgets part of her order. The cooks are the least dependent on others, but they have to be nice to the waitresses to get the secret drinks we bring them from the bar. The waitresses have to be nice to the busboy to get our dishes and glasses and silverware on time. We need each other too much to get on top of each other. We all know that if one section doesn't come through the whole system will fall apart like a house of cards."

Another factor promoting a sense of equality among the workers, even though there were different job levels and pay, was that—at least during the working hours—there was hardly any class distinction: "We all do manual work, we all have wet or dirty hands, we all labor to exhaustion."

Finally there was what Ingrid called the "We Against Him Factor." The fact that Tony's unpredictable temper could and frequently did unload on any one of them (sometimes it was simply a matter of who was closest) acted as a unifying force, with the number one question of the day: "How's his mood?"

At ten minutes to twelve he would arrive. Tall, dark (although starting to bald), athletic (although starting to spread). Somewhere between forty and fifty. Somewhere between dapper and flashy. The show—Ingrid likened the serving of the meal to a theatrical production—was about to begin. Frank would bring up the ice and the glasses. The bartenders would take their places behind the bar: Joey on one end, Arnie on the other. The waitresses would go to their stations. (Ingrid's was one of the largest: ten different tables—two four-seaters, eight deuces, a total of twenty-four seats in all.) Tony would take his place near the door, and welcome the customers as they began to trickle in. By twelve fifteen the place would be nearly filled.

They came from the advertising agencies and commercial art studios and public relations firms and insurance companies and banks nearby. Middle-level executives and high-level clericals. A crowd as mixed as the menu. Three-martinis-before-lunch tables. A hamburger-and-coffee-and-a-check tables. Regulars and strangers. Ingrid would begin with the standard: "Would you like a drink to start?" A menu for those who did not. Back and forth from table to table to table to table to table to table to table to table to table to table. Or from table to bar, where she would prepare the setups (get out the correct glasses from the sideboard adjoining the bar, pour in the club soda or the tonic or insert the olive or the lemon twist—wait for Joey to pour in the booze) then put the glasses on a tray, carry them back to the tables. Or down the stairs to the kitchen once she had a number of orders to call in to the cook in a voice that had grown louder and hoarser throughout the years. Then back up the steps, back to the tables, back to the bar, see the hands waving, back to the tables, back down the stairs, placing the new orders, picking up the old orders, back up the stairs, back to the tables, one table wanting more drinks, one table waiting to order, another getting this order, another wanting mayonnaise, another just arriving, see the hands waving, taking a drink order, taking a drink order, taking two chef salads, one halibut, one chicken curry, taking a hamburger, rare, back to the bar, getting the setups, other waitresses lined up waiting for Joey to pour, Tony all the time watching, making sure you're fast enough, why are those people waving?, down the stairs to the kitchen, placing the new orders, where is the chicken curry?, there shouldn't be french fries with this fish, hurry please or the people will think I've gone home, back up the stairs, delivering the orders, see the hands waving, writing out a check, taking a drink order, removing a menu, taking cash, getting change from Joey, back to the tables, delivering change, clearing a table, carrying the dirty dishes over to the busing tray, see the hands . . .

Forget the theatrical metaphor. A better one, Ingrid believed, was that of a fox hunt. "They don't kill you; they just keep you running, running until your tongue is hanging out and you are ready to drop, and in the meantime all they see is the plate in front of them, the glass in front of them—and if one is empty, then where the hell are you?"

But of course there were different kinds of tables, different kinds of attitudes. And throughout the years Ingrid had learned how to handle most of them.

The-I-Want-Service-Now-Or-Else Attitude: At first when she was a young beginner like Lisa she would get upset if she wasn't able to help everyone immediately. "I would feel miserable. I would apologize and apologize. I felt stupid and guilty, inefficient and ashamed." Then she came to a realization: "I have only two hands, two legs. I'm human, too. I'll do the best I can."

The Male Customers Who Look You Straight In The Breasts: "That happens, not every day but it certainly happens. And when

112

it does, I get—I don't get anything. Except polite, you wouldn't believe how icily polite I can get. I'll just say, 'Olive or twist in your martini?' And then usually they'll stop. Or they'll say, 'C'mon honey, relax.' 'Olive or twist?' I'll repeat. And then if they don't stop, I'll just walk away. If the man is really offensive, Tony will intervene if I ask him but that almost never happens and otherwise he kind of takes pride when the customers find us sexy."

Women with Women: "I hate to tell you this but among waitresses, women have a reputation for being the pickiest customers and the lousiest tippers, particularly older women. And then they'll spend a half hour with each other dividing up the check." Maybe, I countered, that's because they're not on expense accounts like a lot of your male customers and generally don't have as much money. "That's probably true. But I'm just telling you how a lot of waitresses feel."

One Man Sitting Alone: "Probably I like that least of all. They often want you to entertain them. But I'm not there to keep them company if they're lonely, I'm there to serve food as efficiently as possible. The worst thing a customer can say to me when I'm pouring water with one hand, and putting bread on the table with the other, is: 'Honey, why aren't you smiling?' I'll say, 'What will you have to drink?' 'Smile.' And I'm gone."

A Man and Woman Together: "Sometimes that can be hysterical. The man is trying to make a big impression on his date, see. Won't let her talk to me. She has to tell *him* what kind of dressing she wants on her salad and then he'll repeat it to me. Like I was deaf. Absurd. Or he'll ask her if she wants french fries with her escargot. I'll just stand there trying not to howl. But also a man on a date may try to impress her by leaving a bigger tip, so it's usually not a bad table to wait on."

The Pickers: "Someone asked for steak and kidney pie the other day, then asked me to remove the kidneys. Someone wanted mixed vegetables then wanted me to pick the lima beans out of them. On and on like that."

The Customers Who Understand: "They're the best, of course. They see what you're up against and don't ask for the impossible. We have a lot of them, too."

Her System: "I don't know if I can explain it. It's experience. When you start out you're totally confused all the time. Which one wanted the blue cheese dressing? Which asked for cinnamon on his rice pudding? And then one day all of a sudden it comes together. You look at his face and you see steak and kidney pie; you look at hers and there's the hamburger well done. Something clicks inside and you have it. Also of course it takes experience before you know how to carry all these plates on your arm. Some of the more experienced waitresses here look down on the young ones, are very hard on them, because they're not as fast as we are, but I don't feel that way. You're not born, after all, knowing how to do all the things we have to do. Some people say that what we do is unskilled work. All I can say is they should come work here at lunch time during the middle of the week and see how well they do."

How to Address A Waitress: "Except for the regulars who know my name, most people call me Miss. That's fine. Don't call me Ms. Also don't call me Waitress. I don't call you Customer or Eater. Miss is better. Or some people will just go *Psst,* like I'm a cat or a dog. *Psst.* Usually I'll keep them waiting when they do it. Or they'll say Honey or Sweetie or Cutie, that's even worse than Waitress or *Psst.* Except if a table is nice—they see you're busy, they understand—well, then, Honey is okay. It's how it's said and who says it."

And so the fox hunt would continue. "From noon until two you wouldn't know if you had a toothache, you're so busy." Up and down the stairs, back and forth from the tables to the bar, taking orders, calling in orders, picking up orders, serving tables, clearing tables, setting up tables, writing checks . . . and then at last it's almost over, it's two o'clock. The place is half empty. No need to rush now, no more chaos in the kitchen. Two fifteen. Thinning out more. You can see the relief in the eyes of the new waitresses who had earlier seemed overwhelmed. Two forty. Nearly empty. Tony takes the money from the cash register, leaves for the bank. One waitress—the only one working a full uninterrupted day—stays on the floor, taking care of the few remaining customers. The others retire to a table in the back to learn how much they have made. Forget the fox hunt. The image now is after-the-poker-game.

In most restaurants where Ingrid worked before, they didn't pool their tips, but here they do. Ingrid's attitude: "Pooling is really more of an advantage to Tony than to us. It means you work together more, you help out at someone else's station if she's busy, which is something you'd never do if you're working just for your own tips. The disadvantage to us is when there are new girls, and here there usually are, you have to carry their burden. I'll do two girls' work and come home with the wages of one. So it all depends on where you are. If I'm working with all experienced girls, I might prefer to pool, but here it's not fair. In general, though, I do think it's better to pool. There's less envy, less rivalry between the waitresses."

So they then sit around the table, removing the dollars and coins and charge receipts (Joey would reimburse them for the amount of the tips written in) from the pockets of their black aprons. And count. Another day, another one, two, how many dollars? "A good day is about twenty-five. Remember, that's for only four hours work. A bad day is eight or nine, but that doesn't happen too often. Usually, it's between fifteen and twenty." The longer dinner shift, when more expensive food is served, is traditionally more lucrative but with business so erratic lately it's hard to say how much more. "The six to twelve shift is usually the best here, because you have the cocktail hour and that's the easiest money since you don't have to run down to the kitchen. I used to average between thirty-five and fifty dollars a night when I worked the long night shift from six to two."

In addition to her tips, Ingrid and the other waitresses receive a weekly pay check, in which they get the minimum hourly wage minus something called a "tip allowance" that Tony is allowed to deduct. "The check is something I really never think about. It's just a little extra. Maybe thirty dollars a week, when I work thirty hours, after everything's taken out. The real money is in the tips."

Another extra is the meal which Ingrid and the other workers get to eat after distributing their tips. To Tony's credit, give the bastard his due, his restaurant is "one of the most liberal places

I've ever worked, regarding food for the workers. A lot of places a hamburger is a lot. They'll even make you pay for a Coke. But here the chef usually lets us have anything we want on the menu that's under four dollars. Unless it's something scarce. Every day he'll scream out something we can't have. *No bacon for the help! No tomatoes!* Or whatever is really costly, like steak or shrimp; only the bartenders and cook are allowed to have those. But there are ways we can get around even those rules."

Ingrid's favorite way: *the-napkin-over-the-food-gambit.* "What you do—this is the old standby—is very simple. During lunch you order a steak, for one of your customers presumably, and then you hide it someplace, covering it with a napkin. (In most places you can't get away with this, because you have a numbered check with a carbon duplicate you have to give the cook when you place your order, and later the bookkeeper makes her living by going through all the dupes and comparing them against all the checks that were paid for. But at our place we don't bother with dupes at lunch, only at dinner.) So what you do is hide the steak and later when you're ready to eat, you take the plate to a table way in the back, keeping your napkin handy just in case Tony should come over and you have to immediately cover it again. I can't tell you the number of times we've had plates landing up in each other's lap when he's come in and surprised us.

"Or sometimes at night the customer will leave part of a filet mignon or prime ribs—they've stuffed themselves earlier on hors d'ouevres—and we're not above putting that under our napkins. Usually the best way there is is to also order something you're allowed to eat, like the day's special or a hamburger say, and then put the filet under that. No one can tell what you're eating. Or then there's shrimp. That's easier because we make the shrimp cocktails for the customers ourselves, that's part of our job, so if we want shrimp the way to do it is take our own all-lettuce salad and put it over the shrimp. Or booze. Since we use yellow tinted glasses the bartender can put scotch in our glass—he's very good about that—and Tony never knows what's in it. The only trouble with all of this is you have to do all that hiding, gulping down your steak and scotch, so usually I'll just sit down with the others and have something we're allowed to have without worrying about his finding out.''

Again it's a time for talking, flirting, comparing notes. Treating each other as people again, not role functions. Arnie resumes his conversation with Lisa. Joey goes to the phone to check the day's races. Frank gives Ingrid five dollars, tells her not to forget to buy the cologne. Ingrid says she won't, she's on her way. She gets up. She goes down the stairs. She changes back into her street clothes, mutters for the thousandth time about the absence of a real locker room, leaves the restaurant, twenty dollars richer than she was a few hours ago. "And the best thing about it is that it's instant pay, you go home with it that very day." Outside the sun is shining. It's 3:20. Almost half a day left to live.

II

"Sure I'd like to meet her," Ingrid said late one afternoon. We were in her apartment and I had just told her about Jeanne King who, along with another waitress, had filed discrimination charges through the American Civil Liberties Union against eleven of the most expensive restaurants in New York, plus Local One of the Hotel and Restaurant Employees Union, after becoming "fed up with the outrageous discrimination against women in first-class dining rooms." Ingrid said, "I'd be glad to meet her, but you have to remember I'm not your typical waitress."

I nodded. Ingrid was sitting across from me in a low slung canvas chair, tracing with one finger the varicose vein that had begun to develop on her long slender leg this year and was now spreading all the way up to her thigh. She looked tired, thinner than usual. In addition to her college studies, she had been working double shifts seven days a week for the past month and a half so that she would have enough money for another trip to Europe this summer. She was exhausted, but she had done very well. In two weeks she would be off.

She was right, of course. She was not typical. Her life had been a series of nothing but the most untypical experiences. Born to the sound of bombs in war-time Germany. A father presumed shot and dead. A mother and a sister with whom she escaped

117

when the Russians came to occupy the remote town she lived in. A year of incidents terrifying to a child, and then surrender, peace, a reunion with her father, a resumption of ordinary life. School. Dates. The idea of becoming a teacher, the decision against it. Traveling alone through Europe, supporting herself as a waitress. Saving money to come to America, no not America, California. Settling in San Francisco. Waiting for the green card to arrive, the official work permit, in the meantime being able to make only the shakiest of arrangements with the seamiest of restaurant owners. Or so they seemed. One of the most memorable was the one who made her check in three times a day at the beginning of each shift—as if she were an actress, a stand-in for the leading lady, except without the pay—to see if any stations were open. Perhaps twice a week there would be, but if she ever failed to check in, she was told her stand-in job would be over.

The green card finally arriving. Working legally at different restaurants. Deciding to come to New York. Finding her apartment. Canvasing the neighborhood for money-making restaurants within walking distance that hired women. Working at two of them—a fish restaurant and a tea room—before getting the job at Tony's. Staying there. Getting involved, uninvolved, with different men. Traveling in the summer. Getting older. Deciding to go to college, although for what purpose she was not sure. What will you do when you graduate? I asked Ingrid the first time we met. "I really don't know. I don't want to teach, and I absolutely don't want to be trapped in any office all day. Maybe I'll go on for my master's." And then what? "Not sure. Maybe, with the way the job market looks, I'll be a waitress with a master's."

No, she was certainly not typical. But then who was? By now I had spent time with a number of waitresses working in very different kinds of places. Could any one be called typical?

There had been Edna, whose ties to the restaurant where she worked were as long and as deep as her ties to America. Longer. The restaurant was Schrafft's and she had started working there over thirty years ago, only weeks after arriving from Ireland—but she had heard of it even before. In those days there used to be a joke that the Schrafft's personnel manager came to meet all the boats from Dublin, since so many of the waitresses who were hired were Irish (even though Frank Shattuck, the original founder in 1906, was not). But the truth seemed simply to be that certain Irish waitresses got there first and then told their relatives and friends back home who told their relatives and friends who told their relatives and friends. Among them, Edna.

At the same time as Schrafft's was gaining its reputation as a good place for an Irish woman to work, it was also becoming known as a respectable place for an older woman to have dinner alone, perhaps partaking of a little sherry or, later, a quiet martini or two or three as well. "The little old lady's restaurant" it began to be called, even though there was always an ample supply of little old men, not to mention people of all ages and sizes and shapes. But the label stuck, bolstered by the reality of the women with the blue-gray hair who did come in alone day after day, usually at about five, expecting always to sit at the very same table and to be served by the very same waitress. Edna and the others would often be treated by these women as if they were their personal servants. "Where's my maid?" the women had been known to call out, and the maidlike uniforms and aprons that the waitresses had to wear reinforced that image. Compensation would often come at Christmas in the form of special presents and tips ("For Edna from Mrs. Halliday") and there were always rumors about which waitress had just been written into which customer's will.

Edna's day at Schrafft's years ago would begin with inspection and instruction. She and her co-workers would first have to line up to show the manager: fingernails that were spotless, shoes that were immaculate, and, after slowly turning around, apron bows that were perfectly, symmetrically tied. Instruction would consist of a recitation by the manager of the day's specials, which he would read from the menu. Then the menu would be snapped shut, the question period begun. *Edna, what is the soup du jour and how much does it cost?* Edna would flinch if she didn't remember. *And how much is pie à la mode?* Edna mortified if she couldn't answer. *And the day's special?* So: constant pressure to listen and learn. Also: frequent lessons in . . . Suggestive Selling. *Would you care for a drink before lunch, Madam? A scoop of ice cream with your apple pie?* And when liquor sales were down there would be special pep talks, combined sometimes with contests offering prizes (theater tickets, candy) to the waitresses who could push the most booze in a given month.

Whether concerning how Edna set up the tables or took supplies from the kitchen or spoke to her customers, there seemed to be always an infinite number of infantile rules and regulations for her to follow. At the same time, way before the restaurant was unionized, Schrafft's had what was undoubtedly one of the best employee health and pension plans of any nonunion restaurant, admittedly not the hardest record to achieve since most had none. In addition, according to Mary Sullivan, who worked her way up from file clerk to assistant treasurer of Schrafft's, there was always a promote-from-within policy, which meant a promote-women policy since about three-fourths of all employees were female. By 1950 women were holding many of the key jobs—planning menus, supervising kitchens, managing about half the restaurants, a situation almost unheard of anywhere else. But then things began to change. Back from the war, new male blood was taking over, full of plans for a great expansion—branches across the country, hotels and motels as well—grandiose plans which apparently led to the company's recent demise. During the 1950s Schrafft's waitresses were organized for the first time—previous union drives had consistently failed—and Edna's benefits were increased somewhat. In 1968, with the expansion in full force—branches in California and Delaware, several motels in Florida, 30 restaurants in the New York area alone—there was a merger with the Pet Food Company. Six years later, overinvested, underpatronized Schrafft's went under. A new company, the National Restaurant Corporation, bought out a number of the New York branches, converting most of them into entirely different kinds of restaurants. Although there was ostensibly an understanding with the union, Local 45, that most of the former waitresses would be retained, all the new-style restaurants employ either women thirty to forty years younger than Edna or, typically, in several of the more expensive places, they employ only men. Whether out of lack of power or lack of concern, the union is not protesting. When I asked union official Al Specht, why, he shrugged, said the new company was impossible to deal with. Edna is one of the survivors because the restaurant where she works is one of the very few that is continuing to carry on the Schrafft's name and motif and personnel, although it is also under the new ownership. Understandably she and the other waitresses are extremely worried about their future.

Years and years ago, soon after starting at Schrafft's, Edna married and had two children. She then proceeded to follow a familiar work pattern among waitresses—a pattern which is itself a major reason why many women become waitresses. She was able to adjust and change her work schedule according to the needs and ages of her children, something which almost no other job would have permitted her to do. When the kids were tiny, she worked the dinner shift while her husband took care of them at home. When they started school, she worked breakfasts and then lunches, arriving home just before they did. Today her son is an engineer, her daughter a suburban homemaker, her husband is no longer alive. Although she doesn't have to, she now works the longest hours of all, a full eight-hour day. As with Margie at the store and so many other older women I met, she is not ready to retire. Her co-workers ("There's probably over one hundred years of Schrafft's represented on the lunch shift alone") and her customers ("Some aren't very nice, but some are wonderful") are her major social world. And it seems senseless to Edna that at a time when her family responsibilities have come to an end ("Earlier I could have used the time off") her job responsibilities are threatening to come to an end, too.

Then there had been Connie, energetic, petite, in her twenties, Chinese, a former clerk-typist. One night about a year ago on her way home from work, she had stopped at a burger-and-ale restaurant (one of the newly reconverted Schrafft's) for a snack. Sat down and ordered a cheeseburger and coffee. The young woman who waited on her seemed very friendly, about her own age. As she ate, Connie watched her and the other waitresses, a number of whom were also Oriental. It had been a tense day at the office, another reprimand from her supervisor, another warning about making too much noise. Here everyone seemed totally relaxed. The restaurant wasn't busy and the waitresses were talking with each other, laughing. They seemed to be having a good time. Not taking everything so seriously, portentously, the way they did at her office. Connie thought, why I could do this, too.

The next day she went in to apply, and a week later was a waitress-in-training. And while her parents were shocked and disturbed that she'd prefer waitressing to a "nice, clean office job," she found: "I loved it. I loved it most of all because I think the people you work with in restaurants are different from the ones in offices, they're more real or something, they're not so uptight. They have other interests besides their job, and I'm not the kind that thinks you should put your whole life into your work." She made good friends with many of the waitresses, and found, as Ingrid had, a spirit of cooperation among the women that she had never seen in all the offices she had worked in since graduating from high school. The only thing she minded at first was the absurd uniform she was required to wear. Little Bo-Peep in sneakers.

The job itself was far easier than Ingrid's. For one thing the room was much smaller, everything was on the same level. For another, the menu was much simpler, mainly an assortment of different kinds of hamburgers. In fact, she told me (as if to underline the old cliché that everything in life is relative): "Sometimes since I've been here I don't really feel like I'm working. It's too pleasant." Her mother and father worked in a laundry and "I guess I grew up with the concept that work was something really backbreaking, you know, sweating and straining, and here compared to that, it's really easy money." When she figured out the money she was saving by not having to buy clothes for the office, or lunches, or pay as high taxes, she was coming out ahead of her previous $110 gross a week.

But six months after we met Connie quit. The money was no longer easy. The manager had been instructed to hire more waitresses to increase the pace of service, and as a result Connie's tips were cut practically in half, hardly enough to live on. Again no fight from the union. Married by then to a hospital attendant also out of work, Connie and her husband decided to leave New York, look for jobs elsewhere.

And there had been Joan, the one who probably came closest physically to the old Hollywood stereotype of a waitress. Tall, blonde, willowy, divorced, forty-plus and the mother of four, she had worked in almost every conceivable kind of place since starting out in her native Kentucky at age sixteen. Her mother had been a waitress all her life, too (her father was a truck driver), but Joan had never planned to follow in her footsteps. She always thought she was waitressing just-for-the-time-being, and so in contrast to her mother, who had recently retired with the modest union pension she had always counted on, Joan had mostly avoided union jobs. "Why should I pay all those dues? I won't be doing this much longer."

Her first job: a carhop at a drive-in movie. Then a cocktail waitress at a local bar. Through a friend she found a better spot at the airport cocktail lounge (the only time she ever joined a union). Through another she found work serving at banquets where she was trained in formal silver service, a lucrative job typically reserved for men. Then one day she decided to try New York. She arrived on a Greyhound bus with sixty-two dollars: "I don't know where I got the courage." A week later she was spending the day as a switchboard operator in a small brokerage house ("It wasn't bad, they gave me a lot of responsibility") and the weekend as a cocktail waitress again ("The fastest, easiest money, no worries about food"). In between she was enjoying being young and single in New York. "I was having the best time of my life, going out with a lot of these wealthy businessmen I was meeting on my job—those were the years people had money and spent it—but I was also keeping up my contacts with the construction workers I was meeting in Astoria where I was living."

Several years later . . . "Because, I don't know, because he was sexy and I was stupid," she married one of the workers. And then immediately . . . "because he was Catholic and I was still stupid," had one child after the other. After which, like Edna, she regulated her waitressing hours to the ages and demands of her children.

123

In her case, though, she worked mainly at diners. "Diner work is probably the hardest. You usually have to do more cleaning than in other places, sometimes they make you do the floors, and you have to wear those ugly uniforms. But I did it, like a lot of women, because it was so close to home. You could leave and be home in ten minutes, and your kids could come by and see you." As Edna had, Joan worked nights when her children were babies, sometimes all through the night, while her husband stayed home "passed out usually, but at least he was there." Then when they were older she began working split shifts. "I'd go in in the morning, work until 2:30, go home, cook, be with the kids until I went back to work at six. So the split was a good deal for me, something you could never get at an office. Also, when you're on split, there's not so much cleanup—the full-time girls do that—so that was another good thing."

It was his drinking, she said, that led to the divorce. And afterwards the strain of the breakup, the worries about money and the children and the future, led to what she now thinks was probably a nervous breakdown. "I've always had a lot of stamina, but then I just couldn't work, couldn't get myself to move." Frightened, she went home to Kentucky to live with her mother for a while. Slowly she began to feel better. When she returned to New York she decided to look for work in Manhattan again, since she now needed more money than she could ever earn in the diner. "It was hard. After you work in the neighborhoods, at little places, it takes courage to come into the city restaurants, you'd be surprised. A lot of the waitresses I worked with would never try it, they're afraid. They just stay where they are." It was hard also because of the lack of good opportunities in the city for a woman Joan's age. She wanted to return to cocktail waitressing, she had always enjoyed that the most, but the cocktail lounges where she had once carried trays of drinks with one hand high above her shoulder, wearing the shortest of skirts, black mesh stockings, three-inch heels, were now either out of business or only interested in women under thirty. Determined, she continued to look and look, finally landed four nights a week at a dimly lighted spot with a four-dollar minimum and a tinkling piano and a reputation as a hangout for third-level Mafiosi. She was working there when we first met and also serving weekend brunches at a nearby restaurant, combining the two jobs on a schedule of forty hours in four days, ending at four in the morning, making good money, not minding the clientele at the lounge; in fact, some were the best tippers she had ever known. But seven months later she gave up the job. There had been a shooting, two men killed, and although she hadn't been on duty that night, it had unnerved her. Also she was finding the schedule exhausting, with all her household responsibilities, too. Also two of her kids had been acting up at school, the guidance counselor had suggested a psychologist, and, although she was holding on to her brunch job, she was beginning to think it might be better to find work in her neighborhood again, maybe even go back to the diner.

Diners and coffee shops, she told me, are "where waitresses often start out, where they work while they're raising their kids, and where they return to when they're too old to get the sexpot jobs." But if she was considering going back, she wasn't discouraged. There was a new man in her life, married but generous, and she had a feeling she wouldn't be working anywhere as a waitress much longer. Although "of course I said that twenty years ago."

Finally there had been Jeanne King, twenty-eight, the instigator of the ACLU suit. Like Ingrid, she lived alone in a small apartment on Manhattan's east side. Like Ingrid she had walked through the heart of the midtown restaurant district looking for work, passing one haute cuisine restaurant after another which refused to hire waitresses. Unlike Ingrid, she became incensed.

"Why not?" she had asked the ruffled French, Italian, "Continental" restaurateurs, who were not used to being questioned about their hiring policies. Because, they had answered: "Women don't want to work late hours"—an obvious falsehood to anyone who had followed the career patterns of waitresses such as Edna or Joan or Ingrid and the women they worked with.

Or: "Women are unable to do the hard work our waiters do or to lift heavy trays"—another joke to anyone who had watched Ingrid carrying those plates on her arm up and down those stairs, or had learned from Joan how one is *trained* to lift those heavy

125

silver trays in banquet work, or seen how at the most expensive restaurants, the bus staff do much of the heavy work. (Jeanne had also applied for busing work at these restaurants, and been consistently refused.)

Or: "Women can't fend off the amorous advances of men."

Or: "Women can't do French service."

Or: "We have no facilities here, no rest rooms or locker rooms, for women workers."

All of which could be translated, according to Jeanne and to ACLU lawyer Kathleen Wilert Peratis, very simply: "We don't want to hire women. Waiters are classier."

The daughter of a salesman and a secretary, Jeanne had "fallen into" waitressing ten years ago, after graduating from high school. In the years since, she had traveled across the country, worked at dozens of different types of restaurants (except those with a waiter-only policy), married, divorced, supported herself on her tips through college. It had taken almost ten years but she had finally gotten her BA just in time to join the ranks of the educated unemployed. She had once had notions of an "interesting job in communications," but her degree proved to be worthless for anything but a secretarial job, compared to which—both in terms of money and hours as well as atmosphere—she found waitressing infinitely preferable. Particularly if she could find work in the more lucrative places, places where it was common to find waiters earning over $20,000 a year, where they were treated with the utmost dignity, not forced into silly or sexual or servant-like uniforms. And so she had decided to fight. Was Jeanne typical of a new breed of waitress?

It seemed to me that, of course, she was not, Joan was not, Connie was not, Edna was not, Ingrid was not, nobody is ever truly a typical anything, hard as our educational and business and advertising worlds may try to make us that way. But what *was* typical was how they had been segregated into different kinds of restaurants depending upon their age and race, not to mention sex. What was typical was how their family responsibilities, those who were mothers, had shaped their work patterns and schedules. How the overriding need of so many for flexible hours had been a prime reason for getting into the field in the first place.

How the ever-depreciating value of a BA in the job market was forcing college women to enter the traditionally non-college occupations, making the competition even rougher for those with less education. How the end result as usual, with so many women vying for the better jobs, was that employers could and did treat them as the most easily replaceable parts.

"I agree you're not typical," I said to Ingrid that afternoon in her apartment. "Neither is Jeanne King nor the other women I've been meeting. But I have a feeling if the two of you get together, you'll find you have a hell of a lot of experiences in common. I'd like to hear your ideas about how things should be changed."

"Fine," Ingrid said. "Set the date."

III

Jeanne: I really wish everyone had a chance to be a waiter or waitress at least once. Because you can really see the difference when people come in between those who have the sophistication and those who have no concept of what we're up against.

Ingrid: Yes, the people who just see their plate or glass and nothing else. You're running around with your tongue down to your knees and they're waving at you madly and finally you get over to them, and you ask, would they like another round of drinks? Now, however, someone's telling a joke and they're all laughing and you have to ask three times before they hear you. Finally one orders a drink and you make a point of asking, "Anyone else?" No. Not right now. You come back with the drink, another one is ready to order. No, no one else. You come back, and then another wants one, and on and on like that. The place is packed and you have to make five trips for this table just to get their separate drinks. They don't even realize how much harder they're making things for you.

Jeanne: Yes, that's the main thing I'd tell people: Order as much as possible at the same time. You want cigarettes, Worcestershire sauce, onions, tell me ahead of time. Because when I'm busy and I'm called back for these things I could scream.

Louise: What about sexual harassment?

Ingrid: It depends on where you work. You get it more as a cocktail waitress, and I think I told you once I would not work at

127

a cocktail lounge. Because I don't want to be flirted with all the time. Other waitresses don't mind it, I didn't when I was younger, but now I get really sickened by it. At our place most of the regulars know I'm not interested in their proposals, but you do get some strangers, particularly those on conventions, who seem to assume right away because you're a waitress, you're a hooker. You know, they'll be asking you, honey, when do you get off? And to head them off I'll always tell them three in the morning and that I'm going directly home. That kind of thing; it's not even obscene, it's mainly stupid. But then there are some customers who are really nice, you see them all the time and they become your friends.

Jeanne: Oh yeah, they're such a variety. Some can be crude, look you up and down, but then they're crude when you're just walking down the street. It's a hassle with men everywhere. But my biggest gripes are not with the customers; they're with management.

Louise: Why don't you talk about that?

Jeanne: Well, there are the little things and the big. Sometimes the little things bother you most of all. Like you'll be waiting for lunch to start, hardly anyone is in yet, and two or three of you will be standing around talking, and the owner or manager will come over and start yelling: "Hey, get to your station, get to your station!" And it doesn't matter how experienced you are, they'll yell at you in front of everybody.

Ingrid: I could give you a hundred stories about that.

Jeanne: Also, if one of your customers compliments your service, you'll never hear about it. If somebody complains, however, the manager will walk up to you in front of five other people and say, what happened, you screwed up at that table. Oh God, there's no grace, no tact about it. But never a compliment. It's a twelve-year-old mentality; you'll spoil the kid if you say anything nice.

Ingrid: The yelling is so incredible, you'd think I'd be used to it by now. I've worked for this man eight years now. But I'm still shocked. It's not only with women; I've seen him do it to delivery men, old men in their sixties bringing in fresh bread. "Hurry up, you fucking dummy." Things like that.

Louise: Has anyone ever told him off?

Ingrid: I haven't heard it. Most of them know he never carries a grudge. But, as I said, it's the new girls who get it the worst.

Jeanne: I worked at a place once. It was so chaotic, you couldn't get anything for your customers. There was nothing available from the menu, nothing from the wine list, and I was going crazy cursing under my breath, and finally the owner got wind of it, and he came over to fire me. And after he did, he said, "If you don't mind my saying so, you walk like a slut." He put his hand on me at that point, and I said, "If you don't remove your hand I'm going to get you on assault." Then he told me he wasn't going to pay me. He said, "Didn't they tell you the first night is considered training?" And I told him I'd go to the labor board if he pulled that; so finally he came through. But I was so angry I was shaking.

Ingrid: I think we should also be talking about safety. As I said, at my place we have stairs. And often you're so hurried—you have so much in your hand, a dish tips a little, or the busboy is sloppy bringing down the glasses—there'll be water or oil on the stairs. Which of course is very dangerous. In fact, I'm always amazed that we don't have more accidents. Now I've seen girls go down—I've gone down myself several times, but never got anything more than a few bruises—and really hurt themselves. One girl had a concussion. Another broke her ankle. I remember that. We were serving a private party downstairs, and she was trying to balance a tray with five Irish coffees and a couple of Heinekens from the bar and she slipped going down the stairs. Now there was never a word from Tony about her being in pain. Or being out of work. All he talked about was this clumsy bitch, forty dollars on that tray down the drain. That was his only concern. And then when she was ready to come back he told her he couldn't use her anymore.

Louise: How much unemployment insurance would she . . .

Ingrid: I don't think we have that.

Louise: You have to. It's included in the deductions on your pay check.

Ingrid: Well, I never heard anyone go claim it, maybe a cook, but not a waitress.

Jeanne: It's not worth it when your official wages are $1.30 or $1.50 an hour.

Ingrid: Yeah, what would you get? Nothing.

Louise: Well, I don't think it's unimportant, particularly since you're both now working at nonunion places. Because practically the only restraint on nonunion employers from continually and arbitrarily firing their workers is that their unemployment taxes rise when employees are able to collect. But if waitresses don't file, then there's not even that small penalty.

Jeanne: That's true, I agree with that. Also, you know, I think the most obnoxious thing owners do is charge you for your mistakes.

Louise: In what way?

Jeanne: That, for instance, if you add up your check wrong, and the customer has paid too little, the owner will make you pay the difference. On the other hand, if you've charged too much, they of course don't give you that.

Ingrid: Oh yes, that's a common thing. I had something like that happen where for three months I got no pay check, just trying to pay it back. This had to do with a credit card though. The people hadn't signed the receipt and I ended up paying for the whole thing. You know what happens is, you run it through the machine, then you take it back to the table, and you don't want to stand there, it looks like you're waiting to see how much of a tip they're going to write in. Sometimes they just forget to sign it and you're stuck. I've since learned to get them to sign it first, before I go to the machine. However, there's still the problem of bad credit cards. You're supposed to look up every charge card in a special book that's got small print, like a phone directory, where all the bad or stolen cards are listed. Now you've seen what it's like where I work. My station is the most hectic in the house, and there are a lot of singles, which means a separate check for each one and a lot of charge cards. So there's just not the time to look up every card—because I get screamed at if I get behind on my tables while I'm searching for the bad numbers in the tiny print in the book. So I've gotten to the point where I don't look up anything under fifteen dollars anymore. But a lot of things can go wrong and do, and then you have to pay for it.

Jeanne: Then there are the places where there are a lot of walk-outs, and they make you pay for those, too, even though it usually happens when you're in the kitchen and couldn't possibly see them leaving or do anything about it. But still they make you pay.

Louise: That can't be legal.

Jeanne: Oh no, it's not legal. But it happens almost everywhere, and since it's such a hassle to fight the owner, you stay silent. If you want to protest, you have to go to the state labor board, and file statements and then go appear. I tried to do that once at a place where I knew I was getting paid less than the minimum, and when they also charged me for a mistake on a check I got furious. I called up the state labor board and they sent me a flyer listing all kinds of things I was entitled to, things I'd never heard about. For example, a laundry allowance for your uniform, I had never heard about that. And call-in pay. If they tell you to come in, and there's no work, they're supposed to pay for at least three hours even if they send you right home. Anyway I read the whole thing and the way it turned out I was owed at least thirty dollars. So I filled out all the papers and mailed them in with carbons of my checks, but they wrote me I'd have to appear at a hearing downtown which would have meant losing a day's work at the new place I was at, and maybe the job, too, so I let it go.

Ingrid: You're very unusual to go even that far. I don't know anyone else who's done it. Me, I guess I'm the kind that's inclined to say, well, it *was* my mistake on the check. They shouldn't take it out on me, but after all I did make the mistake.

Jeanne: It's your mistake, but in no other profession do they make you pay. . . .

Ingrid: I know, but that's the way I'm inclined to think. And I figure that it's going to be a big hassle or maybe I'll lose the job if I complain. And then I think about the good features about the job—it's close to where I live, the atmosphere is very friendly except for Tony's screaming; it's one of the most liberal places when it comes to getting food and even drinks. . . .

Louise: In other words they treat you like a person some of the time, and you're so grateful you don't complain when they—

Ingrid: I know. But wherever else I go, it's going to be the same thing.

131

Jeanne: Or worse.

Ingrid: Yes, so why not be quiet and stay there.

Jeanne: If I were you, I'd stay, but I'd also keep a list of everything I was paying out. And then when you have that big fight and leave, if you ever do, walk down to the Labor Board, and try to get what's coming. Meanwhile keep a record of everything, the dates, the amounts you paid out, everything.

Ingrid: Yes, I should.

Jeanne: Well, to me that's the shame of the tipping system. Because it puts you in the position where, first of all, the customer feels he's paying your salary so he can treat you any way he feels. And then the owner and the hostess and the bartender and the kitchen help—everyone's jealous of you when they see you picking up that money from the table. They all want a cut of it, they think you're so rich you can afford to give it to them. You know if you got $300 a week in a paycheck, it would be one thing. You worked for it, it's coming to you. But here, everyone thinks they should have a piece of it, too.

Ingrid: At our restaurant all the waitresses are expected to buy presents for the bartenders at Christmas, although they don't buy anything for us. And in addition each waitress gives the busboy one dollar from her tips each shift.

Jeanne: The usual arrangement—and the legal one—is that the busboy is entitled to a certain percentage of the tips, whatever the house says, usually about fifteen percent. But there's just this feeling of everyone else all the time—the bartenders, the cooks— that they should be getting a cut too, and they can make your life very difficult if they want.

Ingrid: They can really screw you up, you're so dependent on them.

Louise: If tipping creates these problems, would you prefer something like the European system, where a flat service charge of fifteen or twenty percent is added to the check? Would that make a difference?

Jeanne: Well, a service charge would still give you the same problem. Whether you're picking up cash from the table or from the cash register, everybody wants it. There's something different about it. And you spend it differently, too, than you would if you were getting the same amount in a check every week, at least I do. You never quite budget.

Louise: So would it be better overall if there was no tipping at all? It would mean that customers would have to spend more for the meal itself, maybe fifteen or twenty percent more, but then you could get paid a real salary, a decent salary.

Jeanne: I used to think that would be better. But I'm afraid that if that ever happened here management would wind up getting the biggest cut. The waitresses would lose out in the long run. The owner would be charging more, but we'd be earning less. They wouldn't pay us the difference. And management would have even more power over you than they do now.

Ingrid: I wouldn't go for salary either. Maybe it's in my mind, but I think I'm better off this way. But I would go along with a service charge. If it was a straight fifteen percent, it would work out to about what I make now. Twenty percent would definitely put me ahead. But no salary.

Louise: But aren't there nights when hardly anyone is there and you come home with practically nothing?

Ingrid: Sure, but then you have nights when you do incredibly well. It seems to average out.

Jeanne: Have you had months when business was so bad you had trouble paying the rent?

Ingrid: No, not quite. I do budget my money very carefully. And our place is pretty steady at lunch; it's dinner that's so erratic, but like I say it seems to even out, usually. Now maybe another reason I'm against a higher salary is that it would be taxed and I'd end up with a lot less.

Jeanne: That's why I'm for it.

Ingrid: Because, you see, most of what I make now is not taxed.

Jeanne: Well, you know, I'm against reporting $25 a week in tips when you make $125, because this way when you want unemployment compensation or social security you're not going to get enough. I'd rather pay the extra few dollars a week and be protected.

Ingrid: Extra few dollars! It would be so much more.

Jeanne: It wouldn't be that much, I don't think.

133

Louise: And as it is, as you said before, you're really stuck if you should ever get fired. Or sick. What would happen to you now for example if you couldn't work for some reason?

Ingrid: It's true, I have no protection. No sick leave, no unemployment benefits to speak of. Usually I don't think about it. But when I do get the flu or something, I do start to worry.

Louise: Maybe the best arrangement would be something like a salesperson's arrangment: a flat guarantee of so much a week that would have to be paid as a minimum.

Jeanne: Supposedly that's how the tip allowance is supposed to work. If your tips plus what he gives you don't bring you up to the minimum wage, he's supposed to give you the difference. But I've never seen anyone say, hey, you owe me eight dollars this week. I wouldn't do it.

Louise: Why not?

Jeanne: Well, again it's a hassle with management. And that gets you out of a job quick.

Ingrid: And it's not worth it, you feel, to lose a job for just a few dollars. Because then you'll have to go somewhere else and be the new girl, and in this business there's nothing worse than being the new girl. You're going to get the worst station in the place, the worst days and shifts, you're not going to be able to get the hours you want, like I can. So you don't stand up for your rights.

Louise: Maybe we should start talking about unions now. Because if your restaurant was organized, the union would be protecting your rights. Supposedly. And Tony couldn't hire and fire the way he does now. Supposedly. And you'd have a medical plan. And sick leave. And a pension.

Jeanne: Comes to about twenty dollars a week, that's all. I have friends at one restaurant and they finally retired after fifteen years in the union, and that's all they got in their pension. I guess I'm just not anxious to join.

Louise: Why not?

Jeanne: Because they're powerless. I worked at Schrafft's briefly about six years ago. It's probably not true, but I always felt that Schrafft's ran that union, the way it acted. They'd snatch the money out of your salary because it was a union shop, but when it came to really listening to your grievances, doing any-thing about them, they treated you like you were a silly stupid child. It was one of the worst places I ever worked, a thousand rules for everything. Most of the other waitresses were in their fifties and sixties, Irish immigrants mainly who'd been there for-ever but they were still afraid to complain, they took anything. It really had to be something horrendous for them to speak up, and then if they did the union representatives would say, well we'll see what we can do about it, dear, and that's the last you'd hear. They'd just try to appease you.

Ingrid: I thoroughly agree.

Jeanne: Yes, you know we've mentioned the union in our sex discrimination charges, too. Because a lot of restaurants will tell you, sorry, we only hire through the union and the union will only send the kind of people the owner says. And in the best places that means men.

Louise: I talked to a female labor official about the distrust of unions I'd heard from a number of waitresses. She said I should tell you that if the leaders aren't doing a good job you should come and join the union and kick them out. She said you have to realize that any union is better than none.

Jeanne: Well, I don't agree. I think it's a false security that way. Because if you've got a union that you think is helping you, and it's really dishing it out to you and sidling up to management, and you're *paying* them to do that? . . . well I'd rather have no union.

Louise: But she would say, don't forget about the medical in-surance and the fact that you can't be fired as arbitrarily or have your hours continually switched, the things Tony gets away with.

Jeanne: Well, I don't know. I've never stayed on a job that long, and I guess even though I've been doing it so long, I've nev-er really identified myself as a waitress. You can be in it for twenty years and still think it's a temporary thing.

Louise: I've heard that a lot. One woman I talked with is in her thirtieth year and she still refuses to join a union because she's sure she won't be working much longer. But by now she would have been entitled to benefits, too.

Jeanne: Maybe part of the reason some of us do that—you

know, look upon ourselves as *not really* waitresses—is because of the thing I object to about this job more than anything else. It's the way a lot of people look at you when you're off the job and you tell them you're a waitress.

Ingrid: Oh, yes.

Jeanne: They just give you this look. And I say, hey, what's the matter? I'm working. I'm making money. I'm making five, six dollars an hour and I'm working hours that are convenient to me. But, you know, people's snobbish ideas about what a waitress is.

Louise: Even here in New York where it seems half the budding actors and actresses are doing it?

Jeanne: Oh, yeah. Most people on the outside look down on you. Middle-class people, I'm talking about. You know, a couple of times I've told people I'm a waitress and they've said, far out. You'd actually stoop that low in some people's eyes because you know it's really a good deal moneywise, and you can arrange your hours and come and go as you want. And they appreciate that. But most people don't. They say, gee, when are you going to get a *job?* And I think that's one of the reasons waitressing is hard, because so many people look down on you for doing it. Or have this impression of you. When that guy called me a slut, I walked home and thought, Jesus, what am I doing it for and it took me all night to get over it and say to myself, oh come on Jeanne, you're doing honest work, there's nothing wrong with you, let's go get another job.

Ingrid: It can be very subtle. At parties for example. You'll meet someone and you'll be having this interesting conversation, and then he'll ask you what you do. I could say I'm going to school, but I don't. I say I'm a waitress. And then this funny thing happens. The whole tenor of the conversation will suddenly change, drop to another level, as if I'm too stupid to understand anything above the third grade. It's the class thing. I feel it. A lot of waitresses today go to school, many are far smarter than their customers. I think people ought to be careful with waitresses, you never know who you're getting. But there are also other people who admire you. Particularly if you can come up with the story about going to college or auditioning for a play.

Jeanne: Yeah, they love the student routine. They're getting tired of the actress bit, though, they think that's a cop out, you'll never make it.

Ingrid: But you know, at this point, I never volunteer about going to college. I just say I'm a waitress and wait to see what's going to happen. Because in a way I think it's rather amusing, I really do. Now maybe you think I should get angry about it, but you know I just think, who the hell are you to feel superior to me? You're sitting in some stuffy office all day and you suddenly think I'm less than you because I'm a waitress. Then disappear, if you feel that way. I don't want to know you.

Louise: I don't know if you saw the movie, *Alice Doesn't Live Here Anymore.* Well, it seems the producers of the movie, Warner Brothers, thought it would be terrific publicity if they could get waitresses to endorse the movie, tell how it authentically, sensitively depicted their lives. They invited a group of waitresses from the Hotel, Motel and Restaurant Employees Local in Michigan—where the International also is—to a private screening. But instead of the raves they expected, it turned out the waitresses were infuriated. In an article in the union newspaper they wrote that the movie did a "great disservice" to waitresses everywhere. They particularly pointed out a scene where Alice, recently widowed and unsuccessfully looking for a job as a singer, has to tell her son that she has been forced to take a job as a—and here she starts to cry—as a—the tears are really flowing now—as a *waitress.* The union women were furious at the suggestion that she had thereby sunk to the bottom of the barrel. They also resented the implication at the end that she had been saved "from this horrible fate" when she decided to marry a handsome young rancher. The article concluded with the point that waitresses, like all workers, have a right to dignity in their labor and pride in their profession. And that the union—again this is in Michigan, where until her recent death, the secretary-treasurer of the local was Myra Wolfgang, one of the very few women not only to go that high in a local but also to become vice-president of an International—that the union was dedicated to fighting for improved respect for waitresses as well as for improved security.

Ingrid: I agree with the point, although I kind of liked the movie. I thought the most unrealistic thing about it was that the owner of the diner was too nice. But to get back to unions, I'm beginning to feel a little better about them now. You know my biggest gripe about unions used to be that there were so many in the restaurant field, almost like they were little businesses themselves. And that if you joined one, like I did once, and paid the initiation fee, you'd find you were only eligible to work in a handful of restaurants, so if you got a new job the chances were you'd have to pay another union another initiation fee and on and on like that. But, Louise, you've told me that the unions are now starting to merge.

Louise: Yes, that's what I've heard. Apparently there are a number of merger movements underway. One is to get waiters and waitresses into the same union; in some cities they're still kept separate just the way they are in most restaurants. Another movement is to get different kinds of restaurants under the same union coverage. And a third movement is to get different crafts—bartending, waiting, and so on—under the same union aegis so that people can be trained and promoted within the union. And all that seems to be happening at different paces in different parts of the country.*

Ingrid: Well, if they would consolidate geographically, so you'd be covered in more than a tinv area—let's say at least on the Eastern seaboard—then I'd be ready to join.

Louise: You'd like to see an organizing drive at Tony's?

Ingrid: Yes. Absolutely. Let's get some power over that man.

Jeanne: And also if they stop the sex discrimination. If they would be willing to not only take your money but to also send you to the best places. You know, ideally, I love the idea of unions. Caesar Chavez, people like that. But in New York, no.

Louise: Again, I talked with Myra Wolfgang shortly before she died, and she said the biggest problem in her view was getting women like you to aspire to union leadership and to challenge the entrenched men. And as always a big part of the difficulty was that so many women were mothers, running back and forth from their jobs to the baby-sitter or the kitchen, with hardly any free

*On July 25, 1976 the *New York Times* announced an agreement between the Labor Department and the Justice Department to begin a major investigation of the internal management and financial affairs of the Hotel, Motel and Restaurant Employees and Bartenders International.

time for themselves, let alone for union politics. I'd wanted two other women I talked with to come today, but they were both busy with their families. But single women and older married woman do have more time.

Jeanne: I'd love to run a union.

Ingrid: You would?

Jeanne: Yeah, and come down on all those owners that have been dumping on me. Look out, gang.

Ingrid: Great.

Jeanne: And get rid of uniforms completely. I think they are really degrading. Everyone says, how are they going to know you're a waitress if you're not in uniform? Well, buddy, the ones carrying dishes out of the kitchen are waitresses. The ones handing you the menu are waitresses. How do you know who's the salesperson in a department store? You look around and figure it out. I think uniforms are a class discrimination kind of thing.

Ingrid: I like the way it is now at our place; you can wear any white top and black skirt of your own. And you wear it every day and so you don't have to spend a lot of money on clothes.

Jeanne: I just prefer that you can wear whatever you want. If you want to dress up and switch around, that's your prerogative. If you want to wear the same thing every day, that's your prerogative. That's one of the good things about working at the place I'm at now.

Louise: Tell us about that restaurant, Jeanne. I've been saving it for last because it seems to be a rare example of how different things can be when waitresses are treated with dignity.

Jeanne: Well, it's really a treat to work there. All the people who come in comment on it. I think there's a new breed of consciousness coming in among some of the younger people going into the restaurant business. They're not like the older managers. As I said we don't have to wear uniforms. There's never any of that get-to-your-station business. When we have our own meal we eat in the dining room like everyone else, we don't get shoved into the basement, and we can have whatever is on the menu, there are no restrictions at all. Also, if people we know come in for dinner we can sit at the table with them if we're not busy.

Ingrid: Really?

139

Jeanne: Yes, it's really an ideal place to work. The waiters and waitresses—we have both working there—switch among themselves. When you want a day off, you simply call another to cover; you don't have to go through the owners at all.

Louise: The workers manage themselves?

Jeanne: Yes, in many ways. I'm working there as a hostess now, not a waitress, but I'm only doing that until a waiting job opens up. Hostess sounds like a better job, people think it's better, but it really only pays three dollars an hour, and the waitresses are pulling in something like $50 or more a night. But as hostess I can see what's going on, and it's really a delight to work there.

Louise: What about the work load?

Jeanne: Well, it's a small place; they have one dishwasher and one person who does the odd jobs. But sometimes the waiters will have to sweep or do some kind of cleaning, and now and then they'll complain. But mainly they think, oh, big deal.

Louise: But in other places they'd really mind.

Jeanne: Oh sure. In places I've worked before I'd never sweep the floor; you know, they're supposed to hire someone for that. But this is a small place, they do favors for me, so I do it for them. It has to do with the whole atmosphere of respect and mutual working together.

Ingrid: Yes, it sounds like a great place to work. I know such places exist. But basically I think it partly has to do with the fact that they're not high-pressure places in terms of turnover.

Jeanne: Oh, you should see us some time. Particularly at Sunday brunches when people are lined up outside waiting to get in. It's hectic then, it's really insane, but there's still this friendly atmosphere.

Ingrid: But I'm talking about lunch now. Weekday lunches in midtown for time-pressed office people. You could never get that kind of relaxed atmosphere. In my place even if they would let you sit with the customers, you'd never have a free second to do it. In fact you don't even have time enough to wait on your people properly. Dinners are different, you can give more service, people have time to chat, but lunches what they mainly want is to get in and out. And that's what Tony is always screaming at us about.

Louise: What about wages and fringes compared to other places?

Jeanne: It's just about the same. Except, of course, you know he's not going to fire you for breaking a glass or any arbitrary thing. Like I said, the main difference is how we're treated.

Ingrid: Well, I'd be the last to say we shouldn't be treated better. But the pleasant places are definitely in the minority.

Louise: If you had a daughter would you advise her to do it—be a waitress?

Ingrid: I'd be afraid for her, I think. Not because of the work itself, and not because of the prestige, the class thing, but because if she's fairly young she might get hooked on it.

Jeanne: Yeah, I know what you mean. I'm a living example of that.

Ingrid: Let me explain. I've seen young kids coming in to work at our place for the summer. They've never had much money. They're amazed to find out how much they can make. They figure, well, I'll delay going to college or I'll drop out next term and save up a little more and then I'll go back. But they never do. There's one young girl at our place now, she's been with us for three years, she's forgotten all her other plans. She doesn't see a reason to go back to school. Now it may come to her years from now, like it came to me, that she's not getting anywhere, that she's still where she was when she started. And that she doesn't have the strength and energy she had then. But she's hooked.

Jeanne: Sometimes I wonder where I'd be now if I'd started off doing something else. You get hooked because of the money, and the fact you can do it whenever you need to. But I know guys who started out when I did, maybe in some crummy job like a messenger, and they were making much less than I, but then their jobs led to all kinds of other things, they've moved way up, and waitressing just sits there.

Ingrid: Most jobs for women just sit there.

Jeanne: Well, at least until we win the ACLU suit, I know I couldn't find a better place for me in this field. And I'd still much rather be doing it than working in a typical office job.

Ingrid: It's certainly much more essential work than they do in a lot of offices. Advertising junk and all that. At least we're really performing a service that's needed.

IV

Three weeks after our meeting, a postcard from Ingrid in Europe: *Recharging my batteries. New York seems so far away and almost unreal.* At the restaurant where she is hostessing, Jeanne is glowing. She will definitely get a waitressing job there in the fall and soon after that the ACLU suit should begin.* In Queens Joan is packing; because of her sons' school problems, she has decided to move further out on the Island, will be looking for a restaurant that will take her full-time. At Schrafft's Edna is pouring the—what could it possibly be?—one millionth cup of coffee since she started working here so many years ago. A thin elderly man takes a seat at a table nearby. Sends Edna a cold angry stare. Edna replaces the coffee urn on a serving table. Walks slowly over to the man.

"What can I do for you today?"

"I'm here to complain."

"Fine. You'd better see the management."

"The service here stinks."

"I suggest you write a letter."

The man's eyes glitter. A look of outright hate. Then, slowly, a smile. "How you doing today, Edna?"

"Not bad, Frank." She smiles, too. It is their daily routine. "What can I get you, the usual?"

*In November 1976 Jeanne King became the first woman ever to work as a waitress at New York's famed "21." The job was a direct result of the lawsuit she helped initiate.

5

Office Worker

The awards were about to be presented. The audience was sitting and waiting and tittering in the banquet room of the hotel. Up at the podium the master of ceremonies was explaining the procedures. There would be a different person to assist in handing out prizes for each of the categories to be honored today. In format, he suggested, it would be something like the Academy Awards. Then a hush. Shoulders in the audience hunched forward. A pause, a slip of paper . . . and . . . the audience burst into applause as the winner rose from her chair. She was slim and blonde and her cheeks were lightly flushed. She wore a pale blue blouse with a matching skirt that swung as she hurried to the podium. She smiled proudly as she accepted the award for filing in the annual competition of the office education program of the Chicago public schools.

"Filing! Oh what frauds," Vickie would say later when I told her about the school ceremony I attended. It was partly because of Vickie that I was staying in Chicago for a short while. She had offered to introduce me to a number of the clerical workers in the massive insurance company (or paperwork factory, as some termed it) where, until recently, she was employed. "An award for filing," Vickie repeated. "What a con job."

But Diane, one of her former co-workers and a graduate of a similar high school program, didn't agree. She said everyone needed recognition, including file clerks.

"But don't you see what a fake it is," Vickie protested. "The schools want these girls to think what they've been learning is really hot stuff, when they know damn well they're going to go out and get stuck in lousy no-money jobs."

Diane shook her head. "Not necessarily," she said. "That didn't happen to me. Hey, remember they're all just beginning."

"Beginning or ending?" muttered Vickie, who had quit her clerical job to enter college.

At the hotel the school ceremony had continued. Other categories, other winners, almost all of whom turned out to be female, which was not exactly a shock to anyone in the room since so were nearly all in the office education program. "We've tried to encourage more boys," a school official told me, "but most still think it's a sissy field, I'm afraid." (Although somehow in pre-typewriter times over a hundred years ago when the position of clerk carried its highest status and highest relative pay, almost all clerks were male. And somehow in those days such work was of-ten deemed—by the male clerks—to be "unsuitable" for wom-en.)

For typist, the emcee, who was also an official of the program, called out.

For accounting and general clerical . . . and a procession of young Chicago women, seventeen and eighteen years old, in party dresses and pant suits stepped up to the podium to receive their awards.

I stood in the back of the hall, listening as the applause got louder and louder. In a way it was like a sports event. The stu-dents—there were close to a thousand—were seated according to their individual high schools and each time a name was an-nounced the contingent from the winner's school would respond with the loudest yells and cheers. As if it were the big game of the season; as if for one day typing had replaced basketball, steno

144

had replaced softball in the traditional schedule of exciting school events. And so it had.

For stenography . . .

Except of course it wasn't a game, wasn't a sport. "These are mainly Terminal Students," the school official told me, apparently finding nothing wrong with that cheerful board of education label for those who would not be going on to college after high school graduation. Instead, in a matter of weeks they would be out in the full-time job market seeking to apply the clerical skills they were now celebrating. In doing so they would be joining what is today not only the largest occupational group of American women—that has been true ever since 1940, but what also as of 1970 became the largest occupational group of any in the country. (Prior to 1970 that distinction had gone to the catchall job title of "operative.")

For bookkeeping . . .

The statistics looked like this: In February 1976 there were fifteen and a half million Americans—repeat fifteen and a half million Americans—employed in Labor Department terminology as "clerical and kindred workers."* More than one-sixth of everyone with jobs at the time. One of the fastest-growing groups of workers for many years, the total was expected to climb to twenty million by 1985 when it would then probably represent one-fifth of the American labor force. Already more than one out of three of all employed women were so engaged. And if you concentrated on women who like the students in the banquet hall would graduate from high school but not from college (in short the vast majority of American women) then the ratio in clerical jobs would have been closer to one out of every two (47 percent of women with no college at all; 48 percent of those with one to three years). An astonishing one out of every two.**

Among female college graduates the proportion was far less but it was still a sizable one out of every six. And that figure

*U.S. Department of Labor, Employment and Earnings, March 1976 (Washington, D.C.).

**U.S. Department of Labor, 1975 Handbook on Women Workers (Washington, D.C.).

would have been higher, too, had it included all those who had taken positions with loftier titles, such as editorial assistant or broadcasting aide, only to find out they were doing essentially clerical work only. Of course such jobs could and many times did lead to other opportunities, that was the whole idea, but all too often as an editorial assistant (with a master's degree) at a major publishing house told me, "The only difference between my job and those who are called secretaries here is that the secretaries earn more money." (But to get either job in that office you now had to have a college degree.)

For dictaphone transcription . . .

Of all clerical workers, men accounted for less than one out of every four (22 percent), and, typically, when you compared the earnings of female and male clerical workers, women earned only 64 percent of what the men had. But these figures were a little deceptive too since in large part men were employed in non-office clerical positions (as postal clerks for example). Or, as in other primarily female fields, the men had somehow found their way to one of the most lucrative areas, in this case as court and conference stenographers where they were in the majority. Or they were working in "youth" jobs, as shipping and receiving clerks among others.

In the front office itself, despite the women's movement, despite well publicized exceptions here and there, the clerical labor force continued to be overwhelmingly female. Women still represented 97 percent of all receptionists, 99 percent of secretaries, 97 percent of typists, 88 percent of bookkeepers, 86 percent of file clerks and cashiers, 93 percent of keypunch operators. Although the numbers of male secretaries, stenographers, and typists had been rising recently (and once again men were substantially outearning women) the totals were still relatively too minuscule (82,000 men in February 1976 compared to four and a half million women*) to constitute a major new trend, especially since it was also a time when opportunities were so scarce in other kinds of work. However, what many women were fearing was

*U.S. Department of Labor, *Employment and Earnings*, March 1976 (Washington, D.C.).

that men would increasingly concentrate on getting those all-too-rare and coveted stepping-stone jobs, particularly in the communications fields. (And in fact another publisher told me the majority of secretarial candidates in his office in recent months had been male.)

But in most workplaces the only real change in the clerical labor force in the past decade had been in terms of race, not sex. Thanks in part to the impact of anti-discrimination laws, but in far larger part to the soaring demand for clerical help, the ratio of black women in office jobs had been growing every year. (As had the ratio of black females studying typing and other office skills in high school. At the banquet hall nearly half of the students were black.)

For keypunch . . .

But the rub was that the office jobs of the present were often quite different from those of their lily-white past. In 1940 (when less than 2 percent of black women held clerical jobs) everyone took it for granted that women in offices were earning more and yawning less than their counterparts on the assembly line. By 1970 (when the ratio was over 20 percent of black women and climbing fast) neither assumption could so easily be made. Just as white women had been recruited permanently into the office only when the invention of the typewriter freed male clerks for higher managerial roles, so minority women were entering in ever larger numbers at a time when new office technology was said to be making clerical jobs indistinguishable from those in the factory. And, moreover, when the pay for many factory jobs was now often far higher.

Indeed in offices all over the country clerical work was reputedly in a state of dramatic change. Corporations everywhere were said to be searching for ways to cut down on the mounting costs of paperwork, which often meant cutting down on the numbers of secretaries and other higher-paid clerical personnel. At the same time more and more office workers were beginning to see the need for unions for the first time. At least that's what I had been reading and hearing. How true it all was I didn't know. I wanted to learn more about the potential of clerical unions. But first through Vickie's introduction, I hoped to get a closer look at life at a major insurance company, one of the most typical ports of entry for a woman just out of school and also in this case, from what I had been told, an emerging example of the kind of clerical operation that *Business Week* and other management bibles were heralding as "the office of the future."

For cluster skills . . .

"And now the moment you have all been waiting for," the master of ceremonies intoned at the end of the ceremony as the last and highest award of them all, signifying excellence in a broad variety of clerical skills, was about to be bestowed. The prize was a bracelet with an engraved lamp-of-learning charm, and when the winning name was finally called the young women in the audience, the fledgling office workers, began to scream and stamp their feet with excitement. Shrieks of delight as the bracelet was presented. More shrieks, more applause, more cheers. "Now students," the school official said gravely, shedding his genial-emcee role for the day, "you really must contain yourselves."

The Company

The modern mid-American headquarters of a giant insurance company, forty stories high. A spacious, lavish lobby: pale granite walls, terrazzo floors, gold metal finish on the ceiling. A newsstand, shops. Over two dozen high-speed elevators to service the forty floors.

It was raining the first morning I was there and the Chicago wind was defending its reputation. Lowering their spastic umbrellas, men and women hurried out of the raw outdoors into the warm dry shelter of their place of work. Others entered the building more leisurely aboard a gleaming escalator that was carrying them up from the convenient subway station located two floors below. (Still others weren't due for another half hour as part of the company's new flexible-hours program.) *Workers' Paradise USA*, Vickie had sardonically called this place.

In the main the women walking through the lobby seemed quite young, in their late teens and in their twenties, although there were perhaps a third of older women too. In the main, as is notoriously common in insurance companies, the women were employed in clerical jobs and the men were not, although there was now, ostensibly, an affirmative action plan to advance more women into the higher paying positions, such as sales, underwriting, actuarial, and management.

They stepped into the elevator, pushed the square metal buttons for the floors where they worked. On one floor was the Transcription Center, a space-age version of the old typing pool where the very latest in automated self-editing typewriters (or word-processing machines) had just been replaced by an even newer model, once more with speedier and speedier results. On another floor was the Video Display Center, where other brand new machines with automated keyboards and TV screens were used to tap in policy transactions directly to computers located in still another part of the building. In the Computer Division itself several shifts worked around the clock as trillions of numbers (or "data") were stored and computed and printed, again each year in faster and faster time. Or so it was stated in the company's latest annual report, which proudly detailed how computer operations were again being expanded, office technology modernized, business methods streamlined, all of which entailed continued reorganization of the company and its many regional and local headquarters across the nation.

The latest reorganization had to do with the possible transfer of two large clerical departments to another branch of the company in another (smaller) city. That was the rumor in any case that Vickie had heard from her former fellow workers. Who would be going? When would it happen? How many jobs would be lost? Only top management knew the answers and top management wasn't consulting with the clerical workers. "Everyone's afraid Big Daddy's going to abandon them," Vickie told me.

Big Daddy?

With a slight shrug she explained that like many other giant corporations seeking to inspire loyalty (and/or head off unionization) the company was also the most paternalistic of employers. Although Vickie herself was a strong believer in unions (we had originally met at a conference on trade union women) she had been only half-sarcastic when she used that workers' paradise line.

149

There were, to start out with, all the employee benefits that have become increasingly expected of the large corporation: medical, life insurance, pension, stock investment plans. There were the assorted we're-all-one-big-family activities: travel clubs, picnics, baseball games, bowling teams, holiday parties, a company newspaper. There was a tuition-refund program ready to assist you if you decided to go to school at night to increase your skills. There was that beautiful building you worked in. There was that affirmative action plan. There was an expensive management training program to make sure those above you knew how to supervise you according to the latest principles in personnel relations. (Bumblebrain had been replaced by the Harvard Business School.) There was even—contrary to the old saw that there ain't no free lunch—a colorful, carpeted cafeteria where every day you could enjoy two or three courses, hot or cold, at absolutely no charge. (Such lunches or extremely low-cost ones are now fairly common at numerous insurance companies and banks.) Finally, as have dozens of other giant corporations in recent years, the company had just set up a special "job enrichment" division designed to make your current work "more interesting and challenging."

Vickie assured me that when I talked with some of her friends, I'd find there was far less than meets the eye in most of the benefits they received. And that under all the trimmings the company was as discriminatory as any other when it came to promotions and pay. But, she said "most of these women still want to believe Daddy's looking after them, those that stay awhile anyway. He keeps throwing out the same tired line about costs being too high to give higher raises and they keep falling. Christ, I don't know. At least that's the way it was when I was there. Maybe it's changing now. Maybe with those departments being transferred they're finally realizing the company's been looking out for its own interests all these years, not theirs. Who knows, maybe they're ready to join a union or something. I frankly doubt it, but who knows?"

She had arranged for me to meet with a number of her former co-workers, one of whom—Bonnie—later gave me a tour of the office building as well. A small, dark, effervescent woman, Bon-

150

nie laughed at the idea that she was working in a model office of the future. "They keep changing things, that's for sure. They keep buying new equipment, new machines. But I'll tell you the truth. For me personally, a lot about the future seems just like the past."

First Job

She still remembers that morning clearly. Two weeks after graduating from high school Bonnie's first day of work at the company had started with a warm sendoff in her home on Chicago's south side. Her sister, a year older and a secretary at a bank, came by from her nearby apartment so that they could ride to the Loop together, a pattern that was to continue. Her brother, a typewriter repairman, departed from his customary policy of absolute silence in the morning to tell her to knock them dead. Her mother, a janitor, and her father, a laborer, cautioned her not to spend all her salary on new office clothes, but they were obviously pleased and proud. It was almost seventeen years to the day since they had emigrated from Poland with Bonnie, then barely a year old. Now for the first time, with everyone working, two of the kids still home and contributing, pressures about money had finally started to ease. They were thinking about buying a house.

Bonnie had applied for the job at the company during her senior year after hearing that a number of her classmates were going to be working there, too. In fact, so active had the company been in recruiting that there must have been twenty from her school starting at the same time. Bonnie's original decision to take a commercial course in high school had been virtually automatic. No one had ever suggested anything else. Do you plan to go to college? someone at school had inquired when she was thirteen or so, her mother then occupied until late at night with mops and brushes and pails. No? Then you want commercial or general? That had been the extent of the vocational counseling offered and except for those of her friends who had found their own way to other fields (usually because they happened to know someone in them), office work had been the destiny of the majority. Once during a summer vacation Bonnie had sold assorted candies at Woolworth's ("I loved it; nobody could understand why I was smiling all the time, but I just loved talking to the customers"), but aside from that, and all the babysitting she had done, this was her first real job. She couldn't wait to get started.

Eager and nervous that first morning, she arrived at the towering building twenty minutes early. Walked slowly through the grandiose lobby. Which of the many elevators was she supposed to take? Then she spotted two of her former classmates, rushed to join them. They were all to go first to personnel before being escorted to the different departments with the somber sounding names where they would now be spending their days. Claims adjustment. Cost accounting. Actuarial services. Treasury. Transcription. Bonnie was the only one from her class to be assigned to computer systems. The mysterious world of computers. She was thrilled, although what her job was going to be she wasn't sure.

It was six years later when, through Vickie's introduction, Bonnie and I first talked. She was now twenty-three, living alone in a two-room basement apartment in the house her parents had bought, paying rent, helping with the laundry and other family chores, dating various young men, finding most of them "too damn wishy-washy—where are all these strong aggressive men I'm supposed to be resisting?"—wanting vaguely to be married, cuddling babies, as were more and more of her friends. At the company her current position was, well, basically the same as when she had started. "I mean I still do what I did then, except now I do a little more. You know how it is. Once you learn something, and they find you can do it faster, they give you more to do, right? Only now that they know they can trust me, they let me do it my own way. So that's different, that's better." As for the twenty-odd classmates who had started with her on that first morning, only she and four others now remained.

She believed most of them left because they expected far more than they ever received. "Me, I guess I didn't expect that much." In the transcription center, where the majority of her friends worked, every single one was now gone except for a young woman named Claire who stayed on and stayed on and recently was promoted to supervisor. In Bonnie's own case she sometimes wondered if she shouldn't have quit years ago, too. Not that she was miserable or anything like that. Not at all, she told me, not at all. It was just that sometimes if you remained too long at one place you begin to have too much "invested" to leave even if you think you might be happier somewhere else. At first it was hard to imagine a young woman in her early twenties already in such a position. Then one night she described a day at work in detail.

Job Description

"Well, let's see, I'm due in at eight, but usually I breeze in about five after, ten after, they're not hard about that. They know I generally leave a little late at night waiting for my lift. Actually I guess I'm giving *them* time. Well, so. After I take off my coat, say hello to everybody, the first thing naturally is coffee. Sometimes I'll go get it myself from the urn for me and the guy who sits next to me, sometimes he'll go, it's pretty equal. My manager (she's one of the two women managers here, she just got promoted) she used to have me get hers but lately she's stopped. Completely stopped. I don't know why. Maybe all this talk about office workers not being servants has gotten to her.

So. Then I go straight to the first mail, that's one of my main jobs besides answering the phone—opening all the intracompany mail for everyone in my division except if it's marked personal or confidential. I have to stamp each item, there can be over a hundred different things, sort it all out and then deliver it to their desks. We'll kid around a little, usually. Except for a couple of people who can't get along with anyone, we're all pretty close. Maybe once a month I'll bring in some special Polish cookies I bake and then the whole office is all over me. You should see, it's really funny.

"Then, after the mail, around nine usually, it's time for my first morning trip. Our company is trying to avoid having too many personal secretaries, so as much as possible, unless it's too technical or it's confidential, we all send our work to the transcription center where they have the word-processing machines and the dictaphones and all that stuff. The trouble is it takes a while before you get it back and sometimes it's garbled and you have to do it all over. My manager is getting pretty annoyed about that. She really wishes she had her own secretary, but they won't give

153

her one. Anyway I'll leave what has to be done with my old friend Claire and pick up what's ready. Then I'll do the same at the dupe shop, that's where they do all the duplicating. I have friends there too and we'll usually clown around. You know, I definitely find the best way to get things back fast is to socialize, be friendly, you'll get better service. Some of the supervisors who come around and give us nasty looks don't realize that, though.

"Well, so then it's back to my desk and by now there's usually more mail to sort out. But today there was a repair problem with one of the electric typewriters. They always call me first whenever there's a breakdown; they know I'm good with my hands and I can save them a lot of time before the official service guy gets around to coming by. Sometimes I wonder why I'm not getting paid for all this, hah hah. Anyway I fixed the typewriter. Then I did the mail and went to lunch.

"In the afternoon I had to cover for one of the other clerks who was out sick (we're all cross-trained so we can do each other's work) and that meant I had to handle the suggestions. Did I tell you about these before? These are suggestions the company encourages all of us to send in. They could be about safety, about ways of speeding things up, or saving the company money, about anything. They pay us for the ones that get used and put our names in the company paper. Once I won $150 for one of mine. It had to do with something we were doing manually then, some information we had to log and splice up and interfile. One day I thought, hey, suppose you run this stuff on the computer, that would save all this time, wouldn't it? I talked to my manager about it and she agreed and then I talked to a programmer and he set it up. I'm not sure how the amount you win is based. I know I must have saved the company at least $1,500 the year I got my $150, but the rules are so tricky I don't really understand them. One thing you can be sure; the company isn't losing; it's coming out ahead.

"So I worked on the suggestions. You have to number them, put them into different categories, it takes a little time. Then I picked up some more transmissions (that's just our word for letters and tapes and stuff) and brought them to the transcription center and dupe shop again, came back, mailed out some material for our manager and did the last mail.

"That's all I did today basically. Besides the socializing, seeing my friends. And as long as I get the work done, they let me go about it the way I want. Pretty much. Like sometimes I get the attendance early—oh yes, that's another thing I do: check who's there and who's not and whether they're entitled to a sick day and shoot it all down to Personnel. But there's no one pressuring me, looking over my shoulder, and that's because of my manager and the way my department is run, there's an easy atmosphere. I know it's very different for clerks in other departments here. Probably I'd never have lasted if I'd been stuck in transcription.

"Our department is a mixture really. They could joke all day sometimes, then other times they're very busy, they'll be furious if anyone makes a sound. They're mostly computer programmers and analysts and a lot of them are great practical jokers. Like once they replaced some guy's phone with a fake phone and fixed it so it would ring all the time, but there'd never be anyone on the line. Well, as you can imagine, that nearly drove him out of his mind. Hello? Hello? Hello? He was going crazy. And another time they pulled a joke on this woman who has a potted plant on her desk. She just loved this plant, see, she was always talking about it, how tall it was growing, and one guy was always threatening to cut it off. And then on this particular day when she went to lunch he removed the plant and replaced it with the exact same kind of pot, but an empty pot, see, that only had a little dirt in it. Well, when she returned from lunch and found the plant gone she was so upset she was ready to kill him but he was nowhere in sight. And then finally she went to the ladies' room and he snuck the original plant back. Naturally, she was so relieved when she came back and saw it, but she was also still boiling—and then I guess she started to think of all he had gone through, buying the pot and the dirt, and she finally started to laugh with the rest of us. We were all hysterical. We have quite a group of comedians and they do this kind of thing a lot. You wouldn't expect that in an insurance company, would you? Probably our department is unusual that way.

"How do I like it? Well, you know it kind of depends on the day you ask me. In the beginning I really loved it. All the time. Now a lot of the time it's still fine, the people are like your family. In my department they're always saying, if you want to know anything around here, go see Bonnie. So you feel pretty good when you hear that, you feel appreciated. And naturally you feel great when and if you get a raise. But then there are days when you feel, well, it's all right, everyone's nice, but I'm not really getting anywhere, am I? Not that I'm after a big career. I personally don't believe in putting your whole life into your work like my manager seems to do. That's not for me. It's just that sometimes it gets frustrating doing the same thing day after day. Year after year.

"That's the way I was feeling a few months ago. See, when it comes to promotions it's up to your manager where you get to go in your department and my manager likes me where I am. She doesn't want to have to replace me. So when I mentioned I'd like something else she said, okay, here's a little more work, a little more responsibility. But it was really the same job. And as for getting something in a different department, you'd have to be requested by the manager there and most of the time they don't know you from Adam.

"So I decided to look around a little. I went to a couple of employment agencies and told them what I could do. Light typing. Keypunch. A lot of recording and clerical stuff, including distributing paychecks—they trust me with all this money and that means something. You might call me a Gal Friday, something like that. But both agencies said the same thing. They said, 'Look Bonnie, you're making $158 a week now. Do you realize you're going to have to take a twenty or twenty-five dollar cut if you leave there? You've been trained for a particular job, you're obviously valuable to your current employer in that job, but in the general labor market your skills aren't worth that much.'

"That was really a shock to me. *Your skills aren't worth that much.* I thought I was progressing in life. Getting experience. Six years of working steady and they say I'd have to take a twenty-five dollar cut. Well, anyhow, that's what I meant the other day when I said maybe I should have quit before and got started

156

somewhere else. 'Cause right now I can't afford to leave. Not that I'm complaining. I'd probably have missed all my friends if I left. Listen, I'm lucky that move the company's planning isn't going to affect my department—I hope.''

Free Lunch

Fruit salad (canned pears, peaches, bits of cherries), Salisbury steak (ground beef with gravy), mashed potatoes, carrots, vanilla cake with chocolate icing, tea with milk. As do many of the other budget-conscious clerical workers, Bonnie usually makes lunch, the famous free lunch, the main meal of her day. It is almost always good, fantastically good compared to typical institutional fare, and the employee cafeteria itself is as attractive as many fine restaurants. In front of the room near the entranceway is a lounge with couches, easy chairs, chess and checker sets, a color TV. Adjoining the lounge is a Ping Pong room, directly next door a library with current magazines displayed on plastic racks. Over the loud speaker come weekly announcements of future events. Tickets to this weekend's hockey game available at discount prices to members of the Employee Recreation Association. A planned trip to the Six Flags in St. Louis, the midwest's answer to Disneyland. The results of the latest matches of the company's bowling or baseball or basketball teams against other insurance companies in the city.

"They really try," Bonnie said, finishing the last bite of her cake on a day when she was able to arrange a guest ticket so I could join her for lunch and look around a bit. "I think they really want us to feel happy. You should see this place at Christmas. All the decorations. Hams and turkeys for lunch. The president and vice-president coming around shaking your hand. They have us call them by their first names, you know.''

They think Big Daddy's looking after their interests, Vickie had said. "Does all this work?" I asked Bonnie. "Does it make the women feel closer to the company, build up their morale, even when they can't get a decent raise or a promotion?''

"Oh, I don't know. For some people it does, I think others couldn't care less. Personally I really enjoy the trips they sponsor, I'm a nut about travel. And on our salaries we all definitely

157

appreciate getting the lunches paid. The other stuff, yes and no. Sometimes it reminds you a little of school, you know what I mean? But a lot of it is fun. It really is. And it does help break up the monotony of your work.''

I asked Bonnie about the company's affirmative action plan and she said she had never heard of it. "Affirmative what?'' I asked whether there had ever been a union drive and she said she thought that some years ago in another branch of the company there had been some preliminary talks but management had gotten wind of it and somehow managed to squelch any further action. She wasn't sure how. "Some women were called down to personnel, I think.'' As for her own branch she wasn't sure how many other workers would agree, but she definitely would be in favor of a union. "If it was a good one, I mean. Because right now so much that happens to you depends on which department you happen to be in and who your manager is. A lot of it is really pure luck. But with a union then there'd be protection and raises for everyone, wouldn't there?''

So Vickie was wrong about at least one woman here.

Then Bonnie said we'd have to hurry if she was going to have time to show me the dupe shop and the transcription center before her lunch break was over.

I mentioned that it couldn't be anywhere near an hour yet.

"Oh no,'' Bonnie said. "We don't get an hour. Since they give us lunch in the building they figure we only need forty minutes.''

Tips for Typists

Claire, the supervisor, was demonstrating the new word-processing machines. "There's no way I could go back to a regular electric typewriter after using this. Just watch.'' She inserted a small plastic card, pushed a button and in less than a minute the machine typed a full page perfectly.

"It's really something, isn't it?'' Claire marveled.

In parallel rows young women, about half of them black, sat silently typing away. Or watching the typewriters type away.

"How many do you have working here now?'' Bonnie asked, knowing the answer.

"As of this month we're down to ten.''

"And just a few years ago there were how many?" Bonnie continued.

"Twenty-three."

"And I bet you're getting out as much work as before."

"Oh, yes. Probably more."

Although she was exactly the same age as Bonnie, Claire looked years older. Perhaps it had something to do with her position, with her slightly prim manner, the totally serious attitude with which she approached her work, the dedication even. She considered herself not simply a supervisor, but also a teacher, she told me a few days later when we met outside the office for a talk. Ever since the company had sent her to a lecture series on How-to-Supervise she had become "a nut about training," about "developing my girls," but for reasons beyond her control things rarely seemed to work out as she planned.

Thinking of the students in the banquet hall, I asked what it would be like to be starting out in her department.

"Okay, it's your first day. You're probably scared to death so I'd try first of all to make you feel at ease. I'd take you around the department. Introduce you to everyone. I'd assign you a lunch partner so later you wouldn't have to go out all alone.

"Then I'd sit you down and explain our training program. This is something, frankly, I'm rather proud of. It's something I worked out myself, using as a basis our company's own *Tips for Typists* pamphlet which has an index of insurance terms. First to get some general ideas about your skills, what kind of practice you're going to need, I'd start you on a sample letter on a simple electric typewriter. I wouldn't be too concerned about your mistakes at this point, more about the setup of the letter. Frankly our executives are extremely fussy about how things look and to be honest I think they have a perfect right.

"Then for about your first week, I'd give you a choice of simple jobs. There's a bin of handwritten stuff we all have to type up, reports, letters, charts, memos, everything you can think of, and usually we take these things in rotation. You finish something, you take the next, that's the fairest way. But since you're new, you'd be able to pick out what you want.

"As a beginner here you'd be starting out at grade-level two.

159

For some reason, maybe they think it would be insulting, we have no grade-level one. With our latest salary schedule that means you'd be getting $108 a week to start.

"Probably I'd keep you on this simple typing for about a month. Then if everything was going smoothly I'd put you on the word-processing machines. Now you'd be learning all about our different form letters, about inserting different standardized paragraphs with others, and I'd be encouraging you all the time, following your progress. You'd stay on this for a while, coupled with ordinary work on the regular typewriter.

"Then, usually in the beginning of the second month, I'd start giving you training on the dictaphone. This is very important. We get tapes from all over the field, some are transmitted on the telephone as well as by hand and through the mail. It takes a while to learn how to do it, the voice can be fuzzy, or they're mixing things up, but I'd be right there helping you out as much as I could.

"In about a month after that, say about the beginning of your third month, if you're progressing okay you'd be advanced to level three, which means a five or eight dollar raise, so that now you could be up to $113 or $116. You really should be if everything is going right. Certainly by six months you should be at level three. If there's a problem I'll try to work it out with you.

"By the way, when you get to the dictaphone stage, I wouldn't have you doing that all the time. So that your day will be varied as much as possible I'd rotate the different kinds of work—word processing, simple typing, dictaphone. That is my policy anyway. At the moment, however, we've been having a lot of sickness in the department, colds, flus, I don't know what's the matter with everybody, we've been very shortstaffed and that makes it difficult to spread the work around the way I like. But if it's at all possible I do.

"Now you'd be building up to level four—that's a senior transcription clerk. And that means you'd have more responsibility and could handle the most difficult jobs. To get to level four should take you between a year, say, and a year and a half."

"And then?" I asked.

"Well, frankly, the trouble is after level four there's nowhere else for you to go. Nowhere except for assistant supervisor and supervisor—and the people who get these jobs generally stay forever. I was a senior transcriber myself for over three years before the assistant supervisor got pregnant and left and that was unusually lucky for me. And then a few months ago the supervisor quit, another incredible break. As I say it rarely happens. Supervisors hardly ever leave around here."

I asked Claire about the company's affirmative action program.

"What's that? Oh, yes, I think I heard something. They've made a few women assistant managers and two have become managers. And I think they've started hiring some women college graduates for other kinds of jobs. But that hasn't anything to do with our department. The girls in our department don't get to go anywhere else usually."

I asked about the company's tuition refund program.

"Well, I think someone in our department used it a few years ago to learn steno, but that's the only one I can remember. And since we have so little call for secretaries here—you have to be on a really high level to get one—it didn't do her any good. At least not here. She left. And now with those two departments moving there'll probably be less call for secretaries."

I asked about the turnover in her department.

She surveyed her fingernails, as if checking each for the answer. "Well, to be frank, that's something I feel awful about. Even though you know it's not your fault you start feeling like it is." She pursed her lips. "Okay, last year we had fifteen girls come and go in just twelve months. In a department of only ten or so you can see how bad that is."

"Why did they leave?"

"A couple were pregnant. And I think a few were driven out by the previous supervisor. She was a very bossy, tense woman. Frankly she was a bitch. She wanted things done *her* way, she didn't care beans about the development of the girls the way I do. But most of them left, I have to say, because they were at level four and they knew that's as far as they would go. I'll tell you the truth. Right now I have three at that level, and I'm just praying they'll last out the year."

A motherly sort of sigh. "But if they want to go you just can't hold them down, can you? You know I'm still in touch with many of the old girls and some are really happier. A few are secretaries and there's one who's working in a travel agency, that's something I always wanted to do, and there's another who's working for a different insurance company, a very small firm. You know in smaller offices you often get to do a lot more different things than in big places like this, you're not on the machine all day, you're walking around, answering the phone, everything isn't broken up into so many departments like here, although sometimes the pay and benefits aren't nearly so good. Anyway this girl, Lois, seems to like working in a small office a whole lot more. But then there are others who haven't found anything they like; they miss the people here, a few are really sorry they left. And then there are some who say when you figure the price of transportation and clothes and lunches in other places, unemployment insurance would pay better than what they're getting for working."

"How would you change your department if you could?"

"Let's see. Well, first I'd give them a full hour for lunch so they'd have time to go out if they wanted to. And I'd raise their salaries so they could afford to—particularly those who have been here for a while. What they're getting . . . it's really not enough with today's prices, is it? And then, last, I'd create another level, a new level five between senior transcriber and assistant supervisor. Maybe then they wouldn't be leaving us all the time."

Claire obviously assumed that the company really wanted all the women in her department to stay for years and years. Yet, as I told her, I had long been under the impression that giant insurance companies (as well as other large corporations) traditionally expected, no, traditionally *depended* on what they blithely called A&P (attrition and pregnancy) to keep their clerical salary levels down. Except for a select proportion—the cream—who were to be groomed, like Claire, for somewhat higher roles, they counted on the exit of many noncollege employees after several years and the entrance of new high school graduates to take their places at beginners' wages. Which is partly why they usually preferred young women to older women (who were less likely to quit) for such "entry" (dead-end) positions in the first place. And partly why an exception like Bonnie found herself overpriced when she went back into the general labor market.

I had first seen this corporate strategy stated baldly in a study by Ivar Berg* in which "one highly placed executive in a mammoth insurance company commented that 'tender minded' academics were 'downright naive' in their concern about worker turnover. . . . It was his 'informed judgment' that clerical personnel "are easily trained for their jobs, that if they stayed in larger numbers they would become wage problems—we'd have to keep raising them or end up fighting with them, they would form unions and who knows what the hell else."

Claire frowned. "Probably they do expect some to leave but not as many as we've had, I don't think. And as far as getting the girls cheaper, I hear that's why they're moving those departments. The small town where they're going has lower salaries, generally."

"Will your department be affected by the move?"

"I can't say. It's all pretty uncertain. Just a lot of rumors so far. No one knows what's going to happen."

"What about your own future?"

"Don't know. I don't see moving by myself, all alone. There's nothing else going on in that town. I'll tell you the truth. I like my work. I think the company's great, but sometimes I can't help wishing I was married, taking care of my own kids at home."

And if and when you do that, I thought, will the company be able to find someone cheaper to replace you, too? Another happy statistic for the A&P file? No, at your level they do believe in paying for experience—don't they? "By the way," I asked, "how much are you paid for all the responsibility you now assume?" (I'd read that the president, whom Claire and Bonnie were privileged to call by his first name, made well over $200,000 a year.)

"I just got a raise," Claire said. "Before taxes, $177 a week."

*Ivar Berg, *Education and Jobs: The Great Training Robbery* (New York, Praeger, 1970).

163

Job Enrichment

"One of the tenets of the company," the job-design man said, "is that there is no job, no job in the world, that can't be made better." He was an attractive man with a terrible cold. He reached for a Kleenex. "We feel the principles we're using could apply to any line of work, but we believe they have particular relevance to clerical workers in huge corporations like our own with so many departments and divisions and subdivisions. Excuse me."

He blew, he wiped, he continued. "Basically we're saying three things. Number one, that people like to see the beginning and end of what they do—in other words they want to do a complete job and not just an isolated task. Number two, they want and need regular feedback on their performance. And third, they want more control over their work, they want to participate in decisions about how the work is done, instead of simply being ordered from . . . from . . . achoo! forgive me . . . above."

In theory the sophisticated management philosophy he was describing was light years away from the typical do-it-my-way-or-get-out school of employee relations. Not to mention preachings of Frederick Taylor, the nineteenth-century father of scientific management whose stopwatch principles are still alive and well in factories across the country, and, lately, more and more offices too. In reality what had I seen so far? Bonnie did feel she had a great deal of freedom in the way she performed her job. That, along with the socializing, was the aspect about it she liked most of all (although she was increasingly troubled that the job itself was never going to lead anywhere else). In the transcription center the workers had in Claire a supervisor who truly cared about their progress, but they certainly had very little "control" over their work. They hardly could move around. And the very nature of the word-processing and dictaphone machines they used—the reason the company had purchased them in the first place—served to divide the work further so that there would be less need for other (more expensive) employees (secretaries) to "perform the complete job and not just an isolated task." Just as old man Taylor would have prescribed.

"Of course we've really only just begun," the job-design man continued. "And we're by no means the first company to get into this. I'm sure you've heard that increasing numbers of large American corporations are setting up their own job enrichment divisions, too."

Yes, and the stated reasons for such programs were invariably humanistic concerns about "worker satisfaction." Or "combatting worker alienation." But if you looked deeper into their backgrounds you could usually find additional concerns, older concerns—most of all, increasing worker productivity and/or reducing the threat of unionization. Which were not in themselves reasons to dismiss such corporate efforts out of hand (after all, who wouldn't like to see everyone's job "enriched"?) just to be cautious, somewhat cautious, before immediately starting to cheer.

"Eventually," he said, "we hope to get to every department in the company but so far because of a monstrous increase in the volume of work last year we've only made headway in two departments, group claims and treasury. In group claims we took a large office of eighty clerical workers and broke them up into smaller units of ten each. Now each clerk is handling the records of individual customers from beginning to end, instead of just fragmented pieces of the job. We think that's much better. In treasury we did something similar. The main job of clerical workers there is reconciling bank accounts, which requires an infinite amount of checking. Formerly there were four phases of the job, each handled by different staff members—proofing, posting, reconciling and something called control checking. Now we've combined these jobs into one, with each worker handling fewer accounts but doing the whole thing from start to finish. Again, much better we think."

I asked how he would improve the jobs in the transcription center.

"Well, again, we haven't gotten there yet, and we'd have to ask the typists themselves what they wanted. As you know we already try to rotate the different kinds of work as much as possible. But, applying the principles I've already stated, we might also consider having different workers be responsible to fewer departments. That's what's been done by a number of corporations, like McGraw-Hill, where they started out by installing really huge word-processing centers and then found the typists were miserable and rebelled until they split up the centers, made them smaller, more personal."

I asked whether promotion and higher pay were considered to be related to job enrichment.

"No, those are separate issues; important issues to be sure, but separate from what we're talking about here—which is improving the job itself."

"What will be your criteria of success?"

A light cough. "Oh, first, that the women are happier. Second, that there are less absences. Right now we've got a horrendous absentee rate in some of our departments, and this is true even though the workers have to have a doctor's note if they're out for three or more days. Then, a third measure of success in some cases might be a decrease in turnover, but turnover is a tricky subject, it's not always bad. Young people right out of high school usually change jobs several times the first few years and that's often a good thing; they're exploring the world of work, finding their way. Oh, and fourth, our last measure of success would be an increase in productivity. That's about it, I would say."

He sneezed again, his eyes teared. He really seemed terribly decent (he was a favorite of Bonnie's), and I felt like saying, go home, don't worry, I will forge your doctor's note. But then I figured that such an infantile requirement would only be made of the clerical workers, not of someone who was enriching their jobs. So instead I asked how the company had fared in the two departments he mentioned, using his own criteria of success.

"Well, I really can't give you an answer yet. First, it's too soon. Second, as I mentioned before, there's been a tremendous increase in the work load and the supervisors haven't had the time to fill out the questionnaires we prepared. We're really still in the experimental state. Elsewhere in our different regional headquarters they seem to be having varying results, some good, some not so good. It seems to depend quite a bit on the attitudes of supervisors, but none of the evidence is very conclusive yet.

Here or at other corporations. Let's face it. Job enrichment is still more of an art than a science."

Then he added that it was particularly hard to draw conclusions in his own branch since so many of the workers were worried about the impending move, and I agreed it would be difficult to feel that one's job was enriched or that one had more "control" when at any moment you thought you might lose it.

The Cream—Mother and Daughter

The daughter (Diane) said, "It's ironic. Here I'd give anything if I could afford to quit working for a few years and my mother would give anything to continue working. So what happened? The exact opposite."

The mother (Nora) said, "At first I was going to try and fight it. But then when I realized I was just another statistic to them I stopped caring. The hell with them."

The daughter said, "Not much she didn't care. After they retired her she was depressed for months. She's only coming out of it now. Speaking for myself, I still enjoy my work; that's not why I wish I could leave. I'd like to have another baby, a daughter, if possible, before I'm too old. And I'd also like to spend more time with my sons before they're all grown up and don't need me. Don't let anyone tell you being a full-time working mother is all that easy."

The mother said, "The company doesn't make it any easier."

The daughter said, "Oh, they're pretty understanding about a mother's problems. Within limits. As long as you're not out too much. Lucky for me my kids are so healthy, knock wood. Colds, something minor, they can stay by themselves or I'll get a sitter. Only twice there's been a serious problem. Both with my oldest. Pneumonia once and then a broken leg. Naturally, both times I felt I had to be with him, so since they don't let you use your sick days for your children I had to take my vacation days instead. Either that or be docked."

The mother said, "So two years straight she missed her vacation."

The daughter said, "Mother's just bitter because she feels the

167

company betrayed her. Forcing her to retire and then as she'll tell you her pension turned out to be lower than she had expected. But most of the time she was there she thought it was a wonderful place to work. It was she who encouraged me to apply for a job, too."

The mother said, "It's true, I used to think it was wonderful, that's how much I knew. Diane was still in high school when I started. My other kids were grown, I thought I'd have no trouble finding a job. I had worked in offices before, and I could still type very well. Plus I knew quite a bit about bookkeeping. I thought I was a great catch."

The daughter said, "Until she started looking."

The mother said, "The employment agencies, God bless them, warned me not to expect too much at my age. Which at the time was fifty. They said employers wanted sexy-looking girls and besides they were afraid of having to pay benefits to older women like me. All my past experience counted for very little. You may laugh, but I remember being mainly upset by that remark about sexy girls. I had gotten all gussied up. A new dress, new shoes, new hairdo. I had lost ten pounds. I thought I *was* sexy. I hadn't realized I was a zero because I was fifty. Then someone asked if I'd be willing to take something part-time for a while. That's how I got started at the company. They put me in the actuarial department where they have a number of part-timers as well as temps and after a while they put me on full-time. And as I say I loved it. The actuarial department—that's the brains of the insurance business you know. You have to understand your concepts very well: cash values, premiums, dividends, everything under the sun. I was a calculator. A human calculator. And I was as content as can be until they started giving everything to the computers."

The daughter said, "After my high school graduation I came straight to the company. I started as a file clerk, like those students in that ceremony you saw, and then they transferred me to personnel where my job was helping to get information about employees for the IBM cards, adding up dependents, figuring out benefits. I liked it very much. Very much. Then the next year I married Bob, who's from Norway, and we went back there to live for several years, during which time I had my two kids."

OFFICE WORKER

The mother said, "The computers changed everything for me. Ask the other old-timers in my department, I think they'll tell you the same thing. Before we were used to doing perfect work. Careful work. We took pride. I remember when they started making the changeover. Instead of asking our advice the men programmed it themselves and for months afterwards everything was coming out wrong. I told them, Look, if you put garbage in, you'll get garbage out. So then one of the young executives, half my age, said I should realize that there were four things you needed in order to be a good calculator. Facts, figures, accuracy and speed. I said I agreed with everything but the speed. Why was that so important? A human calculator can never beat the speed of a machine but we can be as accurate. We can give personal service. But speed is what comes first today. Whatever that man told you about job enrichment."

The daughter said, "When my husband and I came back to America it was a hard time for us. The babies were small and no one wanted to hire him, a foreigner, even though he speaks English very well. So we moved in with my parents, and Bob took care of the kids for almost a year until he was finally able to get work. And I went back to the company."

The mother said, "We used to go in together."

The daughter said, "It was a necessity for me to work but to tell you the truth I probably would have been bored at home at the time. Which may surprise you after what I said before about wishing I could leave now. But you see then we were living in an old neighborhood. There weren't many women my age. There wouldn't have been anything much to do outside. But now where I live it's totally different. There are so many activities I'd like to be involved in—scouting, gardening, our PTA. I believe in parent involvement in the schools but right now I simply don't have the time. That's my main problem; time, the same with most of the mothers with small children I work with. Just finding the time to do all things you have to do; let alone time for yourself."

The mother said, "I was with the company not quite fifteen years when I left this past April. That was exactly one month after my sixty-fifth birthday, which is the longest they allow you to stay. Then I learned, as Diane said, that my pension wasn't going

169

to be nearly as much as I had assumed. Had planned. Thank God, my husband is collecting his own pension. Honestly, I don't know how the single women and the widows are managing. You know, once a few years ago I complained to personnel that the pension plan wasn't fair to women, men got much more. A year later they equalized it by—guess what? By lowering the men to the women, not raising us to their level. So now we can't complain about discrimination with the pensions; we're *all* low. Except, of course, the higher your salary the higher your pension, and the men are, of course, usually far, far higher."

The daughter said, "I'm in group claims now, where they've started the job enrichment program. I think it's probably a step in the right direction, though it bothers me that they seem to think we all want the same thing. I don't think that's true. I think some women, some *people*, want more responsibility and some don't. Some like to work slow and careful and some quick and forget it. Some want to be with other people. Then there are those like me who prefer to work alone. But they act like we're all alike. I know a girl who works on one of those video-display machines— they're basically keypunch machines with TV screens—and she says the best way you could enrich her job would be by letting her get up and move around more often, have some freedom, but since they're mainly interested in production that's the last thing they'd allow. The same in transcription. In my own job, I frankly have no complaints. I'm on a pretty high level now. I appraise the doctors' charges. Make sure they're not out of line. And I really enjoy my work like I say. I think the company is probably as fair as any you'll find today. The only change I'd ask for personally has to do with maternity leaves, since that's what I'm interested in. Right now they let you come back, but they don't pay you while you're gone."

The mother said, "I'm guess I'm much more modern than my daughter. I'd ask for a hell of a lot more than that. I feel they should advance women much further than they do. All the women, not just the college crew. Between you and me, a lot of us resent that these young college women they've started bringing in are getting jobs they never gave us when God knows, we know the business much better than they do. In some cases they're getting jobs we used to get. You can't say that's fair to women. They should use all of us better. As for those computers, sure they should use them, but I would see that people come first. And I'd also see that workers weren't forced to be so competitive with each other. That happens in offices everywhere, I know, not just here. Women are trained to compete with each other to get the few promotions, the few really good jobs, and that's becoming more true all the time. Instead of sharing your knowledge and experience you feel you have to protect your precious little bit of information. Everyone competes, even departments compete with each other and I think it even hurts the company in the long run. I believe there should be more human attitudes generally. And you already know how I feel about putting older women who are perfectly able and healthy on the shelf. Many of us would like to keep working."

The daughter said, "It's too bad my mother and I can't change places with each other for a few years, isn't it?"

Why Clerical Workers Won't/Will Join Unions

It'll never happen, went the old argument. These women—secretaries, typists, bookkeepers, all the others—are impossible to organize. The young ones think they're only working until the babies come along and the older ones think they're part of management. They're too loyal. Too timid. Also they think unions are for the working class and they're better than that. (Basically the same argument used by union officials to explain why more saleswomen aren't organized.) It's hopeless.

But now there's a new argument. Things aren't the same anymore. Women's attitudes toward work are changing and the office itself is changing. Becoming more mechanized. In addition, many of today's clerical workers (like Bonnie) are the daughters and sisters and wives of blue-collar workers: they know firsthand the difference a union can make, particularly in terms of the paycheck. And for those still worried about the class stigma of a union there are now the successes of teachers and nurses and other recently organized professionals to point to. You'll see. Twenty years from now the majority of clerical workers will be in unions. It's inevitable.

The most notable fact about both these arguments is that, as with so many other issues concerning women, the main emphasis is put on the "special attitudes" of women instead of on the outside forces affecting our situation. On the supposed subjective factors instead of on the obvious objective ones. In the case of unionization there are at least three very specific outside forces having little to do with one's sex or "special" psychology: (1) the particular employer; (2) the particular union; and (3) the particular state of the job market in one's industry and line of work at the time of the union drive.

As it happened, of a dozen women I eventually talked with at the company, only three thought a union was needed in their kind of work place with their kind of benefits. (But those were three more than Vickie had predicted when she gave me the list of names to call.) However, to say the least, the issue was academic. There was no union drive in the offing. There was only the scheduled transfer of those two departments and the insecurity that it was causing. How the workers would have actually voted after being spurred by a strong union campaign (and no doubt an employer counter-campaign) is really impossible to say. Only the smallest fraction of clericals in insurance companies have been organized yet. Indeed, to ask any woman office worker (except one working for government) why she isn't in a union is still to risk the cliche rejoinder of the aging bachelor to the old question, Why have you never married, sir? "Nobody ever asked." (Or: "Nobody I wanted ever asked.") Although the very first local union of clerical workers was federally chartered in 1904* and the first international, the Office and Professional Employees Union in 1945, the vast majority of American secretaries and typists and bookkeepers and file clerks and keypunch operators have yet to be asked.

The word is that this situation is finally changing. The American labor movement is now aware that its very future depends on organizing clerical and other white-collar workers as the propor-

---

*Based in Indianapolis, it was called Stenographers, Typists, Bookkeepers and Assistants Federal Union Local 11587 and survives to this day as Office and Professional Employees International Union Local 1.

tion of the labor force employed in the traditionally unionized factory jobs continues to decline. Unions simply have nowhere else to go. So it is said. So it has been said for nearly a quarter of a century. But in the past ten years there has been greatly increased action as well as words.

The most pronounced increase of course has been in government employment, where clerical workers, along with other public employees, are now part of the fastest growing group of union members in the country. But lately there also has been a record number of union elections among office workers in private industry as well. And by a record number of different unions.* All in all according to *White Collar Report*, there were over 2,000 separate elections involving clerical workers in the private sector in the four years between 1972 and 1976. And, as they had consistently in previous years, the unions won a majority of the elections held (about 55 percent). At the same time however they won only a minority of the workers involved (35,000 out of 90,000) and that was because, again as in past years, the unions fared better in the smaller clerical units than in those with more than forty workers. In the larger election units a rough estimate is that unions generally seem to be winning about four out of every ten.

*In fact there is almost no predicting which union is going to be organizing which kind of office worker and in which industry anymore. To be sure the Office and Professional Employees Union is still one of the most active, but you can also find boilermakers organizing bank tellers, carpenters organizing switchboard operators, distributive workers and service employees organizing secretaries in publishing and on the campus. (Oddly enough the Insurance Workers are organizing . . . insurance workers, but so far their main focus has been sales agents.) Both the United Steelworkers and the United Auto Workers now have their own white-collar divisions. But by far the busiest union of them all at the moment is perhaps the most unlikely one of them all to be appealing to workers presumably preoccupied with questions of prestige and status. That union is the elegant Teamsters which in the past five years averaged more than three times as many clerical elections as any other union and had a success rate at least as good or better. Among the new Teamsters are clerical workers at various branches of such uppity places as American Express and the Brentano's bookstore chain who obviously decided (as did newly unionized nurses and other professionals) that there's nothing better for one's status than a bigger paycheck.

Looking ahead there is no doubt that there will be continued activity. Clerical workers in every kind of office in every kind of industry will be increasingly the focus of union drives. So union leaders assure us. But the rate of that increase will be important to watch. For although greater than ever before, the present pace of organizing is hardly sufficient to maintain even the currently small percentage unionized given the enormous increases expected in clerical employment in coming years. In 1960 about nine percent of all clerical workers were in unions. In 1976 about nine percent of all clerical workers (although a much greater number) were in unions. These figures cover both private and public sector employees. For the private sector alone it is still much less.

"We're making progress, yes, indeed, but it's very, very slow when you look at the total picture," a male researcher at the Office and Professional Employees Union told me. "Think of the huge corporations you have today. People don't understand the gigantic costs involved when you tackle one—the time, the money, the energy, the manpower. Say we attempted a drive at an insurance company like the one you visited, where the workers are isolated in fifty different departments, where they do have some benefits and a nice atmosphere to work in, and where management is ready with the carrot and stick the moment they hear about your campaign. I don't know if you've heard, but all over the country corporate officials have started holding conferences on 'How to Keep your Company Union-Free.' They're obviously worried and they're getting very very sophisticated, particularly the giants. In the public sector you have it easier. There the workers know they've got civil-service laws to protect them from employer threats or vindictive firings during a campaign." (In addition to the often slow-moving National Labor Relations Board which is supposed to protect us all.) "There's no question it's harder where workers are insecure about their jobs. I'm not saying we're not moving ahead. We are. We and other unions have had some great victories lately—a number of universities, hospitals, publishing houses, and for that matter a few insurance companies, almost anything you can name. I'm just saying it's a tough, slow process, especially when you take on the biggies, and it costs a hell of a lot of money which many unions are not that willing or able to spend.

174

"And then, of course," he continued, "there's the added problem that most clerical workers are women and as you know women are always the hardest to sell when it comes to unions."

Ah, the old shibboleth again. Which as it happens many pro-union women (like Vickie) also believe. But which, interestingly enough, was found to be decidedly not the case in a careful study of *White-Collar Unionization* by the National Industrial Conference Board. After analyzing the results of 140 recent union elections the researchers concluded:

> "The factor of sex . . . appeared to have little bearing on whether units voted for or against unionization. . . . One half of the predominately female units in the survey voted in favor, slightly more than the male units. Moreover in a few of the mixed units employers report that the female employees were the union's principal strength. . . . These results would seem to cast doubt on the proposition that one of the problems of white-collar unionization stems from a preponderance of female employees."*

Instead, the most crucial factors determining how workers voted appeared to be related to, of all things, salaries. And job security. And employer-employee relations. And health benefits. And grievance procedures. And the reputation and credibility of the union.

"I agree it's not who she is, but where she is," another organizer of clerical workers, a former secretary herself, Margie Albert of District 65 of the Distributive Workers of America, said to me. "Women in factories are just as in favor of unions as men. But offices with their elitism and competitiveness have fostered anti-union feeling among both women and men. And let's face it, there's the other fact. Should women be interested in unions, unions have really not been very interested in them until lately. Now the funny thing that's happened in our own case is that it's been the women you would have expected to have the most illusions about status and individualism who have come to *us* first—

---

*Edward B. Curtin, *White-Collar Unionization*, National Industrial Conference Board, New York, 1970.

college graduates working as secretaries in universities and law offices and publishing houses, the so-called prestige places to work. In their case they're feeling the contradictions between the high expectations they entered their jobs with and the low realities they face: the puny salaries, the limited promotions, the mockery of affirmative-action programs. But it is the low salaries in particular that are going to change women's minds everywhere, especially as the nature of the office keeps changing. For example, those word-processing machines you saw. Did you know that there are typographers who work on the exact same kind of machine all day and get ten dollars or more an hour to do it? Yet your insurance women got less than three. And now they've even started talking about a typewriter someday that will type automatically to the sound of your voice. They're using more part-timers and temporary workers all the time, too. Our own view is that you can't stop the machines, but you can help see that the workers don't get the short end of the stick. As management continues making gains in productivity we should be gaining too. In our paycheck. That's what I would call job enrichment."

How fast will office unionization actually increase? How widespread will it be? Twenty-five years ago C. Wright Mills predicted that as soon as the labor movement was ready to go "all out" it would be only a matter of time before offices are significantly unionized. But for all the current activity we are still waiting for the labor movement to go all out. "When that time comes," Mills foresaw, "management may think it can stave off unions by giving its employees what the unions are out to win for them. My hunch is that it will not succeed." But then he hedged slightly: "Besides, if management really does succeed then the aim of the unions will in a sense be realized, too."*

The Future of One Office
But to return to the company, there was no union drive in the

___

*Only up to a point of course. But it's interesting to note that in the Conference Board study almost all workers were in better financial shape after the union election was over, whether or not the union won. Either way, management had been compelled to pay more. Over the long term, however, it's likely they paid far more with a union.

immediate offing. What did lie ahead? Shortly before leaving for New York I had a talk with the personnel manager or, rather, I asked him a number of questions, to which he replied:

—Yes, of course we have an affirmative action plan, what large corporation doesn't?

—No, I'm not free to divulge it; that is between the government and the company; besides it's very complicated.

—Yes, most of our clerical workers are women, but those are the ones who apply.

—We've always been committed to moving our workers ahead, we're doing it right now, but you have to understand that this is a pyramid. We have far more clerical jobs than any other kind.

—Naturally we're taking advantage of the latest developments in office technology, just as you would expect. There isn't an organization this size that's not greatly concerned about increasing the flow of paperwork today. But in our own case as we go about making improvements we're also deeply committed to our job enrichment program. Deeply.

—Yes, the demand for certain traditional clerical jobs, like routine filling and billing is lessening, but at the same time others are expanding. As you know computer personnel and machine operators are in great demand everywhere. And in places like ours we obviously still need clerical workers for a wide variety of other functions. Furthermore, don't let anyone tell you the private secretary is dead. Like many corporations, we've begun to cut down, to use our transcription center more, but that doesn't mean we have no secretaries at all, not by a long shot. And in smaller offices everywhere there's hardly been any change at all. The secretary is still by far, by *far,* the most common clerical occupation in the country.*

*True, at least for the time being. In 1975 twenty percent of all clericals were secretaries and stenographers and the Department of Labor's *Occupational Outlook Handbook* predicted that their numbers would continue to grow rapidly in the 1980s (although stenography itself would probably give way more and more to the dictaphone). But if the smaller office was expected to be a chief mainstay of the old-style private secretary it was also true that smaller, less expensive computerized equipment was becoming available. And that the long-range trend was toward larger, more complex business establishments. So: as the personnel man

—High turnover is inevitable among beginning workers.

—You may think our salaries are low, but if you'll check you'll find they are at least competitive with those of other insurance companies in this city and usually they're higher. We keep in close touch, you know.

—No, no I would doubt that our clerical workers would be interested in a union. Those who stay with us generally feel this is an exceptionally fine place to work. Far better than many other places they might go to, and they know it.

—Have you heard about our free lunch?

The Move

Some months later I called Bonnie, the clerk in computer systems. I wanted to talk to her about Women Employed, a group of Chicago women that, like similar groups in other cities (Nine to Five in Boston, Women Office Workers in New York, Women Organized for Employment in San Francisco), had been pressuring government agencies to enforce equal opportunity laws and corporations to reveal publicly their affirmative action plans as the law required. Typically, government agencies were almost as lax as the companies themselves (The federal Equal Employment Opportunities Commission, for example, had a backlog of over 120,000 charges.) Women Employed in Chicago had been particularly active in exposing the sex discrimination rampant in local insurance companies and in one case had succeeded in winning a large back-pay settlement.

Bonnie was interested in talking about Women Employed, but she also had her own news to report. First of all she had finally been given a promotion. She was now a secretary, one of the rare secretaries, in fact she was secretary to her whole department. "It's pretty much what I did before, I guess, except now I open the confidential mail and I type the stuff my manager doesn't trust with the transcription center." But the change in job title had come with a raise and for the most part she was feeling quite pleased.

said, the job of secretary did not appear to be on its way out. But the work itself seem destined to change and the proportion of secretaries in comparison to other clerical workers to diminish.

Until she heard the second piece of news. After the transfer of those two clerical departments the company announced that within the next two years it would be moving out of Chicago entirely except for a small skeleton staff that would remain. The beautiful building would be rented or sold. The new headquarters was now being built in a small suburban community in nearby Indiana, about an hour and a half away from Bonnie's house. Bonnie was planning to commute (she didn't want to have to forfeit an annuity coming due in several years) but the cost of the transportation would wipe out much of her recent raise. She doubted that clerical workers making less money could afford the commute and that those who were mothers would have the time. "Some are really upset." There were many other workers who would be moving to Indiana (the company was providing relocation expenses and low-cost mortgages) but usually they were on a higher level, which meant that usually they were male.

I asked Bonnie the reason for the company's decision. "Job enrichment," she said, with a gruff laugh. "They think we'll be happier working in the country. No. I'm kidding. Taxes. They say the taxes in Chicago are too great. They say more and more companies are leaving. You'd better tell those people at Women Employed to come out to the small towns and suburbs. Remember when we first met? Maybe you were right after all. Maybe we really *are* the office of the future. What do you think?"

179

6

Homemaker

The conference for homemakers was held on a Saturday, an eye-opening if troubling event. I spent a good part of Sunday in my hotel room going over notes and on the phone making appointments, finally gave it all up to explore the lively downtown streets of Madison, Wisconsin. But the conference was still on my mind. Monday morning I made some more calls, then set out for Joyce's place of work.

When I arrived it was almost eleven, and she had been on the job, as usual, for a full four hours. The two girls had been fed before leaving for school. The husband had been fed before leaving for the office. Jason had been fed and washed and dressed. The cat had been fed. The beds had been made (although, true, the girls did their own), the dishes done (by hand, no dishwasher). A chicken was browning in the oven. A second batch of wash was ready for the machine.

"S'cuse me a minute while I get rid of this last load," Joyce said, inviting me into her living room with a wave of a narrow and angular arm. She appeared narrow and angular in all places— face, legs, hands, feet—that weren't visibly affected by the new life growing within her. Still extending her arm, she smiled but only slightly. "Some conference, wasn't it? I've been thinking about it ever since."

Then she went down the basement steps and I sat on the couch watching Jason watch *Mister Rogers' Neighborhood* on the color TV. Jason was nearly three. Tousled dark hair, Joyce's pale blue eyes, skinny tiny-boy body. Sprawled on the shag rug in front of the set, he was wearing one red and white sneaker on his left foot, one red and white sneaker between his lips. Mr. Rogers obviously had him in rapt attention, so I turned my own to the view outside the window, a truly extraordinary view as it happened. Beyond the street facing Joyce's small house was a shimmering ribbon of blue-green lake. Beyond the lake were the buildings of downtown Madison, a twenty minute drive away. Beyond the buildings you could just begin to make out the yellow-orange-brown patches of the autumn countryside.

It had seemed an absurd distance to travel at first, all the way from New York to Wisconsin simply for a one-day conference for homemakers, but I had decided to go ahead after reading the literature and calling the organizers on the phone. This was to be the last of six such conferences held around the state by the Wisconsin Governor's Commission on the Status of Women. To my knowledge it was going to be the most thorough attempt by an officially appointed body of women to really analyze the job of homemaking—to discuss seriously its pros and cons as an occupation, a real occupation not some dubious pastime, an occupation furthermore in which for better or worse the majority of American married women (57 percent) are still employed full time. And what's more, among the people participating in the conference would be the true experts, the occupants of the job.

So I had flown to Madison with the hope that in addition to attending some possibly enlightening discussions about a growing number of proposals to aid homemakers, I'd also find out how some of the job holders themselves reacted to the proposals, and hear their own views about the lives they led and the work they performed, their own ideas about what was needed, if anything, to help. And all that happened and then some—the conference had raised issues I had never before considered. That's why I wanted to stay longer and try to get to know some of the home-makers better.

Soon Joyce returned from the basement carrying a basket of laundry still warm from the dryer. Lowering her body very slowly she started to join me on the couch, when Jason playfully grabbed her left ankle, causing some of the garments to fall. Then as we both bent to pick them up the phone started ringing. "Sorry again. That's the way it is around here. Anyway, I forgot to turn off the chicken. Jason, take that sneaker out of your mouth."

Held on the campus of the University of Wisconsin, the con-ference had opened with a few welcoming addresses by the com-mission brass about "this invisible occupation" and then we—there were about 150 women in the audience—had all broken up into individual workshops with topic headings such as *The Law and Me, Money Management and Me, Sex Roles and Me, Educa-tion and Me*, and the one I decided to attend, *The Economy and,* yes, *Me*. According to the flyer, this workshop would "explore the dollar value of housework and its contributions to the Gross National Product and whether such common fringe benefits as paid vacations and health insurance could become a homemak-er's right."

In the room where this workshop was held, sitting around a long wooden table, were ten women of all different ages, but only four, it turned out, were actually full-time homemakers. Since Madison is not only the home of a famous university but is the state capital as well, the conference had also drawn a number of faculty and government employees interested in possible legisla-tion. In fact, the discussion leader was a representative of the Wisconson State Assembly, Mary Lou Munts, a tall handsome woman, who told us she had recently returned to professional life after fourteen years as a homemaker herself. She opened by ask-ing us each to introduce ourselves, tell why we were here, and several of those from the university and government defined themselves as "retreads"—women who had stayed home until their children reached a certain point, then gone back to their original vocation or to graduate school. Apparently each of these women had been to college or started on a professional career be-fore being married. I paid particular attention however to the four who were still full-time homemakers.

Joyce introduced herself in a shy but firm voice as a "home-maker who really enjoys what she's doing. I have to say that right away. I mean I'd like some more time for myself, who wouldn't? But I guess I feel there's no one who could better take care of my kids if I weren't there and I like being there. And as perhaps you've noticed another is on the way. I guess the reason I'm here is because I saw the ad in the paper and I was curious, but not because I want to change anything."

Next to Joyce sat one of her closest friends, Bea, a woman in her thirties with short fluffy hair and lustrous skin. The mother of two daughters in elementary school, she said her chief difference from Joyce was that in addition to being a homemaker all day she also worked thirty hours a week at night as a data processor. She liked the night job, met other interesting women there, but home-making was definitely her main occupation, the one she pre-ferred. "So like Joyce," she insisted, "I'm really just here out of curiosity."

"Well, not me," barked a small slender woman named Faye with a voice as gruff as her black leather jacket was sleek, a kind of Bella Abzug timbre in a middle-western tongue. She could have been forty-five. She could have been fifty-five. ("Let's just say," she wisecracked later, "that I've got children older than I am!") She pointed a platinum polished fingernail in the direction of Joyce and Bea. "You two may only be here out of curiosity, but believe me I'm not. I'm the one this session was made for. I'm here for pay, vacations, insurance, you name it."

"Are you working?" Mary Lou Munts asked.

"Yes," Faye said. She paused. "Very hard." She paused again. "At home. You see, even you fell into the trap. Because I haven't been paid for the work I've done for the past quarter cen-tury—raising a family, managing a home, diapering them and dressing them and feeding them and drying their eyes and you know the rest—what I've done doesn't count. It's not real work. So much so that now that my kids are grown—I've got a daughter who's really living the liberated life, but it looks like I've raised a couple of male chauvinists just like my husband—well, now they all have the gall to say to me: 'Why don't you get a job, mother? Why don't you *do* something?' After all these years of slaving for them, they seem convinced I'm some kind of parasite because

183

I'm still at home. So I'm here for one simple reason. I'm boiling mad."

As Faye spoke, Joyce and Bea listened without expression. But one woman was nodding vigorously. She was the fourth homemaker in the group, a very tall and slim woman about forty whose looks, with the exception of her long, flowing gray hair, reminded me of Pat Loud of *An American Family* fame. A Pat Loud without all that money. Her name, let us assume, was also Pat, and when her time came to introduce herself she said she very much agreed with what Faye had said about people not giving homemakers the credit they deserve. Because in her own case she feared she was a representative of what was rapidly becoming an obsolete species. Certainly an endangered one. She was a full-time homemaker *and* she was divorced. With two children at home, with a small farm house in a rural area where she grew her own vegetables and fruit, with cooking and cleaning and laundry and carpentry and a thousand other things to keep her occupied fifty hours a day, she didn't want to also have to go out and work, at least not now, even though she was increasingly strapped for money. "I mean I do work. I probably work harder than most people. I just don't get paid for it. So that's why I appreciate what you said, Faye."

"We all work," Faye shot back. "We all work and we have to clean up the language and the people that refuse to recognize it."

"That was my friend Bea on the phone," Joyce said, returning to the living room with a tray of coffee for us, chocolate milk for Jason. "She said she'll be home all day until five, if you want to see her later. Here, Jason, be careful not to spill this."

Again she sat ever so slowly. She leaned back on the pillow of the couch, sighed a half sigh. "I seem to be carrying lower this time. Maybe I'm too old to be having this one." She was in fact twenty-nine. "You probably think I'm crazy having a fourth."

I shook my head, not knowing what to say.

"Well, it *was* an accident."

Wondering why she felt she had to explain, I remembered she had mentioned at the conference that she was Catholic.

"Yes, I am, I take it seriously. But that's not why I'm pregnant. I mean I do use contraception, I'm one of those who do. It's just, I guess, I forgot one day."

"And you never considered abortion?"

She stiffened. "No, I certainly did not. Would not. After all it *is* a life. And besides that, who knows, maybe it was really on purpose? I didn't plan Barbara, my first, either. An accident. But what a great accident. Both times I was really glad. I'm from a big family myself, it's something I've always dreamed of having. So you see I'm not really sorry."

Joyce and I had first begun to talk at length during lunch at the conference, so I knew already that she had grown up in a small town outside of Madison, the oldest of five children. If she had learned early about the pleasures children can bring to a household, she had learned just as quickly about the pleasures that have to be sacrificed as a result. Her father was a mechanic, her mother a waitress who worked nights all through the years Joyce and her brothers and sisters were small. In the early days it was Joyce's father who served the dinner, tucked the children into bed, turned off the lights, but then as Joyce grew older, old enough to have a hundred other things she would have much preferred to do, it was her turn. There was never a question, ever, about why her mother was working. "We wouldn't have made it without her money, pure and simple." Which partly explains, she told me at the conference, why she now feels *so lucky* that in her own household it's not necessary for her to go to work. We had each caught the word at the same instant, remembering the discussion we had just heard: "Yes. Right. I mean paid work. That's one good thing they said."

Now, sitting alongside her on the couch, I asked about her other reactions to the conference.

"Well," she said slowly, "to tell you the truth I was a little depressed afterwards. I think Bea was, too. We drove home together and we were both sort of quiet at first. Then Bea turned to me—I was driving—and she said, 'You know, Joyce, if we didn't think we had a problem when we got there, we sure did by the time we left.' "

I asked what had disturbed her the most. She glanced at Jason who was producing exotic sound effects with a bent straw and near-empty container of chocolate milk. "I . . . well I guess it's a little frightening when you realize how vulnerable you are. Or could be. So many things they brought up, I never thought about before."

It seemed to me the same must have been true for the majority of homemakers attending. For among the questions that had been raised in the conference literature and in the workshop discussions were the kind that few of any group like to think about before being forced to:

What if I become ill or incapacitated? Who cares for me if I'm laid up at home? Who cares for the children? How do we pay for all this?

What if the source of family income is lost? Why must the entire family be deprived if the wage earner can't provide? And why under our current system must we lose not only our day by day economic security but also our medical and health insurance if our family's sole bread-winner is out of a job?

What if my home breaks up by desertion or divorce? As more and more do. Will the courts demand and enforce adequate support? Is it true that a boomerang effect of new no-fault divorce laws is a lessening of economic protection for divorced mothers and their children?

What if I want more control over the financial management of my life? What recourse do I have if my mate, who has income, is stingy. (Most male-controlled courts refuse almost automatically to get involved with on-going marriage problems related to money, although there is still a legal obligation on the part of the father to provide.) Would salaries for homemakers make sense?

What if the homemaking job gets too much for me to handle? If we have a handicapped child or if my aged parents move in with us, what community resources are available to help me? With other jobs, time off and vacations are considered necessary for the employee's general health and well-being. How about my health and well-being?

186

What if I need to refresh myself and grow? Where and how can I continue my education? How can I rearrange my life and my family responsibilities to have time to pursue my very own interests?

What about those so-called golden years? Why are so many old women poor? When my children leave home, how will I spend my time and talents? Will there be sufficient income to provide for medical needs? For everyday needs?

What if my mate dies? How will I live if insurance is small or non-existent? What kind of a job will I be able to get? Where and how could I get training? Did my mate's will make adequate arrangements? Did my mate's pension plan provide for my receiving benefits after his death?

"All those *what if's*," Joyce said. "Remember that divorced woman, Pat—what she said at the end: that it can all look hunky-dory until something goes wrong. Suddenly he gets laid off or sick or wants out and then you realize how dependent you've been all these years on his good fortune."

"Or good will," I added. Then I asked if she was worried.

"No, not really. Oh maybe a little this moment, but that's probably because I'm pregnant and I'm not feeling as strong as usual. I'm kind of tired today. But I'm not worried about our marriage falling apart or anything like that. And Bob's doing okay right now, so I'm not really worried about money. So it's not myself. It's just when you think about all the women who do need help, it's very sad. I keep seeing that woman on crutches who talked about homemakers not being able to get low-cost disability insurance like other workers. And who needs insurance more than a mother with small children? If I'm laid up at home after an accident, not only do I have to find someone to take care of me, but also my kids. So what do I do if my husband can't afford to take off from work?"

What often happens to a middle-class homemaker in this situation, so we have learned, is that she and her family will go into debt to hire a surrogate homemaker if there aren't relatives around to come and take over the job. What happens to poor families is that the state can and not infrequently does come to take the young children away if there are no adults there to replace the sick mother.

"I've been thinking about it, too," I said. "What else bothered you?"

"Well, then, all that stuff about social security. How if your husband dies your payments are reduced to 85 percent of what they would be if he were retired and alive. Now why should that be? You still have to meet your expenses. You still have to pay for the rent and heat, for clothes and food. And all those poor widows they talked about. Who are too old to get jobs. That's just not fair."

One fact that had startled me, I told Joyce, was learning that a woman can be married to a man for twenty years—managing the home, raising the children—and then should they divorce at that point, she's not entitled to a penny of his social security benefits when he retires. After all those years. (Beyond twenty the woman *is* entitled to a portion.)

"I know, that was news to me, too," Joyce said. "I'll tell you the truth, after I stopped being depressed I started feeling a little angry. Anyway, when I got home my husband could see I was upset, and he asked me what happened. He does taxes and he knows about these things. Though, come to think of it, he had never heard about the disability or the social security rules either. Who thinks about that? Anyway he reminded me we have life insurance. Except that with inflation it doesn't look like so much anymore."

That had to be true in most homes, I thought, remembering still another sour fact from the conference: that in the majority of homes where the husband has life insurance the amount of the insurance is equal to less than two years of his annual salary. "So where does that leave a woman with children," Mary Lou Munts, the discussion leader, had asked, "if her husband dies at 45?" As for private pension plans, most men fail to take out the "survivor's option" since it would reduce their own payments after retirement, with the result that the overwhelming majority of widows receive no money from their husbands' pensions after these men die.

"I mentioned it all to Bob," Joyce said. "First I talked about the disability. About that woman on crutches. Then I brought up social security and the suggestion that homemakers should get it, too."

"And his reaction?"

"Well, at first he argued a little. He said, 'After all, we're a partnership. What's mine is yours.' But then finally he said if I was so concerned he'd consider it. And I said, 'But that's the whole point, Bob. You *can't* consider it. Because they don't allow homemakers to have things like social socurity yet—and that's why I'm so upset. The fact is homemakers need more protection than we're getting.' "

We continued—Joyce and I—to talk about the conference until it was time to retrieve the last load of laundry and then the three of us, Jason leading the way, headed for the basement. Joyce said she'd have to hurry now because very soon her daughters would be home from school—school was closing early due to a teachers' conference—and then she would take her younger daughter, Amy, to the hospital. Just six years old, Amy would have to stay there overnight before getting a series of tests tomorrow for a bowel problem that had been bothering her for weeks. In the meantime, while Joyce was away for the afternoon, her eleven-year-old, Barbara, would be home minding Jason, with assistance if needed from the next-door neighbor who had agreed to be on call.

Socks. Shirts. Shorts. Assorted children's clothes. Sorting them out on a table next to the washer-dryer, Joyce told me more about her childhood. She went to a small elementary school, then to a slightly larger high school, where like most of the other girls in her class, she automatically signed up for a business course—typing, steno, bookkeeping. There was never a thought about going to college. The short-range goal as with most of her friends was to become a secretary until the long-range goal of having a family was possible. And at first everything went perfectly according to plan. After graduation she landed a job at a "one-girl office," a job which for the most part she enjoyed. Two years later she became engaged to Bob, the son of a small dairy-farmer, a student at a local college. They were married while he continued at school and she continued at the one-girl office. During those years they "sort of" shared the housework, although she supposed she did a little more.

Her first baby, her first great accident, was born shortly after Bob had graduated and started work as a fledgling accounting clerk. It was an extremely low-paying job and Joyce had fully intended to keep her own job, too. But the baby proved more work than she had expected. And perhaps more to the point, her desire to be at home with the baby proved stronger than she had expected.

So the next problem was to figure out a way she could both be home *and* bring in the necessary dollars. The solution was arrived at after long consultation with Bob, the farmer's son. She'd raise chickens.

They moved to a chicken farm in a remote Wisconsin town. Bought six thousand broilers. "You get them when they're chicks, see, and you have to feed them individually while they're babies. Later when they're bigger you can use an automatic feeder. Anyway that's how we did it then. But the hardest part for me wasn't the feeding, it was changing the water all the time, lifting it and transferring it, and, well, the whole enterprise wasn't a success to put it mildly." Late to bed feeding the baby and early to rise feeding the chickens made Joyce very tired but little else. "All that work and we couldn't make any money. Nobody wanted them. It was a disaster."

They moved again. Although they had liked living in the country the cost of suburban living, when everything was figured, was more within their means. So they settled on this house where they have lived ever since, and although it took a while, "I've grown to like it here, too," Joyce said. "There's more to do, more people around although frankly I'm not the coffee klatch type."

But after moving to the suburbs there was still the same problem. Wanting to be at home with her child and needing more income to get by. The second solution: foster children. "I took in two kids, then three kids at different times and since I love taking care of children that was really fine. I enjoyed it." Enjoyed it but still not enough money. Needed more money.

Solution number three: Sell Tupperware. "You've heard of that, haven't you? A lot of housewives like me do that. That and taking in foster kids. It's something in between working outside and not working. Either that or be an Avon Lady, and the Tupperware seemed to pay more. You know what happens is, you have to arrange parties in people's homes and you bring the Tupperware over and serve the food in it and tell everyone it's wonderful."

She partly loved the work. "The great thing was that you'd be able to fit in the work with your own schedule. You could do the preparation for the party during the day while your children were napping, and then at night, while your husband was minding things at home you'd go out and have a change of pace."

She partly hated the work. "What would happen is you'd see these women, women who have even less than we did in those days, and you'd think, just the very minute before you knew you were going to make the sale, you'd think, gee, lady, you shouldn't be buying this junk, you shouldn't be wasting your money. At least that's what I would think."

Eventually it didn't matter whether she hated or loved the work—she found she wasn't earning that much after all. So she tried another night job, selling cheese at a gift shop for a while. Until finally by the time her second daughter was born ("That was no accident. I'd waited five years for her.") Bob was doing well enough so that for the first time in her marriage (and ever since, except for having a foster child now and then) she hasn't had to find new solutions. "And you can't imagine what a relief that is. What a relief! Now you see I really knew what I was talking about at the conference when I said I preferred to be a homemaker. Don't tell me about how liberating other jobs are."

I asked if she thought, as some have said, that the women's movement with its emphasis on careers as the road to self-fulfillment had made it harder for her to state her own preference to stay home, had made her defensive about being a homemaker.

"No, not really . . . oh, maybe a little. But in another way it's made things easier. I mean it's good, really, to know there are women out there trying to create better job opportunities so that if I ever need them or want them, they'll be there. I really feel that. And it's good, too, in the sense that if I choose to stay home, as I do, then I know it's really a choice. I mean I'm not trapped. And if you realize you're not here because it's your *place* to be here, but because you really want to be, then you enjoy it more."

She paused in the middle of folding a tiny pair of dungarees. "At the same time I do think what that woman, Faye, said was right. That homemakers or housewives or whatever we're called, we should get more credit. Just a housewife! Just! People think it's all so simple now, with all the machines, that there's nothing left to do. But let me tell you, I don't ever seem to get caught up. There's the children, the marketing, the cleaning, the cooking. There's the yardwork, which I do myself. . . . "

"Because . . . " I interrupted.

"Because," she continued, reading my mind, "I enjoy it. Bob would help there if I wanted him to."

"And the rest of the house?"

"Okay, I have to admit when it comes to the inside he's not much of a help. Except if I'm sick or something. I guess you could say, except for the first couple of years of our marriage that he's pretty traditional about man's work and woman's work."

I asked if that ever bothered her.

"No, not really. He usually comes home pretty tired for one thing." She folded a red cotton sweater in half. Frowned. "And there's another thing. Last year he was working so hard he started to get an ulcer. He was very, very sick, so now I want him to relax when he can."

"So you don't mind his not helping you?"

"No, not usually. Although sometimes at night, well maybe for a few minutes. I mean, I'll know he's had a hard day and he's tired, but I've had a hard day, too, and I'm practically ready to drop and there's still the dinner and the dishes and getting the kids to bed, and meanwhile he's sitting on the couch looking at the TV. So for a minute I'll feel like saying something, but then I'll remember he's been under all this strain, a lot of money problems, and I'll think, is it worth it? Basically I guess I'm not the kind to complain. And as I said before it's just finding some free time for myself that's so hard. Otherwise I really have the life that I want.''

I asked how she felt about the suggestion that had been made at the workshop that homemakers be given time off and weekends and vacations like other workers.

"Well, sure, what homemaker wouldn't like that? But how do you get it? One thing in my own case, Bob and I do get away weekends maybe once every other month, to go skiing or camping by ourselves.'' That was thanks to another woman, her mother, who lives a half hour away and enjoys taking care of the children. ''And then as far as the housework goes, I think it's going to let up as the kids get older. I'm a strong believer in children sharing the work, too—that's something the women who write about housework don't talk about—and my older daughter already helps out quite a bit.''

Right now she tries to set aside ''one day a week just for me. I go to an exercise class and I also belong to a mothers' group at my church where we talk about our problems with our children, things like that. Besides that I like to read, but I seldom find the time, even though I've put Jason in a play group two mornings a week, so that both of us can have some time away from each other. That's very important. Otherwise you go crazy. But there are still all the unexpected extras. Things you can't plan on. Something in the house needs fixing. Doctors' and dentists' appointments for the children. Like today, as I mentioned, I have to take my daughter for tests. Imagine if I was working outside. Who would do it? It might be very hard getting out of an office or making arrangements with another person to take her. And I'm the kind who wouldn't feel right if someone else took my daughter to the hospital. After all she's only six. I know she's frightened and she'll feel safer with me. And remember things like this are *always* happening when you have three kids. And I think—I *know* —it would be extremely difficult to get a boss to understand.''

How about her friends, how many have outside jobs? "More and more. We never talk about why, but I know they mostly have to. Some of them sell Tupperware or go to a night job, like Bea, so they can still be with their children during the day. Then some of them have full-time jobs, but I can see it's often a hassle.

193

Like a close friend of mine wasn't able to go along with her child on his first day of school—most of the other mothers were there—and she felt awful, her kid was crying, but there was nothing she could do, she had to keep the job. And all last winter another friend had to drop off her son in front of the school before it opened in order to get to her job in time. The school refused to let him in earlier. Then one freezing morning he lost his glove and by the time they let him in the school door his hand was practically frozen. They had to send him to the hospital. Well, you can imagine how my friend felt about that."

Jason and the cat, who had recently put in an appearance, were now off on a chase and I asked Joyce what she planned to do when the children were older—would she then want another job, or to go back to school, or to continue as she was?

She folded a yellow sweatshirt, flipping the arms across in the shape of an X. "Well, I don't know for sure. Later on it probably would be good for all of us if I got involved with other things—I don't want to be an over-possessive mother. And I notice the housewives without outside interests seem to get older looking much faster. But what would I do? That would mainly depend on whether we needed money. If we didn't I might prefer to volunteer, probably at my church, and do something that wouldn't be done otherwise. Something that also wouldn't take away a paying job from someone who really needs the money. I've read that women's liberation doesn't approve of volunteer work, that there should be salaries for these kinds of things, and I agree there should be, but in the meantime you see so many areas where if someone doesn't volunteer it won't get done. So many children sick and alone, old people alone and dying who need help and attention this minute."

"And if you found you did need the money?"

"Then I guess I'd have to take a refresher course and be a secretary again, wouldn't I? But I don't think that's what I'd really like. And to do practically anything else I'd have to have a college degree, which of course I don't. And if I went to college myself—I know a lot of older women are doing that and I think that's fine—I'd have to start out from scratch, and I don't think that's right. I mean I'm not an inexperienced beginner, although that's

194

the way they'd treat me. You know, we should have talked about that at the conference—that you get a ton of priceless experience running a household but nobody gives you credit for that experience and knowledge. I mean, what you learn about child development. About planning meals. Nutrition. Budgeting money. About decorating and gardening and planning for the future. Working in your community, or with the Girl Scouts or the schools. So many things we do as a matter of course that nobody gives us credit for.

"Let me give you a silly example. Last spring our church put out a cookbook, and I was the one who collected all the recipes from my friends and then I organized the recipes into different sections. And then I wrote a little introduction and took the whole thing to the printer, the one where Bea's husband works, and when they were finished I helped distribute them and sell them to our members. Well, I guess you could say I was the editor of that book, but could I put that on a resume? Most employers would laugh at me, wouldn't they? So, maybe the whole deal is to start educating *them* about how much experience homemakers have. Again it's a matter of giving us the credit we deserve."

"Had you gone to college before getting married, would things be different now, do you think?"

"Well, of course the general attitude in my home in those days was that a girl doesn't go to college, she gets married. I didn't expect to go and I didn't miss it. But probably if I had it would have been money in the bank for later. Maybe I would have become a social worker. Or maybe I'd have gone into religious education, and then after the kids were grown I could have picked that up. If I do go back to school later, that's probably what I'd be interested in—education."

About college for her daughters: "I wouldn't push them either way, but I'd definitely encourage them to learn *some* kind of trade, maybe not requiring college, but some trade so they'll be protected after they get married and have children—yes, I guess I assume they'll want to get married and have kids, too," she said, and as if in answer there was a burst of shouts announcing their arrival upstairs. Joyce handed me a pile of laundry, took the rest herself, and then she and I and Jason started up the basement stairs. I had one more question.

195

"What about the famous isolation of the housewife that everybody keeps writing about?" I asked her midway up.

"I'll tell you something," Joyce said. "At the end of the day, there's nothing sweeter to me than the word isolation. I only wish I could manage some. That one day a week I told you about, with the exercise class and the mothers' group, and those weekends away with my husband—that's plenty for me in the way of outside activity. Remember I'm just talking about me, and like I told you, I'm not the coffee klatch type. Other women may feel differently. But for me, with the kids running in and out all day, and their friends running in and out, and their mothers calling for them, you know I'd say a little isolation would be the thing I'd appreciate more than anything else."

Then we reached the landing and Joyce introduced me to her daughters, one blonde and slim, the other dark and slim, a female version of Jason. "Come, Amy," she said to the younger one, "we've got to hurry if we're going to get to the hospital on time. Barbara, you know you're minding Jason this afternoon. Mrs. Warren will look in from time to time, but call her first if anything's wrong. There's chicken in the refrigerator for dinner if Daddy gets home before I. . . . "

"What is the value of a homemaker?" Mary Lou Munts, State Assemblywoman and discussion leader of our workshop, asked us. She meant in purely economic terms and she referred to several estimates that have been made. The one most often quoted was made by Chase Manhattan Bank in 1972, which figured that the American housewife, with no outside jobs, spends some 99.6 hours a week at twelve jobs in the home, among them laundress, cook, dishwasher, nurse, seamstress. If all these services were paid for on the open market, according to the bank's calculations, using 1972 wage levels, the cost would come to $257.53 a week, or $13,391.56 a year to duplicate. Other investigators have questioned these figures: some find them too high, some far too low, but the most glaring problem with the estimate (and those like it) is that it fails to make any distinctions among different homemakers. Those with large families and those with no children, those with infants and those with teenagers, those with husbands on

Wall Street and husbands on welfare, and those with no husbands, are treated as all alike. As any gardener will tell you, Gertrude Stein was dead wrong; a rose is not a rose; there are over 3,000 varieties. As any divorced mother trying to raise four kids alone will tell you, a homemaker is not a homemaker.

"It's almost like comparing apples and oranges and bananas," Mary Lou Munts said, and then referred us to another study in our conference packet that did try to analyze some of the differences. Conducted in the late 1960s by Kathryn E. Walker and her colleagues at Cornell University, the study is considered by many to be a landmark, the most carefully conceived of its kind. After interviewing some 1,300 homemakers in upstate New York (of all income classes, but predominately lower-middle and middle income) Walker found a tremendous variation in the time spent on household work. Some of the differences were no doubt related to varying attitudes about how much housework was really essential and how much could be left undone, but the researchers found that the most significant factors determining how much time was spent were simply these three: (1) the number of children in the household (the more children, the more time spent); (2) the age of the youngest child (the younger the children, the more time required); and (3) whether or not the homemaker is employed outside the home for more than fifteen hours a week (if she is, she spends slightly less time on household work).

"So it's obvious the job changes significantly at different stages of a homemaker's life and the time she has to spend on it changes too," said Mary Lou Munts. "I guess we all knew that."

"But what doesn't change," said Norma Briggs, the executive secretary of the Wisconson Commission on the Status of Women, who was also attending our workshop, "is that, unlike her husband, the homemaker never gets any guaranteed days off or holidays or paid vacations or. . . . "

"Or unemployment insurance if she loses her job to a twenty-year-old blonde," said Faye of the gruff voice and sleek attire.

"Or just wants to quit," said Pat of the long gray hair and Pat Loud face.

"What particularly interested me in the study," said Mary Lou Munts, "was what it said about husbands. The time spent by the

197

wife on homemaking tasks increases with more children and younger children and it decreases a little when she's got an outside job. But the husband's contribution in the home barely changes with *any* of these factors, it seems. The amount of time he spends is mainly related to only one thing. How many hours a day he spends on his own regular job."

The study found that the average time spent by full-time homemakers on household work ranged from five to twelve hours a day. Or thirty-five to eighty-four hours a week. Among homemakers with outside jobs, the range in the home was from four to eight hours a day. Among husbands, however, the contributions of both those whose wives were and weren't employed outside averaged eleven hours a week, or, if broken down, less than an hour and a half a day. (Even this amount may sound like more than many would have expected of husbands, but it should be noted that the tasks performed were largely the typically male jobs of mowing lawns and repairing furniture, much of which was probably done on weekends. Also, according to other researchers, husbands' help with child care is often largely centered on the more pleasant nonphysical tasks: playing games and telling stories.)

Then Walker and her staff tried to calculate who worked longer hours, the average husband or wife, when you tallied up the total amount spent by each on both the outside and household jobs. The findings were that in families with no children or just one child where the wife remains home, the husband works longer hours. In families with two or three children where the wife is at home, the total for husband and wife is about the same. (But here it should be pointed out that only the hours when the wife was actively performing a certain chore were calculated. Time off for coffee breaks or talking to a friend on the phone—which would be included as part of the husband's work day—was not included in the wife's. Nor were those moments waiting for the kids to come home or lying in bed listening for the sick baby's cry. "Yes, someone could easily dispute those figures on that basis," Kathryn Walker, the director of the study, told me when I called her later at Cornell.)

But what was not possibly in dispute were the inequalities—in

198

terms of sheer hours worked in comparison with their husbands—faced by full-time homemakers with more than three children and, the most overloaded of them all, mothers with pre-school children who were employed outside the home more than fifteen hours a week. Upper middle-class professionals ritualistically urging all women to go out and get a job should look at these figures sometimes. With only a minute proportion being able to afford domestic help (in contrast to the professionals) the typical work week of employed wives (combining outside job responsibilities and household work) varied from an average of sixty-six hours in some kinds of families to seventy-five in others. In comparison to their husbands, the total work week of wives employed outside the home thirty or more hours per week averaged a full fifteen hours longer. Almost two ordinary work days.

"So besides getting more benefits for homemakers, we also have to start talking about changing the family itself—about equalizing roles," said Mary Lou Munts.

"For those who want that. Don't forget there are still a lot of us who like things the way they are," said Joyce's friend, Bea, the woman who worked at a data-processing firm five nights a week.

"When I got back from the conference, I told my husband I was going to join women's lib and he said if I did he'd flip." I was sitting with Bea in her immaculate living room a few days later. "He was kidding of course. He knows I'm not political and he didn't think that would be my style. He also thinks we're a partnership, same as I do. 'We're in this mess together,' he's always saying."

But at the same time, Bea said, she was highly disturbed by a lot of the discussion. "Homemaking is a high risk occupation, they said. And that's true, isn't it?"

"Which of the facts we learned did you find the most disturbing?"

"Well, probably since I'm working part-time, what they told us about social security. I'd never heard that before. That, where I work now my social security payments are going to be a lost cause because my benefits through my husband will be higher than my own—and they only allow you to take one or the other. Yet it's required I pay. I think that's totally unfair. So does my husband. What you pay in you should get back.''

There were also ideas expressed by the professional women at the conference that she didn't agree with: "I got the feeling, you know, that women shouldn't want to be dependent. That we're fools if we do, that we're stupid. But the fact is many of us, maybe most of us, like leaning on our husbands—he leans on us, too, you know—and we don't like to be told we're fools. And there's also the fact, at least I think so, that a lot of women are much better off married and at home then they would be at some low-paying job and they know this: they've usually worked before, after all. So when they hear some feminist writers or lawyers or something like that say that jobs are so terrific, they know that for the average woman that's a lot of baloney.''

Bea said she went to the conference because of Joyce, who was more interested in women's problems than she. She thought there was a decided lack of full-time homemakers at our workshop, which led her to conclude that there's not as much dissatisfaction among homemakers as some think there is. At least among "typical women like me." I mentioned that I had heard that part of the reason for the relatively small attendance was that the conference organizers didn't go out into the neighborhoods where the homemakers lived, but mainly depended on a couple of ads and a flyer to do the job. "Maybe so," Bea said, "but my guess is that a lot of women were afraid it would turn out to be the usual women's lib stuff, telling us housewives how boring our lives are. What monsters our husbands are. And most of my friends are turned off by that kind of talk.''

Like Joyce, Bea's standard of living is now a good deal higher than the one she knew as a child. Like Joyce, her mother was a waitress, except that in Bea's case her mother's earnings were the sole source of support for many years. Bea never knew her father. He died when she was an infant. For twelve years there was no man in the house and then her mother suddenly remarried, had another child; stayed home for a year or two, and then when financial needs pressed in, returned to waitressing. This time she worked only at night. As Bea does now.

Bea's dreams as a child: "First, the usual, a nurse. Then something less usual: I wanted to be a nun. I was in second grade then and my mother nearly fainted when she saw how serious I was becoming, praying all the time. She took me out of Catholic school in a hurry." From then on Bea went to public schools, thinking for a while of going to college to become a medical technician, changing her mind when she tried chemistry and "I just couldn't hack it. And, besides that, where would the money for college have come from anyway?" And besides that, by that time she had decided to get married.

She had known her husband since ninth grade. A year older than she, he was in his second year of a six-year printer's apprenticeship when they set the date. The reason: "It was a mutal wanting to be together." After the wedding they moved into a small apartment in the city of Minneapolis, where they had both grown up, and Bea took a job in the office of a local store, "doing figures," and she liked it, was good at it, so good that after a while her employer, impressed with her work, sent her to an IBM keypunch school. "That's where I learned the basis of data processing which I do now."

A young married woman going to work in the morning, hurrying home at night to prepare dinner ("He'd do the dishes"), bowling or movies or watching ice hockey on Saturday nights, visiting her mother or his on Sunday afternoons—"It was really a pretty carefree life as I remember it now." Days arrive, years depart. Three, four years of marriage. A trip to the doctor: "Those awful tests." Nothing wrong. Five years, keep trying. Six years. Seven. "Finally, one day we look at each other. We're reasonably happy with our life, but we both think, 'This isn't what it's about, is it?'" So they went to an adoption agency. "It took a year, a very nerve-racking year, but finally we got our baby, and I stopped working."

"And how was that?"

"I was overwhelmed." Her voice is mellow, soothing.

I smiled. "With happiness, you mean?"

She laughed. "Oh, yeah, that too. But I meant overwhelmed with the *responsibility*. With the fear I'd do something wrong. Susan was only three weeks old when we got her, and I felt terribly unsure of myself. She was so tiny and helpless. I felt surely someone else could do a better job. Poor Susan, I'd think, stuck with clumsy old me. Boy, she was crying all the time. I'll tell you this: It was sure a lot harder work than punching a keypunch machine.''

It took about six weeks, Bea said, before she and the baby settled down and began to relax and enjoy their life together. Soon after the family moved to Wisconsin where her husband had been offered a new job. Then some time after that, "the common crazy thing after an adoption happened—only generally it happens faster.'' Pregnant. Another girl. And then a down payment on the house they live in now, the necessary furniture, a repair on the car, doctors for the girls, "you guessed it—the bills started piling up.'' And up. So after four years out of the official labor force, Bea proceeded to look for and find the job where she has been working five nights a week ever since. "Anyway, by that time I was getting a little restless in the house.''

The first blow was learning how little the payscale in her line of work had changed since the old days in Minneapolis. "They offered $2.00 an hour for beginners, $2.50 for experienced data processors, which was just about what I was making four years before. I thought, goodness, nothing has progressed in all this time, what's going on?'' Now six years have passed since she started that job. The pay has inched up to $3.00 an hour for part-timers like herself who have been there a long time. In addition, as is so often the case, if you work part-time you don't get the fringes—the sick leave, pensions, medical insurance the full-timers do. "So, naturally, they're hiring more and more part-timers, since they know they can save money on us.''

She works with about twenty other women on the five-thirty to eleven-thirty shift. "They're mostly the same as me. Housewives working nights when their husbands are home so they can avoid baby-sitting costs.'' She repeated what she had said at the conference: that she enjoys her job, she likes the change of pace, that phrase again, and she thinks most of the women she works with feel the same. "Although let's face it, we're there because of the money.'' As for the work itself: "I guess many people would say the work we do is monotonous—we're a data processing firm servicing bookkeepers—but I think it's really more varied than a lot of other jobs." Her employer "treats us okay." And then there are the "good friendships you develop—a lot of us have become very, very close."

Perhaps the largest difference among the women, in her view, is the range of attitudes that their husbands have toward their wives working at night. Some, like Bea's, take the we're-all-in-this-mess-together position and seem to accept it easily. Others have obvious conflicts but go along, often because they have no economic choice. Then others resent it so much they "make life miserable at home until there's nothing you can do but quit or get a divorce, even if you'd really prefer to keep working. That's what a friend of mine had to do last week: she quit and she was really sad to do it."

The negative feelings of husbands in this case are not based solely on the traditional male sense of being threatened or feeling less than a man if he is not able to fulfill his expected role of breadwinner. That, surely, is often part of it, but in the case of a man whose wife works at nights there's also the added rub of not having your mate with you when you come home to relax for the evening, of missing her company when you sit down for dinner, and then to add insult to injury, of having to do all the night household tasks yourself. Unlike the average husbands in the Cornell study, husbands of women who work nights often have to serve the dinner, do the dishes, supervise the children's homework and bedtime, spend far more time on such activities than is usually required of men. And it's important to remember when generalizing about husbands and child care that substantial numbers of women who work—particularly in the working and lower income classes—work nights.

In Bea's case her husband arrives home from the printing shop about twenty minutes before she leaves. By that time she has already prepared the dinner for the family, eaten her portion alone. Later her husband will heat it up, sit down with the two girls, who are now six and ten. "They can help out some, but that wasn't true in the past."

I asked Bea how working at nights had affected her marriage and family life.

"It's hard to say. I guess I've never thought about it. We've been doing it so long now we're just used to it."

"Does your husband ever complain about feeling abandoned at night like the others you mentioned?"

"No. At least he's never said that to me. I think really, you know, it's had a good effect on the family in a lot of ways. Bringing him closer to the children. Giving him a chance to play another role with them, like all the articles are saying men and women should do. Well, he's been doing that and a lot of husbands of the women I work with have been doing that, long before there ever was a woman's movement. And I do think it's probably good for the family. I think my kids enjoy their father and know him a lot more than if I was there at night. And he enjoys them too. So in our home it's working."

"And its effect on your marriage?"

"Well, again, I never really thought about that before. He's usually still awake when I get home, if that's what you mean. At least for a few minutes. And, you know, come to think of it, maybe the fact we see less of each other than most couples makes our time together more valuable. Like for example, I notice we don't go out on weekends as much as other families. We seem to want to stay together. Be by ourselves at home."

"You mean a woman's working at night can be good for a marriage?"

"Well, yes, now that I think of it, maybe it can. Do you think, from what other women have told you, that that could be true?"

I found myself oddly at a loss for words, somehow both moved and disturbed by the way Bea consistently searched for the positive aspects, the hidden benefits, in whatever adjustment she had been forced to make in juggling her different roles as mother, wife, housekeeper, income earner, let alone as simple human being. And that had been true with so many of the women I had met.

"Do you think it could?" she repeated. "Be good for a marriage when the woman works nights?"

I said I really didn't know. I supposed it would depend on the couple, but I was the wrong person to ask, she and the women she worked with were the ones who would know. But I added that what struck me most about mothers of young children in the labor force (in addition to the long total work days as documented in the Cornell study) was the tremendous skill usually required in reconciling the different and often conflicting demands on their time, energy and emotions, and whether they worked days or nights, the wonder was how so many made the best of the results with so little complaint.

"Well, that's all you can do," Bea said and I could sense she was disappointed with my answer. She had turned a problem into an advantage, a necessity into a virtue, and I had mundanely turned it back around. Still I persisted in this vein for a while, asking her what she thought were the special needs of women working at night.

Her first answer was physical protection. Guarded parking lots for those with cars, better and safer public transportation for the rest. "It's not so bad here," she said. "But I remember in Minneapolis, in the high crime areas, there were women who worked nights who were scared to death to go home at midnight when they had to."

"And other needs?"

"Well, okay, there are all the physical needs. The women with babies and really small kids do talk a lot about being tired all the time. Coming home near midnight and then having to get up at dawn or something like that. They're the ones who have it the hardest, no question about that. Most try to take naps sometime during the day, but often they can't manage it, especially if they have kids of different ages. Sometimes they'll have trouble keeping their eyes open."

She added that she tries to take a nap herself for an hour or so after getting the girls off to school in the morning. "Today, though, it wasn't possible." And as she said this I started to wonder for the first time just how much that soothing tone of hers had to do with peace of mind and how much with plain old fatigue. But when I asked whether she was tired, she said no, and then came that most often repeated phrase of all I've heard since I started this exploration of working women: "You get used to it." And also: "It's a lot easier than when the children were small." She said she runs the house on a carefully regulated schedule.

Her husband helps with "the male things" on the weekend and will pitch in with the vacuuming or floor washing "or really anything else I ask him to." But generally she follows a plan giving most of the housework to herself. "It's the old standard routine. Monday washing, Tuesday ironing. You know when I was a kid I swore I'd never get into that rut like the typical woman, but here I am. And you know why? It's really easier that way.

"Then on Wednesday it's the maid's day off. If I can manage the time I'll see my friends or do some personal shopping and I'm also in that mothers' group with Joyce—but often I get bogged down with something at home. Then Thursday it's a good cleaning upstairs, plus the bathrooms. Friday, the downstairs, grocery shopping for the week. Saturday I get my hair done, maybe go clothes shopping with the girls, they always need something, so you see there's always too much to do. That's why you really need a schedule, particularly if you work."

"Suppose you were able to get a good job during the day, and there were also reliable after-school centers for the children. Would you prefer that? Would that be an easier arrangement— less tiring than working nights?"

"Well . . . maybe . . . no, no, I don't think so. 'Cause if I worked during the day, there'd still be the problems of school holidays and summer vacations and the kids getting sick, wouldn't there? That's the whole point of the two-shift family. One of the parents is always there when the children are home so you don't have to spend the money you earn on baby-sitters.

"And then with a full-time job there's another thing. You're probably going to think I'm unliberated or something. But I really like to be there when my children get home from school. To hear how their day went, to see how they are. I know some people say it doesn't make any difference, but I don't feel that way. I also hear that a lot of the kids are acting up at our local school lately, that there's a lot of truancy, and some say there's a reason for that. If more of the mothers were at home. . . . "

"You mean the trouble with the kids is that their mothers are out working? I thought that idea had been put to rest a long time ago," I said. But during the lunch break at the conference I had heard a number of the homemakers express similar attitudes. For all the morning's talk about homemaking being an occupation like any other occupation there still seemed to be an obvious division between mothers who worked in the paid labor market during the day and mothers who worked at home.

One woman I had talked with put it this way: "Let's face it, women who have paid jobs, particularly good jobs, are often the first to use that condescending just-a-housewife line. But on the other hand mothers at home often feel a little critical of mothers who are away when the kids come out of school. I used to be that way myself when I was home in the suburbs with my kids and it seemed like all the children whose mothers were on jobs would land up at my house. Those of us at home would often have to take over the supervision of these kids in a lot of ways. Breaking up fights or bandaging knees or deciding who was going to use what at the playground or just talking to them. Then some of us mothers at home volunteered at an after-school center, and I thought then, listening to how the women talked about the other mothers at work, that it was unlikely that sisterhood could exist between these two groups. It was only when I became a job-holding parent myself that I really saw the double bind a working mother in this country is put into. On the one hand she wants to be a good mother; on the other she wants or needs a job. Usually needs. But how does society help her? Look, here in Wisconsin a state employee gets two weeks vacation a year, but her child gets all summer off. Our school system says it is responsive to the needs of the community, but it doesn't provide alternate care during the summer or other holidays. Likewise our medical system. It's impossible to get a dental appointment for your child around here outside of working hours. So what can a mother with an outside job do unless she's wealthy enough to afford a full-time housekeeper? If I had understood all the problems these women face when I was at home I would have felt very differently, I assure you." The woman who made those remarks, by the way, was one of the key organizers of the conference for homemakers, Norma Briggs, executive secretary of the Wisconson Governor's Commission on the Status of Women.

But to return to Bea, she said she "wasn't sure" that the truancy of the children was related to the fact that both parents were away during the day. "I don't know if it's true or not. I hear that the kids cut school and then go to the empty houses during the day. But I'm not saying that's the cause. I'm really just talking about myself. I'm just old-fashioned enough to believe that my daughters need a lot of attention. I don't want to dump them in a center after they've been in school all day. Maybe I feel so strongly about this because I come from a home where my mother was away so much, where I never knew my father, and I remember feeling lonely when I came into the house and no one was there. Maybe that's why I prefer to work nights so I can always be there. I don't know. I just feel it's a big responsibility being a parent. I take it seriously and I also enjoy it. Later when they're older I'll feel differently maybe, but now I really feel it's the most important thing I can do."

Listening to Bea, I couldn't help but think of Joyce. Two friends with much in common. Both growing up in middle western families with little money. Both the daughters of waitresses who would have preferred to be at home. Neither going to college. Neither preparing for careers. Both getting office jobs. Both marrying young. Both now viewing their lives, with whatever difficulties they presented, as easier than their mothers had known at their own age. All that making a difference. All that influencing their expectations. Joyce marrying a college student, watching him become an accountant, watching him work himself into an ulcer. Bea marrying a high school sweetheart, a linotypist, an apparently easygoing man with whom she was in-this-mess-together. Both when becoming mothers searching for a way to be able to stay home at the same time as they accepted a responsibility to help pay the bills. No pedestals here. No princesses here. Joyce with her chickens and foster children and Tupperware. Bea with her nightshifts in the office, dayshifts in the home. Both after a decade of motherhood continuing to give first place to this role at a time when the accolades go to women with careers.

"You and Joyce obviously share many of the same values," I said. "And you seemed to have similar reactions to the conference."

"Yes, if you mean we like being homemakers. And we don't think our husbands are our enemy. If you're looking for really angry or unhappy homemakers, I guess that woman Faye at the conference or Pat, the one who was divorced, are the ones you should go see. I personally enjoyed the conference. I learned a lot. But I don't think that women like Joyce and me are going to be appealed to by anti-male statements. Or by big sweeping proposals, you know the kind I mean, to change the whole world in a minute. There was a little too much of that kind of talk at the conference for me. But you know if those women who called themselves feminists would just talk about the *fair* thing, you know just stick to getting those social security and other protections we learned homemakers need, instead of telling us all how to live our lives, well, then, you know people like Joyce and me, we just might join up in a minute.''

During the conference the subject of salaries for homemakers was briefly discussed.

"Great, but who's going to pay for them?" Bea asked. "Our husbands? It's already necessary for a lot of women to go to work because there's not enough money to make ends meet. Let alone for a special salary."

"It's more than salary," Mary Lou Munts said. "It's our whole system of benefits and rights. From medical benefits to social security to pensions. As long as so much of our social insurance system is work-attached—I mean you don't get the benefits unless you've been in the paid labor market—then women who aren't in the labor force will always be in a very disadvantageous position—a dangerous one very often if they get divorced or separated or widowed."

"I'll second that," said Pat.

"It seems to me that maybe the most critical thing," said one of the women from the university, "is the fact that we only consider 'work' that which is directly related to wages. And if maybe we started to define homemakers as 'workers' and included their output along with the rest of the gross national product—and compensated them for that work, then we would have solved much of the problem."

"But then we get back to the problem Bea raised before," another woman said. "If the homemaker is a worker, who's she working for? And who's going to pay her? Is her husband going to be considered her employer? And if so, except among the wealthy, where is he going to find the extra money? It sounds like a good idea for the rich."

A husky groan from Faye, the woman in black leather. "I think I should make a comment right here that anything that makes the housewife appear to be an employee—or the husband an employer—should be avoided like the plague. We've just got to move into a situation where the relationship is really equal, where we're really a partnership. Because, believe me, if you start talking about employer-employee in a family situation we're not any better off than we are now. We're worse off."

Norma Briggs: "That word, too, about the *head of the household*, that has to go, also. She's heading it as much as he."

"Exactly," said Faye.

"And that's the chief difficulty with most of these new kinds of proposals," said Mary Lou Munts. "Even those where the homemaker would be considered self-employed and contribute payments toward her own social security—even those require that the breadwinner agree to it. It would be totally up to him to fork up the money for the payments and if he wouldn't or couldn't . . . well, there's no guarantee of a homemaker's right here at all."

"And what if there's no breadwinner around? And no money for the payments?" Pat reminded the group.

"I'm afraid I must speak up again," said Faye. "That's another word I've objected to for a long time. Breadwinner. As if this other person—me—who's in the home is some piteous dependent who's freeloading. I really wish that somehow we could clean our language up in that area, too. This fellow isn't just coming home at night tossing pennies to someone who's been lying around all day eating chocolates. He's getting that salary because she's making it possible for him to focus on his job. He may be out of the house and she's inside keeping the family running, but they're both contributing to the same package."

Norma Briggs again: "There are those who say the government should be the one to pay a salary to those who are managing a household and rearing children full-time."

210

"Full-time or anytime?" asked one of the women from government. "That would be discriminatory if you said it had to be full time."

Bea smiled vaguely at Joyce, as if to say "are they kidding?"

"Yes, you'd have to define the limits of this job, wouldn't you?" said Norma Briggs, "because otherwise everyone could stay home and say, give me a salary, I'm a homemaker."

"That's another part of the problem," said Mary Lou Munts, "and that's why I think some other measure—whether a negative income tax or guaranteed income—might be better than this salary idea. Because if you pay a salary for homemaking, then right away you come up with the problems of definition that you have in the welfare system. People start to say: 'Are they really worth it? Do they really deserve it? Are they really working full-time?' You know, the whole range of questions that get raised in the welfare system and that are so demeaning."

"And it also gets us away from the idea of sharing the household and child care tasks that so many of us feminists are advocating," said a woman from the university.

The discussion continued seesawing like that for a time, someone coming up with a suggestion, someone coming down with a drawback, someone raising a counter-suggestion, someone dropping a hint that it wouldn't work so long as we faced the same basic hurdle: the little matter of the entire American social insurance system, which unlike many other countries is basically financed through payroll taxes, instead of the general revenue, and thus leaves vulnerable anyone who, like the homemaker, is outside the paid labor force.

"That's certainly the largest question," said Mary Lou Munts. "Whether we can move away from a system of social insurance that is based on work attachment to one that is based simply on need. And it seems to me the more we can do that—making old age and medical insurance, for example, the right of everyone— the more we can solve some of the problems of the homemaker we discussed today. But there's also another question, just as related to what we've been talking about here. And that's whether we want to do anything to make it easier for people to move back and forth from work to nonwork. . . . "

211

Faye, interrupting: "You mean from paid work to unpaid work."

"Yes, from paid to unpaid to paid, and to give some credit for that unpaid work in our educational and employment systems. Unfortunately, right now, it's only the crisis situation that forces people to look at this. It's the death of the husband or the divorce or the kid leaving home that suddenly brings home to a woman the fact that there's been no credit building up for all the years she's been working at home. And then in the meantime there are still a lot of women who *want* to be home at least while their children are small."

Of the four full-time homemakers in the workshop, Faye was the only one who was born into the upper middle class. The only one who never had to worry about money in the years growing up and later in the years of her marriage. The only one who went to college—she left before graduation because she had "no burning desire" to be anything except a wife and mother, the most socially valued role for a woman in those post-war baby boom days of thirty years ago. The only one who now considers herself a feminist, to the extent that "if my consciousness gets raised anymore, I'll be on the moon."

And yet she feels it is very difficult for any homemaker to accept feminism totally. And that is because, "let's face it, to most women in the movement, being a housewife is the lowest of the low—and homemakers know it." Outside of some token lip service, she feels there's been almost no consideration given to the woman who chooses to stay home. No real appreciation of her problems *or desires*. That's why the conference was important, she believes. A step in the right direction. But in the long run "maybe the only thing that will really help is for homemakers to get together and form our own movement. Maybe then we'd get the changes we need, the protection we need. Because the whole economy, the whole society, depends on us for its survival, you can be sure of that."

We were sitting in a dimly lit restaurant in downtown Madison several nights after the conference. She was dressed dramatically again, this time in a white wool blazer, black flared pants, a profusion of gold jewelry circling her neck, wrists, several fingers, looking affluent and stylish except for the giant mug of Milwaukee's finest that she was holding in her bejeweled right hand. The beer, like her gruff ironic voice, seemed to be a kind of assertion that she was not simply the well-heeled matron she appeared to be. Not only that. She finished the beer, ordered another. In contrast she barely touched her plate of cornish hen and rice.

I told her she had sharpened my own consciousness about the use or misuse of such words as work and dependent and breadwinner and support. About the need to clean up my own language. "Homemaker isn't so hot either," she said, "but it's probably the best we have. A hell of a lot better than that godawful Housewife."

She stopped toying with the rice, lit a cigarette. She said that part of the problem in gaining recognition for homemakers was that the job varied so much from woman to woman. "Not only what they mentioned in that Cornell study about the differences that depend on how many kids you have and how old they are. That may be the main thing, but it's not the whole story by any means. There's also the whole business of how you function on the job. From the woman who never has a word to say about the financial side of things to those who take charge of everything to do with money, balancing the checkbook, figuring out the budget, making out the tax return every year. Then a great deal depends on where you live. There are the women who keep strictly to themselves because they don't know anyone, or they're living in a big impersonal city. Probably some prefer it that way. These are the women we always hear about. The 'isolated housewives.' But there are also all those like myself who really get involved in their community, who find something they're interested in, whether shaking up the schools or forming a food cooperative or starting a theater group for the old, so many things a lot of us do you wouldn't believe it.

"And then there are the big differences in what individual homemakers *like* to do. Take me. I'm one of those rare birds who'd rather clean than cook. For some reason food has never excited me that much." She glanced at the documentary evidence, the full plate, in front of her. "But when it comes to mak-

213

ing a home look lovely, decorating it and then taking care of it, now I won't say it's my favorite activity—most of my friends at NOW would say I was a robot brainwashed by the Ajax commercials—but the truth is I don't really mind housework at all. In a way, you could say it's my dirty secret: I like to clean."

I laughed, recalling a friend's semiserious theory about why cooking was generally more popular than cleaning. That in addition to the commonly observed 'creative' factors, there was also the immediate feedback and recognition, the oohs and ahs or even the ughhs that you got after serving the dinner, in contrast to the lonely silence after, say, making the bed. "What we have to do," my friend had joked, "is produce a record that will sound wild applause when you've finished the housework. What fabulous hospital corners!, a voice will say. What magnificent plump pillows! Congratulations!"

Faye chuckled. "It's true, when you do the housework basically you're doing it for yourself. That's the hell of it. Who else cares if your house is neat or messy? Who even notices unless there's three inches of dust? Who could care less? But still, call me an idiot, *I* care and I don't mind doing it. That's why, unlike many of my friends, I rarely have outside help."

But of course Faye was anything but an idiot, and of course we both knew that of all the distinctions among homemakers she had just mentioned the largest: the one between those who did and did not have the choice of whether they *wanted* outside help. Or *wanted* an outside job. That indeed what made homemaking so radically different from all other kinds of work (in addition to the lack of pay) was the fact that no other occupation was regularly filled by such a total cross-section of all the social and economic classes (from Happy Rockefeller to a mother on welfare), no other occupation changed so drastically in terms of specific job functions and working conditions depending upon the financial status of the person (assuming there is one) paying the bills.

More to the point, what Faye had said about the individual differences in what homemakers liked to do was surely true. But it was obviously still the class differences that determined what they *had* to do. Among the wealthiest of homemakers all the primarily physical tasks—cleaning and laundry and mending and cooking—are traditionally delegated to other (the least wealthy) women as rapidly as possible. Among upper middle-class homemakers, if full-time help can't be afforded, the first chore to be regularly delegated (in addition to sporadic baby-sitters) is almost always housework, whether on a once a week or more frequent basis. However, among the vast majority of homemakers today outside help for regular household tasks is an unthinkable luxury.

Therefore, when in the mid-1960s the feminist battlecry was sounded to free *all* women from total responsibility for the "drudgery" of housework (by having men share equally) nothing seemed at first more likely to sound a common chord. And nothing *did*—among the mainly single and/or upper middle class and/or career-centered women involved at the time. Few articles were more acclaimed by feminists in those days than the one by Pat Mainardi entitled "The Politics of Housework." Few sentiments more echoed by overworked feminists than those in Judy Syfer's "I Want a Wife."

But as one doing the cheering it is perhaps high time to ask: to what extent were these attitudes shared by the women actually engaged full-time in the day by day job of homemaking? And a more troubling question: to what extent, if any, was the feminist position about "the drudgery of housework" also an expression of class attitudes—of (1) an elitist disdain for manual labor that one also often finds among upperclass men and (2) a commitment to "careers" as the one route to "success," that again is more typical of the upper classes. More specifically, how do homemakers of different economic and educational levels vary in their views of the separate tasks of the homemaker's job? Or do they?

As far as I know, the most extensively researched answer to the question of homemakers' attitudes toward their specific chores comes out of the same study noted before by Kathryn Walker at Cornell. During the course of their interviews, each of the 1,300 women studied was asked to rate on a scale of one to six her attitudes toward the different household tasks she regularly performed. (One meant she disliked the task very much; six she liked it very much.)

Among the tasks rated were:

215

Meal preparation

Special food preparation (baking, parties, and so on)

After-meal cleanup (dishwashing)

Regular house care

Ironing

Physical family care (bathing, diapering, feeding the baby, and so on)

Other family care (playing games, reading stories, tutoring, and so on)

Marketing

Management (overall planning and coordinating of family activities, budgeting, and so on)

"The findings absolutely shocked me," Carolyn G. Jarmon, who analyzed the homemakers' answers in her 1972 master's thesis, told me when I called her recently at Cornell. A married feminist who herself "hates" being stuck in the house, she was most surprised at the overall finding that the great majority (71 percent) expressed high satisfaction with the job as a whole.

As for the ratings of the individual tasks, the ones that scored the highest were "Other family care" and "Special food preparation" followed closely behind by "Physical family care" and "Meal preparation." Each of these four tasks had a median score of 5 or higher, which means, Jarmon said, "that for the average homemaker, playing with children and cooking are considered fun things to do." (Cooking regular meals, however, became less fun as the size of the family increased, as did physical child care as the age of the children increased.)

"Next in order of preference," Jarmon said, "were management and marketing," both of which scored a fairly high 4.8. "And then," she said, pausing for emphasis, "this is the one that really floored me—came regular house care, which got an astounding 4.3, meaning that for the average homemaker in our study it's still much more liked than disliked." Put another way, only 9 percent of the women rated housework in the 1 to 2 (strongly dislike) zone, 50 percent placed it in the neutral 3 to 4 zone, and 41 percent gave it the highest score of 5 to 6.

The two lowest-rated household tasks were ironing and then the most disliked of all, dishwashing. But even those last two scored in the neutral territory of 3.4 respectively, Jarmon said. Certainly not adored, but for the majority of the women—particularly those with smaller families and therefore less dishes—not abhorred either.

"I was really amazed by these positive attitudes," Jarmon said, "and I had to start questioning some of my previous assumptions about the typically unhappy homemaker."

I asked if she had been able to break down her findings by social class and by age. She said that while they did not have an income breakdown, there were some interesting correlations having to do with the homemaker's amount of education and type of previous employment and also with the occupation of the husband. Later she sent me a copy of her study so I could look at the findings myself.

What they found was a slightly negative relationship between a woman's education and her satisfaction in the physical aspects of the homemaking job. In other words, as the education of the homemaker increased there were slightly less positive attitudes about regular housework and, conversely, more positive attitudes about the management aspects of homemaking and about paid work. Also, as the wife's type of employment became more specific and shifted upward on the scale of unskilled toward professional, her attitudes toward paid work, as a number of other studies have shown, became more positive. Again, and not surprisingly, her attitudes toward paid work also moved in the positive direction as the age of the youngest child increased.

In contrast, as the husband's employment type shifted downward from professional and managerial to mechanical and unskilled, the homemaker was more likely to register higher satisfaction with the physical household tasks. In fact, Jarmon wrote, "in all cases . . . as the husband's socioeconomic status decreased, wife's attitudes toward [the physical tasks] . . . moved in the positive direction" with the one exception of dishwashing, the least popular chore for all classes. The crucial factor with dishwashing seemed to be mainly the work load—the more you had to do the less you liked it.

All in all then, Jarmon's findings did point to distinct class differences in homemakers' attitudes toward housework. But, she warned, "you have to remember that the differences were only a matter of degree. They didn't change the major finding in any way." And the major finding: the large majority of the women enjoyed the job of homemaking as a whole. "At least that's what they said."

She added the caveat that the interviews had been originally conducted in 1969 before the women's movement had its fullest impact. However, since then, a number of other studies have pointed to similar conclusions, in particular one conducted in 1972 by the University of Michigan's Institute for Social Research. Based on interviews with 445 homemakers, this study found that, once again, over two thirds expressed high satisfaction with their lives, but that those who were college graduates were somewhat less satisfied than other housewives. Conversely, employed married women with less than a high school degree were less satisfied with their lives than those who were at home. Those with high school degrees registered about equal satisfaction either way. It was only among college graduates that employed married women registered somewhat higher satisfaction with their lives than their counterparts who were homemakers.

According to Jarmon, her own study dealt with the most traditional kinds of families. Very few wealthy, very few poor, very few childless and no single parent families had been part of the sample. Educationally speaking, just 20 percent of the women and 30 percent of the husbands had graduated from college, although a majority of both sexes (and more women than men) had high school degrees and some post-high school training. (In fact, the sample was educationally more advanced than the U.S. population as a whole.)

"So there's always the possibility," Jarmon said, "that since these were women from traditional families they were voicing more positive attitudes about homemaking than they actually held. They may have felt they had to accept the female role and that was that." She noted the sociological saw that "attitudes follow behavior" or in other words that once we start to do something we frequently modify our previous feelings about it, sometimes simply because what's the use of complaining. And in her study she mentioned the fact that homemakers' attitudes toward their work must also be seen in relation to whom they are doing it for. Unlike other workers, the homemaker and those nearest to her are the direct recipients of the services she performs and what's more, she performs them generally under no one else's supervision or time schedule or standards of excellence but her own. And in this sense, at a time when job enrichment is supposedly a public issue, the homemaker's job can be viewed as both less alienated and more autonomous than most.

Finally and perhaps most to the point, Jarmon emphasized the truism that none of our attitudes, no matter who we are, appear out of the thin air. They are always made in some context, against a perceived set of alternatives. So it is not simply a question of homemaker, yes or no. But rather, if not a homemaker, what then?

"Of course there *is* one more interpretation," Jarmon said, just when we were about to hang up. "The simplest one. The women were simply telling it the way it was. The majority really enjoyed what they were doing. To my dismay."

"I don't know why it should be such a shock that many if not most homemakers enjoy what they're doing," Faye said, sipping the foam off a fresh mug of beer. "The energy and talent and wit that can go into managing a home and taking care of a family— there can be great fun and satisfaction that you can't get doing anything else, at least in my opinion. My children have broadened my horizon, no question about that. My husband is like a lot of men who have zeroed in on their work and neglected their family but because of him I'm probably a thousand times more interested in the world than I would have been."

"Really, Faye," I said. "You sound just like Betty Crocker. What happened to that dark lady of fury I met at the conference?"

"I'm still furious, you just don't understand. I'm furious because I think women should get credit for whatever we do, but of course we don't. There's still this ingrained sense that you're not quite as good as a man, especially if you're not bringing in what this society reveres more than anything—hard cold cash. And then when you get to be my age and your children are grown, you find you've got nothing to show for all these years. Plus on top of everything else there's this ghastly blast we discussed at the conference. That homemaking is a hazardous occupation. If he keels over or takes off with some young thing, where does that leave the typical homemaker? For most women of course there's no big settlement, no expensive property to be divided, and many divorced women who felt heady when the movement started now find they're left with next to nothing.

"Or suppose a woman has given her all to caring for a family and suddenly she reaches the age like me where outside she faces the double whammy of sexism and agism in the labor market and inside her husband and children are looking at her like some kind of leech because she doesn't want to go out and get liberated and become a file clerk. She wants to keep doing what she's been doing but to do that she has to go to him each week for money like a nine-year-old child. And as long as we're dealing in dollars and cents, he'll always have the upper hand. So what should this woman do?"

Her great gravelly voice had become softer, almost gentle. She raised her mug, took a long swallow, put it down. Stared for several seconds into the mug that was now, like the old adage, half empty or half full depending upon your point of view. Or maybe just the time of day.

"Something wrong?"

"No. Nothing." She looked up. It had clearly been half empty. "It's just that we're obviously so far from solving these problems. It has a lot to do with giving homemakers credit. And it has a lot to do with money. And once you start to talk about more than a few token dollars—whether for social security for homemakers or salaries or whatever—well, you know how much of a chance we have. And as far as your husband giving you the credit you deserve, forget it. He's too busy with his important work or his latest girlfriend or the football game, anything but you."

I asked how her husband—who was affiliated with the university—had reacted when she told him about the conference.

"Oh, you know, he thinks he's a big liberal. Why *of course* homemakers deserve more recognition. Of course we need more protection. Of course he didn't really hear a blasted word I said." She pushed the mug away from her. "But let's not talk about him. Let's get back to that hypothetical woman I was discussing. What's she supposed to do? Oh, sure, she could go out and have an affair, but since the men around are usually as insensitive as her husband, what's the good in that? Since she's too old to get a decent job, divorce may not be a hot idea either. It could put her in worse shape than she is now. So it's hopeless, isn't it? There's nothing to do but stay where she is."

Oddly enough, or was it naturally enough, the thought seemed to cheer her up. At least her voice was getting strong again. Half full.

> *It can all look hunky-dory until something goes wrong. All of a sudden he's laid off his job or he gets a heart attack or he tells you he wants a divorce or maybe like me you want it first and then you see how vulnerable a homemaker is. How dependent you've been on his goodwill and good fortune all these years. And then you start to shake.*

Vulnerable? Pat? She was clearly the most self-confident woman at the workshop, so you thought as you looked at her. Even when she mentioned the drastic decline in her standard of living since the divorce, even when she predicted she might one day be on welfare, her proud erect posture, her carefully modulated voice, seemed to belie the troubled words she spoke. She was in fact trembling with shyness everytime she forced herself to speak up, so she told me later. "But people are always getting the wrong idea about me 'cause of how I look."

The subject of divorce had been an intermittent topic throughout the conference, an intermittent warning to the overly secure. How the rate is of course at an all-time high. How attitudes toward divorced mothers have been changing in recent years. How

221

judges are increasingly refusing to award alimony, increasingly saying to women with children: "Well, you understand you'll have to go to work now." How the amount of court-ordered child-support payments is on the average less than enough to furnish half the costs of rearing the children involved, according to one estimate by the Washington-based Citizens' Advisory Committee on the Status of Women. How even these insufficient amounts are not to be counted on, with one study in Wisconsin showing that only 39 percent of fathers were in full compliance of the support order after the first year following the divorce. (A federal program to find and collect from ex-husbands who default has recently been started.) How—not surprisingly but seldom mentioned—divorced and separated women are now the most likely of *all* women, including single women, to be in the paid labor force. (Nearly two out of every three are currently employed.) How, even so, the female-headed household has become almost a synonym for the financially strapped household.

At the conference luncheon Herma Hill Kay, Professor of Law at the University of California at Berkeley and a noted feminist expert on family law, told the audience that "something funny happened on the way to the courthouse" after the passage of a wave of no-fault divorce laws in over a dozen state legislatures in the past decade, laws that many women, including herself, had been supporting. What happened—along with more liberal attitudes toward everyone's right to divorce without ugly allegations—was that "judges in many cases stopped awarding spousal support." They decided to take women's liberation slogans at their word before many women were ready or equipped to live up to them. "What they did in effect was to treat these women as if they were their own grandchildren. As if they had grown up in an age when equality was valued between men and women, which, of course, they hadn't."

What needs to be done? According to Professor Kay: "We have to soften the way equality hits the woman not prepared for it." While she felt it "essential" that divorced homemakers be encouraged to be self-supporting, she also saw the need, as have many others, for a subsidized program of counseling and educational assistance—like a GI Bill of Rights for Displaced Homemakers—that would help them make the transition to the paid labor force. Such a bill has been proposed by the National Organization for Women.

But it is precisely this ever growing assumption that a divorced mother *must* make that transition, and quick, that frightens a woman like Pat. What it means is that what she is doing right now—taking care of her young children at home—is less and less to be recognized as having any economic and social value. Exactly what we had been discussing at the workshop. Except that for Pat and women in her position the issue is obviously far from academic. It is a matter of how she and her children will be able to manage their lives.

She picked me up in an aging blue station wagon at the nearest bus stop, ten miles away from the busless (population 700) rural town where she and her children had resettled after the separation. Sitting behind the wheel with that same almost rigidly erect carriage, her long gray hair pulled tightly back with a silver barrette, she drove us slowly through the flat and silent countryside, pointing out the various sites along the way. The local general store where everyone came to gossip. Dairy farm after dairy farm. A new building under construction, possibly a medical center, no one was sure. Dairy farm after dairy farm. The country schoolhouse where her two daughters (one six, one nine) were at the moment attending class. Dairy farm after dairy farm—and then she slowed down at the entrance to a tiny wooden farm house and pointed to what she said was the pride of her life, the several acres of land surrounding it.

"Nature," she said, getting out of the station wagon. "Take a whiff."

She told me she decided to live here because all of her life she had been happiest whenever she was in the country, was uncomfortable and tense in cities, fed up with the suburbia of both her childhood and marriage. Once moved in she had begun the transformation of her life by transforming the inside of the four-room house, repanelling walls, plastering and painting, doing almost everything entirely with her own hands. We sat at a square table in the modest kitchen and she brought out a series of pictures of the house before she moved in. How dark and dim in comparison.

223

And as I looked at the pictures and realized the tremendous physical work she had accomplished, I also began to understand that remark about people getting the wrong idea about her because of the way she looked.

She grew up in a working class suburb outside of St. Paul, the middle of three daughters, "the looker of the bunch." Her father was an electrician, "the kind of man, you know the type, he's there, but dammit he's not a real presence. He's just someone who goes to work and comes home and nods at you and eats his meals and watches the tube." Her mother, a full-time homemaker, was the dominant one, the one who made all the decisions, the one who expected "big big things" of her strikingly attractive second daughter. Without money or aspirations for college, big things meant mainly (1) become a model and/or (2) marry money but (3) take typing and steno in high school just in case.

Tall (always the tallest girl in her class), proud (always aware of her mother's high expectations), Pat grew up feeling different from her classmates, indifferent to school in general. To help support the family she took part-time jobs throughout high school—a smorgasbord of pink collar jobs, once a telephone operator, once a receptionist, twice a waitress, and once during a special back-to-school fashion show she was the model of her mother's dreams. But by the end of high school, no big, big thing, either in the shape of a modeling career or wealthy suitor seemed likely to present itself quickly, and anyway by that time Pat's expectations had started to scale down to those of her female class members. "Mainly we wanted a lot of clothes, a good looking husband and a baby." Two years out of high school, after a brief stint as a secretary, she had the last two.

He was a salesman. Screws. "Really, that's what he did. He sold screws. It sounds like a joke, but except for some other little parts that was pretty much it." He was the son of a construction worker, on his way up, and like Pat's mother he expected big things, of himself, of her and their life together. But after the marriage he was mostly on the road—often two, three weeks at a stretch—and she was mostly pregnant or busy with the babies. Three in six years. "I should have stopped at one, but I was stupid. And once you have three you don't leave so easy, even if you know something's wrong, which I did."

He was transferred to a new territory outside of Chicago. They found another suburb, another house, and Pat resumed her work. She cooked. She baked. She cared for her children. She cleaned. She gardened. She shopped. She had another baby. She joined the community center. She joined the (Methodist) church. She went to parties with her husband given by other employees of the screw company.

At these parties it was very important to her husband that she look a certain way, talk a certain way. "So I'd dress very carefully." Then on the way home, "he'd go over the whole evening and discuss everything I did wrong. What a floozy I was. What dumb things I had said. I didn't have the class the other wives had." And because she had not been to college and many of them had, "I figured he was right. It took me a long time to understand that he was the one who was really insecure, and that's why he was so hard on me."

In 1968 their last child was born. "By that time we couldn't get through a meal without fighting." She suggested they see a marriage counselor. "He wouldn't hear of it." She went to see her minister. "Know what he said? Two people who look as good as you and your husband do together, how could you think of splitting up? Can you imagine that? What a great reason to stay together."

To bolster her spirits, she made friends with gin. To bolster his spirits, he made friends with women. "We were your everyday soap opera. The alcoholic housewife and the cheating husband." Depressed, she'd let the housework slide. Annoyed, he'd badger her more. What the hell was wrong with her? Why couldn't she shape up like other women? One night, half meaning it, she told him she wanted a divorce. He told her he didn't, forget it. "Oh, not because of me, because he didn't want to part with any of his precious money." But she breathed a sigh of relief—How would she have taken care of the children? And the arguments continued. Another night right before they were due to start off on a vacation he blew up at her and in a rage she decided to go off by herself, leave the bastard with the kids. And the fact that she was able to do this—spend two weeks alone after so many years of marriage—gave her some of the courage she needed.

Returning home, she went to an attorney a friend had heard about. At first he thought she wasn't serious. A divorce after all those years? With all those kids? But when he saw she meant business he told her to go home right away and take whatever stocks they had out of the safe immediately. "Well, I couldn't bring myself to do that. I couldn't be that kind of person." Instead that evening she told her husband she had seen a lawyer. "He begged me to take a couple of months to think it over, give him one more chance." Through her own tears she saw his, and she agreed. One more chance. Then he went and sold the few stocks they had, without her knowledge.

"I guess you could say it was the worst period of my life. I was going through emotional hell, scared to death of what would happen to me and the kids, drinking heavily, taking Valium all the time." Like the old saying, everything that could go wrong, did. She smashed her car. Slipped her disc. Injured her hand. And the arguments got worse. Got physical. First a little push, then a shove against the wall. Twice, three times, he knocked her down. "But never anything so bad there were real injuries I could show in a courtroom and in Illinois at the time you really had to be battered before you could prove physical abuse. Also the truth is, I'd always feel I had provoked him in a way. I'd be drinking and he'd be drinking and he'd make one of his insulting cracks and I'd know just what to say to make him come unglued."

"But that doesn't mean he had the right to hit you?"

"No. I'm just telling you how I felt."

So: days into weeks into months. They continued to live together, "and it was horrible. I'd tell him to leave and he'd say if you're so anxious to go, you go, but no one's kicking me out of the house I'm paying for. By that time I was pretty desperate. In Illinois grounds for divorce were still very strict"—they've since adopted no-fault—"and I didn't want to stoop to snapping pictures of him with other women.

"Finally, I did the dumbest thing a woman in that situation can do. I took the advice of a relative, my dear kind brother-in-law,

226

my husband's brother, who said he'd help by finding a common attorney to handle the divorce for the two of us. That way, he said, we'd ease my husband's fears about being wiped out and I'd be protected, too. What a joke. But I thought, to hell with it, anything to get the whole mess over with."

The settlement: "I got this place which we had bought as a last ditch effort to keep us together, this crummy place, which I love, but which isn't worth anything. Also, I got the grand sum of $300 a month out of which I have to take care of the girls" (two other children stayed with their father, one is in college), "pay the mortgage and taxes and keep up the station wagon and everything else. The way prices have gone up for food and everything, we're eating mainly the fruits and vegetables we grow."

But if she is finding it difficult to manage, if she is afraid to think about the future, she also knows that she is far better off than many many women in her position. She knows this very deeply because once a week she drives the old station wagon to Madison and spends the entire night talking with and listening to eight single mothers like herself. "Without these women," she told me, "I don't know how I would have made it. After the divorce you hit rock bottom and then you start to build. I think it was the group"—she read about it getting started in the newspaper—"and working on the house that held me together."

The women are of all ages. "Some in their twenties, thirties, forties and some undetermined." She smiled. "That's what's so good about it. The variety. We all learn from each other. The ones with babies learn from the older ones. You know, we can say to them, don't worry, it's just a phase, it'll pass. And the older ones get a little courage from the younger ones, about going out and trying new things."

They are from different economic brackets, too. "One is an ADC mother, and she has to be. She has an infant and a two-year-old and no skills and a husband who can't be found though the state is looking. Another works full-time, takes her two kids to child-care in the morning, picks them up at night, and it's working out okay except for when they're sick and except for the cost; it's so expensive it's just about bleeding her to death. Then another has a pretty good job and she can afford to take the kids to a baby

227

sitter, but by the time she comes home and does the cooking and puts them to bed, she's so exhausted she finds herself screaming all the time at them and she hates herself for it. Then, let's see, another is looking for a job and can't find anything, she's too old and she's never worked before. And then a couple seem to be managing okay, one started college this year, and one really likes her work, so you see we're all types and all situations.

"But I'd have to say that the women generally envy me very much. That I don't have to go out and take the first job I can find like they mostly do."

On the table a round wooden bowl filled with enormous Wisconsin apples. "From that tree over there," Pat said, proudly, pointing toward the window. "Help yourself." I did, and while I bit in, she told me more about her life since the divorce. That in addition to attending the single mother's group every week she had also taken a series of aptitude tests and begun to get some preliminary vocational counseling at the extension division of the university. "See: that's another way I'm really fortunate. Living near a college like this. What happens is you go in and you have no idea of what you can do or what opportunities there are and you're a little scared and they assign you to a counselor who knows where it's at. And the one I have really seems to genuinely care. She's a woman about my age. And the best thing is that it's all completely free. That's the kind of thing all women like myself should be getting. But they don't."

"And what did she tell you?"

"Well, we're talking about carpentry right now. And maybe something to do with wild life. But the first thing she told me, after we talked awhile, is that I shouldn't feel I have to *prove* anything right away. To take a few months to be sure. She said the big danger when you get divorced is that you often set up a lot of goals for yourself that you can't meet. And then you feel worse. And from talking with the other women in my single mothers' group, I'd say that really has been true for most of us."

"In what way?"

"In almost all ways, really. I'd say we all found our expectations were much, much too high about what was going to happen.

228

Both as to the kinds of jobs we'd get and the kinds of social life we'd have. A lot of us thought, boy, now I'm finally going to live again. Start all over. Show the world. Well, what a letdown. At least, for me. Not that I'd want to be back with that turd for a minute, I'm not a bit sorry about that. But as for the new men you meet when you're my age, well most you'd want to have anything to do with—if you're choosy and I am—they're married and that's not my scene. So loneliness is the first thing you have to get used to usually. For a while anyway. And then as for the great jobs, well we all know what kind of a wonderful market there is for women my age, even before the economy got bad."

Again she looked out the window. "In that respect maybe women's liberation has hurt us. You know, giving us false hopes about how great everything was going to be when we were out on our own. But there are also a lot of things that feminists are saying and doing that I do agree with—500 percent."

I mentioned the gap between homemakers and feminists that I had discussed with the other women. "Yes, there is a gap, let's face it. I really wish I could bridge it, but that means feminists have to understand women like me, too. For example, there are aspects of homemaking I love. Housework is a bore, I think, but I really enjoy my children and I love to grow things and build things and cook. The fact is if my husband had been different, if he wasn't putting me down all the time and we had been able to communicate other than sexually, I think I would have been fulfilled, whatever that means. At least until the kids were older.

"I'm in favor of the movement, but women like me, we can also see how the movement has been used against us. I don't mean by the feminists, but by our ex-husbands who say go out and get liberated and get a job so we don't have to support you. By the judges who say the same thing. Like I said before, I think most homemakers with very small children don't want to *have* to go out, at least not full-time, unless they're interested in a certain line of work, you know they're professionals or something. I think frankly that's why a lot of homemakers are afraid to open their eyes to the good things the women's movement is saying. They're afraid someone's going to say, put up or shut up. Stop

229

complaining or get a job. I think that's why there weren't more homemakers at the conference. They were afraid they'd have to prove something."

"Is that how you used to feel?"

"Me? People have been asking me to prove something all my life. First my mother, then my darling husband. Both times, whatever I did, I never made the grade. In their eyes. That's why now, if I'm trying to do anything, it's to reach the point where no one can do that to me anymore. Where I don't do it to myself either. You know today for me it's a lot like when I was a young girl starting out. Then there was all that pressure to get married. Now there's all this pressure to get into a field. Do something important. *Be* something. But with me, that's just what I don't want—pressure. I don't want to have to go on a guilt trip because I'm not accomplishing enough in someone else's eyes. I don't want to be judged anymore; that's what happened to me all my life and now I don't want any parent or any husband or any minister or any woman's movement or any television commercial to tell me what I should do or be."

At the end of the conference we were all asked to gather in the auditorium to hear the reports from the different workshops. As might have been predicted, however, there were far fewer women present for the summaries than had been there at the opening in the morning. Many had had to rush home to start Saturday dinners or to relieve their husbands of the children—to resume their seven-day-a-week jobs.

Taking a seat near the front I noticed that Joyce and Bea had both left early. So had Pat, whose daughters were spending the day with one of the women from her single mothers' group. I thought Faye had left too until I heard her bellow of approval when one of the workshop discussion leaders announced: "We have today clarified our conflicts."

Each of the leaders from the different workshops was to report on the major recommendations of her group, so I took out my pen and pad.

The workshop on "Money Management and Me" called for an investigation into our entire social security system, since it is blatantly a misnomer for an ever-growing number of older women who are now the most likely of *all* Americans to be living in poverty. Later I learned this workshop had been mostly attended by homemakers in their late fifties and early sixties, many of whom had been shocked and frightened to learn that they would likely *not* be covered by their husband's pensions should the husband die first (as three out of every four do) and to hear as well how little their social security payments would probably amount to. No one had ever told them.

The workshop on "The Law" emphasized the need to revise marriage, no-fault divorce and inheritance-tax laws so that not only will there be equality between the sexes, but the economic value of the homemaker role will be recognized and whoever assumes that role will be protected in the event the marriage ends.

The workshop on "The Political System" declared that the economic problems of homemakers must now be addressed as political issues, along with those of women in the labor force. It called in addition for affirmative-action officials to begin dealing with the nature of our entire work structure that now says a decent well-paying job with all the fringe benefits must be a full-time one. For although more and more mothers are being pressed by economic needs to look for employment each year, the fact is that most mothers of pre-school children still do not *want* to be forced into full-time work. So the participants believed.

The workshop on "Family Roles" reported a great deal of disagreement among its participants. But in the end, those who did feel that changes in the family division of labor were badly needed called for conferences involving both wives *and* husbands. Such conferences are important, the women said, because even after a decade of the new feminism, many homemakers still need reinforcement from other women before they can gain the confidence to press their husbands for change. To which Joyce's comment, "Basically, I guess, I'm just not the kind to complain" could well bear witness.

The workshop on "Education" said that if mothers are to have the time needed to return to school then homemaking must become the responsibility of the entire family, including the children. Support groups for women wanting and needing to make changes in their lives were also advocated. Not only are most women unaware of what educational programs are available, said the participants, but many still have to beat down resistance from husbands (particularly those who have not been to college themselves) should they desire to get a degree. In addition, the workshop recommended that continuing education programs be made available on a part-time basis, since, as with employment, many women who would like to participate do not want to be away from their small children for a full day.

Representing our group on "The Economy," Mary Lou Munts detailed how we had spent the entire day discussing the unrecognized value and worth of the homemaker's job and the many economic risks she faces. How in a system where protection is mainly given to those who have been attached to the paid labor market, the homemaker is left particularly vulnerable in the event of a crisis. It seems clear, she said, that in the short run we must find a way to provide piecemeal measures, such as disability insurance, medical insurance, and old-age pensions for homemakers on a low-cost or publicly supported basis. And to provide scholarships and loans and, most of all, decent jobs to those in the transition back to school and the labor force.

But in the long run, she said, there were far more basic issues that needed to be resolved: The whole question of how the services of homemakers are to be recognized and rewarded. The whole issue of whether a system of social insurance should be based on income and labor-market attachment or simply on need. The whole nature of a job market that puts a premium on continuity in employment, thereby penalizing the majority of American mothers who still choose to interrupt their (paid) work lives, if only for a matter of a few years. And we really have only begun to look for the answers to these deeper questions, she said. But at least we have finally begun.

7

The World of Women's Work: Who, What, Where, When, Why

It used to come easier. Before I set off on this journey, this venture, this quest, whatever it's been, polemic came easier. Before, I was still writing: "It is time to give all women a chance at self-fulfillment and a choice of ways to define it." Or, in an article dealing with the double burdens of mothers compared to fathers in the paid labor force: "It is time to recognize that the home is also a place of work." It is time . . . it is time.

Right now, however (although I have of course not changed my mind), I can still see their faces. The memories are too close for easy rhetoric. I think of the department store. Try to imagine walking over to my co-worker Peggy standing near the $16.66 raincoats: *Peggy, it is time to give all women a chance at self-fulfillment and a choice of ways to define it.* "Sure, honey, get us some chairs." I see Ingrid climbing up the stairs in Tony's restaurant, five plates on one arm, three on the other: *Ingrid, it is time to give all women a chance at self-fulfillment and a choice of ways to define it.* "Great. Tell the bastard to build us a real locker room." Or, leaning over a sink in the back of the beauty shop, Linda, who would prefer to be home with her child but needs to earn

233

money, while in the meantime her husband refuses to be "inconvenienced" in any way: *Linda, it is time to recognize that the home is also a place of work.* "Thanks. For nothing. Would you hand me the cream rinse please?"

The memories are still too close for the old high-flying rhetoric. Not only the memories of the women, although primarily so, most vividly so, but also of the union officials and the employers—no, isn't it also time we dropped the euphemism and got back to that more telling word—the bosses, and their paid representatives, at the various workplaces and union offices I visited. *Gentlemen* (for they were indeed mostly male, if not mostly gentle): *It is time your women workers received far higher pay. It is time they had the same opportunities as the miniscule proportion of men in these relatively few occupations in which most women work. It is time women had true power. Power on the job and power within your unions. It is time you had less power.* "But indubitably. Of course it is time. What time *is* it by the way? Shouldn't those girls be back from lunch by now?"

It is time . . .

What did I "find"? What are my "conclusions"? Death is the only certain conclusion in this world so they say. (Some millionaires still don't pay taxes.) So instead of conclusions I will just try to speculate a bit.

In doing so I shall call on my old friends Who, What, Where, When and Why for help.

WHO

Too many. By far too many waitresses, beauticians, saleswomen looking for work, at least in the local job markets I visited. By far too few opportunities for them. Tony and Bumblebrain being able to hire and fire with no worries at all. Tony even able to "forget" whom he had hired. The department store so flooded with applicants at Christmas that some didn't even dare to inquire about the pay. A certain-sized hard-core staff that can be depended upon over the long haul, and from there on out, easy come, easy go, baby. Replaceable parts to expand when business is

busy, contract when business is slow. Three-platoon staffs.
Temps. Kelly Girls. On calls. "You must have made a mistake;
there are no stations open tonight. Try again next week." At the
insurance company things were more sophisticated. But once you
looked past the better fringes, the better conditions, the pretty cafeteria with the tasty free lunches, the basic pattern was really
quite similar. A certain sized hard-core clerical staff of women
who received modest promotions (but the best were reserved for
college women and, above all, college men) and then the rest—
young single women right out of high school who were "expected" to leave in a few years ("It's good for them") and make room
for new beginning workers at beginning wages. Also a growing
use of part-timers and temps there, too. Also strong indications
that the onrush of new office machinery is going to accelerate this
trend. Yes, to some extent more computer-related technical jobs
but at the same time a reduction in ordinary middle-level clerical
and secretarial positions appears to be in the cards. Granted, the
newspapers are still flooded with want-ads and every other day
you can hear someone mouthing, "My kingdom for a good secretary." But in the long-run this demand seems destined to diminish
somewhat and if the new technology alone doesn't cause it, there
is another cloud moving on to the horizon that surely will. At
least there is in the considered opinion of the U.S. Department of
Labor and at the Department of Labor, you understand, they
don't have any other kinds of opinions. I quote from the *1975
Handbook on Women Workers* again:

A number of factors will significantly affect the outlook
for women workers in the next decade . . . In terms of
supply there are expected to be many more women participating in the labor force—8 million more in 1985 than
in 1972.

Another factor is that the age composition of women
workers will be changing. The Bureau of Labor Statistics
projections of labor force growth for the 1972–85 period
indicated that the major increase in the female labor
force is expected to occur among women 20 to 34 years

of age. The number of women workers under 20 is expected to decline during this period.

Women in the labor force in 1985 will have had more years of schooling. . . . The large increase in the supply of women college graduates in the labor force will coincide with an expected slowdown in the growth of demand for elementary and secondary school teachers; occupations in which a large proportion of college women have been employed in the past. . . . The proportion of all male workers who will have 4 or more years of college in 1985 is expected to be higher than that for female workers—20.8 percent versus 16.7 percent. However, a greater proportion of men than women will have 8 or fewer years of school—8.6 versus 5.8 percents.

How do the Labor Department writers know all this? I'm not sure. They have computers, economists, investigators, census charts, past statistics which they project further. Jeane Dixon comes in now and then, so I hear. They have been known to be wrong. Very wrong. A lot obviously depends on, as the jargon goes, other variables, economic and otherwise to be discussed in a moment. But as a general guide this is the best we have. Now here comes the part you have perhaps been expecting:

The supply-demand situation may be of special concern to women since the supply of women college graduates will be growing at a faster rate than that of male graduates. . . . Despite the apparent surplus . . . it is unlikely that there will be large-scale unemployment among college graduates. Rather it is likely that college graduates will obtain jobs generally filled by individuals with less than 4 years of college. In the past, graduates have reacted to changes in the job situation by taking the best available job and there is no reason to assume that this will not be the case in the future . . .

The availability of more college-trained women . . . is expected to have an adverse effect on many of the less educated. . . . This is essentially a problem of credentials. If the required educational qualifications for a job

236

rise more rapidly than the actual education required to perform the job, the availability of more college-educated women will limit advancement of workers with fewer years of schooling.

Perhaps this is the best moment for a personal interjection, a slight digression. So many women have told so much about themselves in this book that it seems incumbent upon me to do some opening up, too. I am not a college graduate. I do not have a BA. During my senior year of high school my father was stricken with lung cancer, my brother was already a sophomore at an out-of-town college, and so my tentative plans of going fell apart. I wanted to be with my father as long as I could. There was also the question of leaving my mother alone during this crisis and of course the medical bills were piling up and up. So I took a job instead. That was the ostensible reason, the touching reason, but there was another one equally strong. (Actually deeper because of course I could have gone at night if need be.) I didn't want to be in college, not unless it also meant traveling to a new and exciting city. I wanted to be out in the world, not in a classroom. After elementary school I had never really learned much in school, just enough to get reasonably passing grades, but my deepest and most serious learning was never done in an organized setting. I was always an omniverous reader, books piling up and threatening to drive me out of my own bedroom, but these were rarely the books I was supposed to be reading. I had absorbing interests, was compelled to follow them in my own way, at my own pace, one at a time. Seven or five different subjects a day was simply not my way nor was the classroom atmosphere. (Since those days I've tried taking various courses at nights and it's always the same. After a few classes, even with the most brilliant of instructors, my eyes start to glaze over. It's simply not the way I learn. There are people like me everywhere of course. Academics can't or won't understand it but the woods and the libraries and, I might add, the author's index cards are full of us. Not to mention the unemployment lines.)

The first job I found, through an employment agency, was presented to me in the jargon of the time as a Girl Friday job. (Now it's supposed to be simply Friday.) I would be working for an important executive at the then New York offices of Metro-Gold-wyn-Mayer. Now this couldn't possibly have been more thrilling to me, since like many dreamy young females growing up I had often thought of becoming an actress, the most glittering of pink-collar jobs. Girl Friday to an MGM executive. What a perfect place to be Discovered. Hurry and show me the way. As it turned out, however, the executive was the building maintenance superintendent. My job was to sit in a little one-woman office taking phone calls from people complaining about burned-out light bulbs, impacted toilets, leaky faucets. I was to write down the room number and problem on little white message slips for the house electrician, plumber and carpenter, plus do a little typing for the building superintendent. How did I like it? Just fine. It was a lovely job. For a seventeen-year-old me at the time. All through the day the workers would drop into the little office to pick up their messages and, to waste time, they'd tell me tall and funny and sometimes serious stories about their lives—I remember the plumber was from Belgium—and I'd listen fascinated, learning much more about the world than I ever had in school and God knows having a much better time. They were extremely decent men. This book has described mostly other kinds and so, particularly in these days of Wayne Hayes et al, it may be a good idea to point up some exceptions. Give the boys coming up some models. They were very decent men, including the building superintendent. At lunchtime I'd go down to another world, the cafeteria, and listen to the young college women in "publicity" and "the photo lab" talk about the stars. I thought it all very glamorous. Then I'd go back to the impacted toilets. Two months after I started the job my father died, and in my weekly paycheck was an additional fifty dollars, with a note that this was a small contribution to help pay funeral expenses. It was company policy, nothing special for me, maybe years before Louis B. had gotten soft watching one of his own tearjerkers (but not so soft that he was going to really shell out), but I remember being surprised and touched. It was a gesture of concern, I thought. I can see now the paternalistic flavor to it, but at the time it didn't feel that way. Or maybe at the time that was just what I wanted.

Now I'd better do some rapid skipping because there are far more serious matters still to discuss. We've still got What, Where, When and Why waiting in the wings, impatiently. At some point I quit the job. (It's true you usually do want to move around when you're that young, but like most of the women at the Chicago insurance company, I was never given entree to openings in other departments—publicity could have had me in a minute—it was that internal labor market question again.) I found another job, a series of other clerical-type jobs, started studying acting, tried a bit of acting, saw it wasn't for me, I wasn't for it, began looking more and more for jobs in the editorial realm, a perfect place for a bookish person like myself. Most of the want-ads for those jobs said Rcnt Coll Grad. Since there appeared to be no other way to get into those doors, I became a Rcnt Coll Grad, my acting classes shouldn't go to waste. (But nothing fancy, mind you. Not Radcliffe. Not Vassar. I still had my egalitarian values. Queens.)

The Rcnt Coll Grad landed a series of publishing-type or media-type jobs (including a trade magazine, newsletter, advertising agency for publishing houses, public relations agency for political crooks) all in the general euphemistic "editorial assistant" vein, which mainly turned out to be typing and magazine production and proofreading. In the course of those jobs I met my own share of Bumblebrains and Eds, although I must say nobody quite as upfront as Tony . . . oh yes, yes, I do remember one now. Some jobs I would quit, several I was fired from (typically for lateness or lousy typing).

Eventually when I was twenty-three I found a real editorial job at a nonprofit research and advocacy agency called the National Committee on Employment of Youth. The job entailed working on a bimonthly newsletter and quarterly magazine and some four years later I was made editor of both. For our male model file (it should only be that easy) Eli E. Cohen is the name of the rare and fine man who helped me move up that particular internal labor market ladder, and I was just one of quite a number of women he helped advance occupationally, and this was long, long before the days of affirmative action.

Now, finally, the point this is all leading up to: What would happen to a person like myself today? What *is* happening to young women starting out now, twenty years later? I haven't checked, but the way things are going you might have to have a college degree to work in that building superintendent's office. To get some of those pseudo-editorial jobs, I might have to fake a master's now, if not a PhD, and not just from any old school. Frankly my acting was never that good. Frankly I think it's outrageous that I ever had to stoop to lying to get inside those doors in the first place. Now I guess what would happen is that I'd have to graduate from college, there'd be no other choice. If the money in our family was really tight I'd also be in far worse shape than before, since free tuition is now becoming increasingly rare. I guess I'd be experiencing what Marcia Freedman once termed the taming-of-the-shrew syndrome. Like Katherine, you're not permitted to have any mustard for your beef until you already have the beef in hand. At the same time, sorry to say, you're not permitted to have any beef until you already have the mustard.

I want to be very careful about how I put this because the whole subject of higher education is at the moment a very tricky issue. In no way am I a let's-deschool-America fan. In no way am I anti-college. Some of my best friends are academics. (Truly.) More to the point, I have known too many people, women and men, working class and middle class and upper class, who tell me their lives were transformed by their college experience. Jeanne King says that even if she never does anything but wait on tables for the rest of her life she will never be sorry for the money and years she spent matriculating. "For me, it was an incredible experience." Ingrid of Tony's restaurant said virtually the same thing. "Okay, if things don't open up, I'll be a waitress with a master's. It was worth it." So the point for the moment is not that college is superfluous. The point for the moment is the obvious one that everyone knows, that every six-year-old knows . . . people are different. The man was right: many flowers do bloom. Do grow in different ways. Do need different amounts of sun and water and shade. Do hear the sounds of different drummers, different plumbers, the ticks of different clocks. But there seems to be no stopping it. There seems to be no end to the capacity of this mass society, this technological age, this capitalist economy, this

240

sexist power structure, this particular combination of each, this whatever you want to pin it on, to force us into standardized molds. College women over here, non-college over there, please. Ivy League over here, community college over there, please. Master's and PhD's wait in the outer office, the rest of you can leave now. Thanks for stopping by. Older women in that diner, black women in that Nedick's juiceatorium, younger white women would you please turn around slowly so we can see where your talents would be best situated. Ah, here comes our model black woman for our front office, she's really quite pretty, isn't she? The rest will please file back into the keypunch room. Here come our two new female exceptions for furniture and hard goods. . . . And now our trusty *Handbook on Women Workers* wants us to know that:

> The availability of more college-trained women and men is expected to have an adverse effect on many of the less educated. It is likely to mean that, in the future, workers with less than a college education, *particularly women,* will have less chance of advancing in professional positions as many could do in the past, particularly in professions such as accounting. They will have less opportunity for promotion to high-level positions in sales, managerial and some clerical and service occupations. . . . This is essentially a problem of credentials. If the required educational qualifications for a job rise more rapidly than the actual education required to perform the job, the availability of more college-educated workers will limit advancement of workers with fewer years of schooling. [Italics added.]

Musical chairs. The oldest of children's games. Except this is not exactly a game. Who gets to sit where? Who gets pushed aside? *You're out.* We regret to inform you that because of current economic indicators and census projections the chairs we had reserved for you are no longer available.

Many people in high positions are now worried about "overeducated" workers. Many people in high positions are deeply troubled by soaring educational costs. Should these people have their say, and they have already begun to, more and more students will have to forget about college, at least about free tuiton. Guess which prospective students they will be? ("I never could have afforded it otherwise," Ingrid told me.) Guess which side of the social-economic-racial-gender scale will be most affected? And in the meantime those, like myself, who never wanted to go to college in the first place, will have less chance of advancing in the job market without a college degree.

"Particularly women."

No mustard, no beef. No beef, no mustard.

It is "essentially a problem of credentials" the anonymous Labor Department writer states carefully in the Handbook, no doubt fully aware of the growing if largely ignored body of research that has shown that length of schooling in general and educational credentials in particular have little bearing on job performance in all but the most highly technical fields. Other personal characteristics turn out to be far more relevant. Indeed, in quite a number of instances, the relationship between education and job performance appears to be inverse, with the more highly educated worker also the one to become more quickly discouraged because of her/his higher expectations in the first place. And yet the trend over time, as Ivar Berg demonstrates in his important book, *Education and Jobs,* is for more and more people to be employed in jobs using less and less of their education. Berg ends his book (after making the obligatory assurances one has to make in these matters, namely that he, an academic in high standing, is of course not against education qua education, not against scholarship nor the House of Intellect at large) with a warning that "the tendency on the part of employers to raise educational requirements without careful assessments of their needs in both the short run and the long run can benefit neither managers nor the system they extol."

"Particularly women."

I should hurry now. It is high time we proceeded to the next W, so I'll just say one last word about Who. As all faithful followers of Pollyanna know, every cloud has a silver lining (if only we look) and in this particular case there may be a silver lining, too. The fact of so many over-educated workers (a more convenient

242

term to the powerful interests of this country than "underemployed" workers) has already led to some good things for women in traditional women's jobs. College-educated waitresses like Jeanne King with "greater expectations" get angry and file suits against discriminatory restaurants and unions and that's a plus for all waitresses. Most of the office worker groups that have been sprouting across the country (*Nine To Five*, Boston; *Women Employed*, Chicago; *Women Office Workers*, New York, etc.) were initially instigated by college graduates in clerical jobs and then other women began to join in, too. And from what I can gather, although I have no widespread evidence, college graduates in clerical jobs have been more likely to organize caucuses and special protest groups within their companies and to vote pro-union in office elections. So Pollyanna is right again; there may in fact be a silver lining. It's just the whole cloth—the whole system of hiring and allocating jobs—that is still desperately inhumane and in need of basic repair.

WHAT

The editor was apologetic. She had asked to see the chapter in this book on sales workers for possible condensation in her monthly magazine for women, and now she was explaining that "I found it fascinating, fascinating. I guess we've all wondered what it would be like to do that kind of work, but, well, I'll tell you what our editor-in chief said: 'It's quite interesting, yes, but for our own readers, don't you think it would be a little too . . . depressing?'"

I didn't know whether to laugh or hang up the phone. I said, "Oh, so you just want to hear about glamorous workers in glamorous jobs." But to myself I was thinking, no, no, Editor, that store wasn't depressing. Maybe it would be to you with your standards, with your opportunities, maybe it really would be to some of your readers who can afford to spend $1.50 an issue or whatever you're charging, but I doubt if most of the women I met at the store would describe it that way, and I hope my writing didn't lead you to that conclusion. Marlene in robes wished that she could have a chance at real selling (an opportunity more and

243

more rare in the age of self-help stores). Lillian in dresses wished she could find something closer to home. Alice in my department would give anything for Ed's job. And Peggy just waits for the day they will call her back. The place was overflowing with problems, problems that need to be attacked, but, again I doubt that the word to describe working there was depressing. Awful, yes at times. Fun, yes, at times. (Where are you, Diamonds? How's business?) Boring, interesting, convivial, frustrating, tedious, enraging, and sometimes quite pleasant. Particularly in the morning before your feet started hurting. Particularly when you could talk to the other workers. The typical comment of the young female students: "I'm only here for the time being." The typical comment of the women in their fifties and over: "You'll get used to it, you'll see." The typical comment of the in-between women: "It's okay. It's a job. You have to deal with reality, you know." That's the word, I guess. Not depressing. Real.

The new glorification of work and achievement that has replaced the old glorification of marriage and family in our women's magazines seems to me to contain the exact same seeds of unreality. So-called glamorous workers in so-called glamorous jobs will never account for more than a fraction of the work force in our most unglamorous job market. Only 15 percent of women are classified as professionals and most are teachers and nurses. And even for professionals the issue of work (inside or outside the home) is invariably an issue, as it is for everyone else, of specific costs versus specific benefits, the choice of a particular job invariably a tradeoff between certain advantages and certain disadvantages. While we continue to read about wonderful or terrible jobs, blissfully happy or miserably dissatisfied workers, liberated or unliberated women, with nothing in between, it makes sense to remember that work, like everything else, has to be seen in a social and economic context. Most of all the question must always be asked: *Who's defining the situation?*

There is the work you do and everything that surrounds it. There is the actual job and the actual pay. There are the fringes (health insurance, vacations, life insurance, pensions) assuming they exist. There is the amount of job security or insecurity. There are the chances or lack of chances to move up. There is the question of your age and whether you believe there are better opportunities for you elsewhere. There is the specific atmosphere you work in—the working conditions, the health conditions, the social conditions, the way you are treated by those above you. There are the little things. Chairs. Lockers. Pats on the back. If I have been reminded of anything at all on this sojourn, it is of the importance of the little things. Heaven, someone once wrote, is probably largely a matter of details. Hell, too, no doubt. Corns, bunions, hives, hemorrhoids, diarrhea—radical activists have stayed home from the march for lesser reasons. Robert Schrank has written about the importance to workers, particularly mothers, of the right to receive and make personal phone calls, a seemingly little thing. When Ingrid said that of all things the matter with her waitressing job, the locker situation disturbed her the most, she was not being facetious. You feel it first where it pinches the most.

There is the lack or presence of grievance procedures on your job, the lack or presence of a union, the kind of union if it exists. There are the expectations you started your job with. There are the expectations and biases of the impartial observers who decide they want to write about your work. To get mine out of the closet, I'd have to say that in most of the jobs this book explores, including homemaking, the work itself turned out to be far more dimensional than I had expected (and I hadn't been expecting Charlie Chaplin in *Modern Times*). I'd also have to say that in most cases (with the partial exception of the insurance company) the conditions surrounding the work—the pay, fringes, job insecurity, supervision, chances to move ahead—turned out to be far worse than I had expected (and I hadn't been expecting Workers' Paradise or Walden Two).

There is the social value, if any, of the work you do. There is the amount of respect the people you compare yourself to accord your work, and the fact of whether you see yourself as doing better or worse than they. There is the amount of respect the outer society accords your work and the question of whether this attitude is reflected in your paycheck. If you are a sanitation worker you can afford to thumb your nose back at middle-class snobbery, knowing you are doing far more vital work than most, so long as your rate of pay is not on the bottom rungs, too. (Of course there is now a middle-class backlash building in response to the decent contracts that many unionized sanitation workers, along with other public employees, have at long last won. Who do they think they are? Ad men?) If you are a typical artist or writer in this country you know what you can buy with the patina of respect the outer society accords your work. If you are a woman, however, working in an occupation traditionally filled by noncollege women, a pink-collar occupation, the odds are overwhelming that what you do is vastly undervalued, both by the outer society and, more to the usual point, by those who set your rate of pay.

The most dramatic documentation I have ever seen of how blatant this situation is can be found in the report of a University of Wisconsin study of the way traditional women's occupations are listed in the federal government's *Dictionary of Occupational Titles.** Considered the world's most comprehensive source of job information, the *DOT*, as it is known, describes and rates the level of complexity of the tasks involved in some 30,000 different job titles. The accuracy of these ratings are extremely important since the *DOT* is used by a wide range of private and public employment specialists, including the U.S. Employment Service, for many and sundry purposes, ranging all the way from . . . "as window props and door stops" . . . to "the basis on which many large organizations evaluate job prerequisites, career ladder criteria and place in the classification and compensation hierarchies" . . . to "the code" used by Employment Service personnel to sort out their clients' work histories and determine appropriate job placements now. All in all, multimillion-dollar decisions affecting millions of workers' lives are said to be made with the help of *DOT* ratings.

The theory behind the *DOT* system is that each and every occupation requires the worker to perform on some measurable lev-

*Witt, Mary, and Naherny, Patricia K., *Women's Work—Up from 878; Report on the DOT Research Project,* Women's Education Resources, University of Wisconsin Extension, 1975. The study created such a stir that, in the next edition of the *DOT*, now in preparation, the jobs in question are being reclassified.

el of complexity in relation to three different categories: data; people; and things. Usually a job will be more demanding in one category than the others. Next to each occupational title, the *DOT* gives a separate numerical rating for each of the three categories, based on a scale of zero to eight. A zero signifies the highest level of complexity possible. A four is the middle level. And an eight means that the job entails the smallest or no amount of skill at all in that category. One of the top scores in the *DOT* is for surgeon, which receives a 101 (the first numeral One is the score for data, the zero is for people, and the last One is for things). Just about the lowest possible rating is an 878. Here is one example of an 878, which was singled out in the University of Wisconsin study:

> FOSTER MOTHER (dom. ser) . . . 878. Rears children in own home as members of family. Oversees activities, regulating diet, recreation, rest periods, and sleeping time. Instructs children in good personal and health habits. Bathes, dresses and undresses young children. Washes and irons clothing. Accompanies children on outings and walks. Takes disciplinary action when children misbehave . . . May work under supervision of welfare agency. May prepare periodic reports concerning progress and behavior of children for welfare agency.

Rated almost but not quite as low as foster mother was the following occupational title, which received a slightly higher 874:

> HORSE PUSHER (agric) . . . 874. Feeds, waters and otherwise tends horses en route by train.

Now I suppose it would be logical to think that the above examples are just a couple of isolated and absurd errors. Naturally there will always be some mistakes in a compendium this size. But in fact the ratings were absolutely and perfectly consistent with the *DOT* scoring of a whole series of jobs traditionally filled by women. A few more examples which the study pointed out, with male comparisons also listed:

247

CHILD CARE ATTENDANT, 878—". . . House parent, special school counselor, cares for group of children housed in . . . government institutions."

rated the same as

PARKING LOT ATTENDANT, 878—". . . parks automobiles for customers in parking lot . . ."

* * *

NURSERY SCHOOL TEACHER, 878—"Organizes and leads activities of children, maintains discipline . . ."

much less complex than

MARINE MAMMAL HANDLER, 328—"Signals or cues trained marine mammals . . ."

* * *

NURSE, PRACTICAL, 878—". . . cares for patients and children in private homes, hospitals . . ."

only slightly less complex than

OFFAL MAN, POULTRY, 877—"shovels ice into chicken offal container."

* * *

HOME HEALTH AID, 878—"Cares for elderly convalescent or handicapped persons . . ."

about as skilled as

MUD-MIXER-HELPER, 887

* * *

NURSE, MIDWIFE, 378

nearly as skilled as

HOTEL CLERK, 368

THE WORLD OF WOMEN'S WORK

* * *

HOMEMAKER (cross references MAID, GENERAL)),
878
nearly as skilled as

DOG POUND ATTENDANT, 874

Based on the results of its work, the University of Wisconsin study concludes, "that the *Dictionary of Occupational Titles* systematically—although not purposely—discriminates against virtually all nondegreed, people-oriented women's jobs at great expense to the public in general and women in particular . . . Project findings show that jobs suffering most are the salaried derivatives of homemaking and mothering . . . Nowhere is the state of neglect more evident than in the disposition of the most traditional of women's jobs."

It is, then, not feminists who should be singled out (as they sometimes have been) for demeaning the value of traditional women's work. The *DOT* example is symptomatic of an underlying attitude that is pervasive throughout the higher reaches of this motherland, despite the façade of reverence, the flowers and the candy on Mother's Day, the avuncular tributes on television commercials.

It was "non-degreed people-oriented women's jobs" in particular that the study found the most underrated—in other words, non-degreed service jobs. (Women working in assembler's jobs predominantly filled by women were scored accurately in the study's view.) At a time when many in the upper echelons can be heard complaining non-stop about the supposedly poor quality of service in this country ("What's the matter, don't these people have any respect for their work anymore?"), it is instructive to note who exhibits the least respect.

Although it was certainly not the most pressing problem on the minds of the women I met (working conditions and pay usually were), the general public's lack of respect for and recognition of their work, both because of class and sexist prejudice, was a sub-

249

ject that did come up spontaneously again and again. Particularly among the younger women.

Suzy at the beauty shop: *People won't tell you this, they think we don't know what they're feeling, but a lot of them think we're cheap, think we're lower class.*

Jeanne King, waitress: *Oh, yeah. Most people on the outside look down on you. Middle class people I'm talking about. [This] is the thing I object to about this job more than anything else.*

Jackie at the beauty shop: *They think their shit is cleaner than yours. Well, I could spit on them.*

Ingrid at Tony's restaurant: *Some people say that what we do is unskilled work. All I can say is that they should come work here at lunchtime during the middle of the week and see how well they do.*

Joyce in her home in Wisconsin: *You know, we should have talked about that at the conference—that you get a ton of priceless experience running a household but no one gives you credit for that experience and knowledge.*

Faye in Wisconsin: *Let's face it, to most women in the movement being a housewife is the lowest of the low—and homemakers know it."*

And one of the main slogans of the office workers' groups around the country is: *Raises, Rights and . . . Respect.*

Respect. Recognition. How do occupational groups usually achieve either one in this country? How do they at least gain economic recognition of the value of their work? The Sanitation Workers provide one answer. The *DOT* study provides another clue. For as it turned out not quite all "people-oriented jobs traditionally filled by women" got the 878 treatment. Just virtually all. The ones that didn't fell into two main and usually overlapping groups. According to the study: "Quite a few jobs necessitating a college degree are considered 'women's work' such as dietician, home economist, physical therapist. . . . And yet the *DOT* makes no distinction between these entries and degreed jobs associated with men. The equalizer . . . is the prerequisite college education. But just as important as a college education is membership in a professional organization that comes with a specialist's degree. . . ."

Unions· Associations. Degrees. Licenses. In other words, as the old slogan goes, don't agonize, organize. Which is just what teachers and nurses, still the overwhelming vocational choice for college-educated women, have been doing with striking effect in recent years—at least until the current great decline in the demand for teachers and the crisis in city budgets for public services generally. However, when we look at the nondegreed women in the jobs this book explores, the formula of unions and licenses doesn't seem to hold up as well. The beauticians, after all, did have to be licensed. There was also a union in the area that they could have joined—but what a union. I can still hear that barber in the swivel chair explaining why the salaries of women were less important than those of men. And the waitresses also had a union, a union to join and represent them. So long as they didn't insist on getting the most lucrative jobs. Solidarity forever except in the same high-priced restaurant. Except in the paycheck.

And yet it nevertheless seems obvious to me that if women's situation in the work world is to improve, we desperately need to organize and join and shake up and lead labor unions. It also seems important, however, not to underestimate the difficulties at the moment and not to be afraid to talk about them. There are of course unions and unions. Locals and locals. Models and exceptions. Some of the unions now representing women (for example District 1199 of the National Union of Hospital and Health Care Employees; United Department Store Workers; American Federation of State, County, Municipal Employees), are exceptionally fine. But throughout history the overriding pattern of labor, even in those unions where women form the bulk of the membership, has been first and foremost to protect the interests of the white male members and that surely remains the predominant pattern today. Historically women's place in the labor force has been as restricted by unions—organized white male workers—as it has been by management.

There is of course a difference. Joyce Maupin of Union Wage

in California, an organization of women fighting not only to help women to organize into unions but also to end the male domination of unions, puts it this way: "Women are discriminated against in their unions, too, but there's a difference between profits and privilege. If employers exploit, that means profit; if unions discriminate, that's privilege." Well, I guess I understand the ideological distinction, but from the point of view of a waitress like Jeanne King who's been locked out of the good jobs, it doesn't really matter which is which, does it? Joyce Maupin would be the first to say that both management and union treatment of women have to be overhauled; indeed she's dedicated a large chunk of her life to trying to make that happen. The hope was that the national Coalition of Labor Union Women, which was launched with great fanfare in 1974, would also be a major instrument in the pursuit of the goal as well. So far it remains just that—a hope. From where I sit not very much rocking of the male boat has yet taken place, but it is true I have not been sitting very close. Although the actual numbers of unionized women have been rising (thanks largely to public service unions) the proportion of women in unions has been falling. Only 12.5 percent of women workers are unionized today, compared to 13.8 percent ten years ago and 17 percent in 1950. Again this is largely because of the shift from manufacturing to clerical and service work where unions are least active. The question of whether unions will now be spending the time, money and labor power to organize in these areas on the truly grand scale needed also remains just that—a question.

As for homemakers, the issue of organization, of associations, of pressure groups, is perhaps an important one too. For as Faye noted at that little restaurant in Madison: "In the long run, maybe the only thing that will really help is for homemakers to get together and form our own movement. Maybe then we'd get the changes we need, the protection we need. Because the whole economy, the whole society, depends on us for its survival, you can be sure of that."

WHERE

So how is it, what's it like working here? Lillian and I asked Peggy, the experienced one, before starting actual work at the department store.

"Well, you know, like everywhere else, it all depends on which department you're in. Naturally it's how your manager and the other people you work with treat you and that's different all over the store."

Naturally, Peggy said. Never dreaming that all over the country giant corporations were spending thousands and thousands of dollars, perhaps millions, on putative job-enrichment programs and studies that often as not came up with some such conclusion as: The-managerial-factor-appears-to-be-a-meaningful-variable-in-an-optimal-program. (Or, is it an optimal variable in a meaningful program?)

They should have asked Peggy. "Naturally," she would have said.

"We're really still in the experimental stage," the job-enrichment specialist at the insurance company told me: "It seems to depend quite a bit on the attitudes of supervisors, but none of the evidence is very conclusive yet. Here or at other corporations."

Is it only a crude antimanagerial bias of mine, a simplistic reverse snobbism, or is it really true that time and time again the average worker can tell you far, far more about what is going wrong or right in her/his department, and why, than any company official can? Or job enrichment specialist. Or writer of a book like this.

Suzy at the beauty shop: "The pay is lousy, the security is lousy, the benefits are lousy, the union is lousy—but it's nice here, isn't it? It's a happy place . . . And we've also got something good between the girls here and that means a lot. How you get along." Not having had the benefit of a seminar on management techniques, Suzy was bungling along with her own archaic philosophy of supervision: "I'm never pushy, but they know we have to get things done. I think you have to treat your help the way you'd like to be treated yourself. And I think we have a good relationship. My boss thinks it's too good. He doesn't like me to socialize at all with them, but I can't be like that. As much as possible I encourage you to use your own methods, your own ways of doing things. I don't like to be told what to do, so I won't order anyone either. But ask me nice and I'll do anything you say if I know you're being fair. And that's the way I try to be."

And that's the way she was until Bumblebrain fired Jackie and then started turning the screws. And tall, talented Marianne quit, noting: "It wasn't just the pushing that was so bad. It was the way it was being done and who was doing it. When Suzy was there you didn't mind it. You always knew she didn't push you any harder than she had to. Whereas with Bumblebrain, well I'd slow down everytime he started running things, I'd finish that cigarette first if he said to go and get that lady with the wet head. . . ."

Naturally, Peggy would say.

At Tony's restaurant Ingrid said it was "we against him." At the restaurant where Jeanne King worked: "Well, it's really a treat to work there. There's never any of that get-to-your station business. The waiters and waitresses—we have both—switch among themselves, you don't have to go through the owner. It's really a delight. It has to do with the whole atmosphere of respect and mutual working together." You mean, I asked Jeanne, the workers manage themselves? "Yes, in many ways."

Respect. Working together. Self-management in many ways. Naturally.

Bonnie talking about the pranks in her department in the insurance company: "And then she went to the ladies' room and he snuck the original plant back. We were all hysterical. We have quite a group of comedians and they do this kind of thing a lot."

But only a few doors down the hall in the department where Nora worked before being retired (the new euphemism for fired): "It happens in offices everywhere, I know, not just here. Women are trained to compete with each other to get the few good promotions, the few really good jobs and that's becoming more true all the time. Instead of sharing your knowledge and experience you feel you have to protect your precious little bit of information. Everyone competes. Even departments compete with each other and I think it even hurts the company in the long run. I believe there should be more human attitudes generally.''

It's too bad nobody on the job enrichment team thought to ask Nora to pass on her years of insight before she was pushed out of the company. But then, come to think of it, what would the members of the team have done with the information? What real changes in the rigid corporate hierarchy would they have been willing to make to solve the problems she saw? Or, perhaps also to the point, what changes would they have had the power to make? Job enrichment and personnel divisions are usually far from the top of the corporate pyramid, and as the personnel man was careful to remind me: "You must understand that this is a pyramid." For that matter, what would the job enrichment specialists have done with this fundamental perception of their program by Nora's daughter, Diane:

> I think it's probably a step in the right direction, though it bothers me that they seem to think we all want the same thing. I don't think that's true. I think some women, some *people*, want more responsibility and some don't. Some like to work slow and careful and some quick and forget it. Some want to be with other people, then there are those like me who prefer to work alone. But they act like we're all alike.

Just suppose (another office worker at another large company said to me) that the personnel departments of corporations functioned the way the guidance department of your high school was supposed to act, but never did. Suppose they saw their job as helping you to use your strengths and weaknesses in a manner that would be best for you and also for the company? As long as you worked there, you would be able to go in and talk with them anytime you wanted about how you were doing in your current job, any problems you were having, and also about possible openings in other departments and divisions of the company. All such job openings would be posted somewhere centrally, and any time you happened to see one that particularly interested you, why you'd just drop in at personnel and find out what the score was. They would be interested in your progress throughout the company, assuming you wanted to progress. It would be an ongoing relationship—not simply the periodic, usually pro forma, review system many corporations now have. In other words, if this young woman's fantasy came true, office workers would have a personal guide to help them find their way through and up the maze-like internal labor markets of today's giant corporations.

Does such a personnel department exist anywhere? (Remember we are talking about help for people who start as clerical workers not as junior executives.) I've never seen one, but I wouldn't be surprised if someone could dig up a model or two here or there; anything is possible in this most contradictory of all possible worlds. However if we're talking about the usual state of corporate affairs, then it's still the extremely rare firm that even deigns to post its job openings so that workers can know what's available in other departments. Bonnie's experience at the insurance company was the typical one: "As for getting something in a different department, you'd have to be requested by the manager there and most of the time they don't know you from Adam."

Which is why a number of the office-worker groups around the country are now citing job posting within companies as one of their major goals. (Supposedly it is a legal requirement of affirmative-action programs, too.)

And what about Diane's comment: "They act like we're all alike." I can imagine the personnel man's answer: "But of course we do, my dear. After all, machines are all alike; you don't want to be replaced by one, do you? Look, we're trying to be nice, trying to make things more pleasant, but this is a business, not a country club. Profits, productivity, cost efficiency—this is the holy trinity that is still the name of the corporate game and don't you ever forget it."

One hundred years ago when typewriters were first being marketed the women who were hired to use them were called typewriters, too. Today, in the age of word-processing machines, there are want ads in the paper for word processors. Will the continued inevitable increase in mechanization necessarily mean even less room for individuality among clerical workers in the future?

Although it certainly seems likely, certainly seems to be an issue that will become increasingly serious in coming years, it also, again, seems to be partly a question of . . . Where. In fact in my travels I managed to find one office, one model, where the introduction of word-processing machines was having the exact opposite effect on the different clerical workers. The office was the art and design division of UNICEF Christmas Cards, a multimillion dollar business, which is also, of course, a part of the mammoth and super-hierarchical and super-sexist United Nations. However the man in charge of this particular division, whose name is Roy Moyer, happens to be an artist and an iconoclast, a man temperamentally and philosophically opposed to the pyramid structure of modern corporations. "It should be more like a circle," says Moyer, who is particularly disturbed by the corporate propensity for dividing everything into departments. "Every time there's more than two of anything they have to make a new department, with a new supervisor." Moyer is also cynical about job titles, another maverick position in an organization that next to the military and the federal government has probably contributed more to the proliferation of grades and titles and subtitles and sub-sub-sub-sub titles than any other organization in the country.

When the first word-processing machine arrived in Moyer's office, all new and shiny and equipped with its own video screen, Moyer or someone else there named it Ella. (I liked his philosophy so much I forgot to needle him about automatically giving it a female name. Hey, Moyer: why not Elliott?) Because of Ella almost twice as much of the formula correspondence could be handled in the same amount of time. In addition, Moyer declared a personal war against unnecessary paperwork, still another revolutionary attitude in UN memoland. "It's so much easier to just pick up the telephone."

Then, with those two time-savers established, Moyer called a meeting of the clerical workers in his and the promotion department, which was headed by a kindred spirit named Bonnie Berlinghof. On a card that everyone received was listed all the different tasks that had to be accomplished in both departments within the next several months. Okay, Moyer said. Who's interested in

257

working with Bonnie on the brochure? Who wants to work with me on the budget? And so it went. The plan was that the office workers would spend part of the day with Ella and on other regular clerical duties and part of the time on the particular project she/he had personally selected. As a method of job enrichment Moyer's approach was the opposite of most I've heard about in that he reveled in people's differences. Says Moyer: "Some people are highly critical, cranky, fussy, never satisfied. Wonderful. We need that kind of mind to help us ferret out mistakes. Then some people are more accepting, tolerant, a little shy maybe. Fine. There's so much enthusiasm and care a person like that can bring to a project. I'll tell you something. The people managing these giant corporations think their methods are so efficient. So productive. My strong belief is that probably at this moment eighty percent of the potential of most workers is not being used."

Of course Moyer is assuming that the corporations really *want* to use the potential of their women workers. Maybe Moyer hasn't heard about the corporate dependency on A&P (attrition and pregnancy). In any case while Moyer continues trying to turn the pyramid in his own office into a circle (how far he gets only time will tell) here is what is happening to a secretary in another office three thousand miles away, a medium-sized office of radical lawyers noted for their socially progressive work, a unionized office in which the issue of job power and participatory decision-making has been discussed for some time. I quote from a letter this secretary wrote to the particular lawyer she worked for:

Dear ——— :

I really resent the assumptions from which you apparently proceed. Without giving me a chance to do certain things, you assume from the front that I can't do it, it's too complicated. "These things you only learn from experience" type comments. It is true that I cannot do easily and confidently many things that are routine in the work that you do. But they won't be learned by your doing them all the time. There are many, many things that

258

you do that I could just as easily do, but you dictate them. You dictate almost every letter, pleading, etc., right down to telling me what kind of paper to use, every comma, etc. It's partly an insult to my ego and largely unstimulating, boring, degrading and half a dozen other things.

I also resent when I come into the office once in three weeks late by twenty minutes your accusation "You're late." The assumption is not that there was a good reason, since I beat you to work almost every day and am rarely late. Or: "When are you going to do that tape?" and so on, which implicitly assumes that I'm not doing it because I don't want to, have been fucking off or whatever. If you thought about it for five minutes you'd realize that yesterday, as an example, when you commented on the tape not being done, you had interrupted the work I was doing half a dozen times to ask me to do something else.

My initial reaction was, fuck it. If that's his attitude I'll be here 9 to 5 sharp, do what I have to do to get by and he won't get a damn extra bit of interest or initiative out of me and eventually I'll find some place else to work. But realizing that was juvenile and I had not really tried to struggle the whole thing through long enough to be really giving up, I decided instead that I will get caught up as fast as I can and then just start doing some things before you get a chance to say no.

It's always much easier for people to retreat into stereotypical roles and assumptions than it is to develop new ones with the daily pressure of work not letting up a bit. But I can't function like that—I sense from your efforts to change since I've been here that you don't want to either. So let's try again and see if we can make some more progress.

My kingdom for a good secretary. The relationship did not get better; got worse. In the lawyer's view the problem was not the secretary's desire for more responsibility, more equality, but rather her "difficult personality." After a while another job

259

opened up, she grabbed it. He hired someone else. "The exact opposite," he told me. "Blonde, gorgeous, passive. But also highly skilled." And how is that working out? I asked some months later. "Well, pretty good. Okay. Except, well, frankly sometimes I wish she'd use more initiative. She waits for me to tell her practically everything first. Funny isn't it? I guess the ideal would be someone in between the two women."

You mean, I asked, someone who would take over more of the responsibility but not challenge your power? He smiled slightly. He was a lawyer who had spent, still spends, a good part of his professional life defending the powerless, and the irony was far from lost on him. "Yes," he said softly, "someone who would not challenge my power."

I do not need to comment on which attitude is the norm in the work world today, Moyer's or this lawyer's. But as a token exception it was particularly unsettling to realize that a man like Moyer could exist and to some degree shake up the rigid structure in his own office in a monster bureaucracy like the UN (although, again, how far he gets still remains to be seen) and that in contrast the power relations in a modest-sized free-swinging radical law office could be as traditional as at Dun and Bradstreet.

Naturally, Peggy would say, "It all depends on which department you're in and how your manager and the other people you work with treat you." In other words, in terms of satisfaction, the question of where and with whom you work can be almost as decisive as what you do. And this, so I learned, is no less true for women in the job of homemaking. Although typical discussions, whether pro or con, exalting or demeaning, seldom take this fact into consideration, Faye, sitting in that restaurant in Wisconsin helped me to understand that:

There's the whole business of how you function on the job. From the woman who never has a word to say about the financial side of things to those who take charge of everything to do with money . . . Then a great deal depends on where you live. There are the women who keep strictly to themselves, some because they don't know anyone, they're living in a big impersonal city, probably some because they prefer it that way. These are the women we're always hearing about. The "isolated housewives." But there are also those like myself who really get involved in their community, who find something they're interested in . . . so many things a lot of us do you wouldn't believe it.

The last thing to be said about Where is that for mothers in the paid labor force the geographical location of the job, the closeness to home, is often one of the most important things about it. When her sons began having problems in school, Joan felt forced to give up her more lucrative waitressing job in Manhattan and try to find work nearer by, even if it meant returning to the diner. When the Chicago insurance company announced it would be moving an hour and a half away from town, it was only the men and the single women and the few mothers on a high-enough level to be able to afford outside help who could even consider commuting. As for relocating to the new site, a Bureau of Labor Statistics survey of unemployed persons found that 82 percent of unemployed married women said they would not be willing to move if a job were available elsewhere. The comparative figure for unemployed single women was 60 percent; for out-of-work married men it was 40 percent.* As economist Beth Neimi has noted, "a married woman's geographical location is still typically a function of her husband's employment rather than her own personal job opportunities." And it is this geographic immobility that is the additional and sometimes final roadblock that seals her higher rates of unemployment and chances to move onward, in Neimi's view. There are, of course, and once again, models and exceptional instances, including at the insurance company, where the husband moves to help his wife's career. But invariably such sacrifices occur among the higher salaried, where the woman's income in comparison or in addition to his is significant enough to make the relocation logical on economic as well as on feminist grounds.

*Robert L. Stein, "Work History, Attitudes and Income of the Unemployed," *Monthly Labor Review* 86, No. 12 (December, 1963): 1405–13.

For the majority of women, however, the question of Where remains a question of cost and time. "You still want to work here?" Lillian asked Peggy at the department store, "Of course, I do. For me it's a one-fare job."

Indeed for most mothers in the paid labor force, at least while their children are small, the question of Where is only topped in importance by the next W coming up.

WHEN

Like the obsequious butler in the cliché murder mystery, the question of When seemed of only shadowy significance at the start of this pursuit, but by the end there was no doubt it was playing a pivotal if not *the* pivotal role.

When over the course of their lives do most women work outside the home?

When over the course of their lives do most women *want* to work outside the home?

What difference does it all make?

There are currently three major patterns followed by women after leaving school:

Pattern A: Working in the paid labor market for a few years before marrying or having children, and then settling into the homemaker job for the rest of your life. (This was the predominant pattern for white middle-class females until World War Two and of course is still followed by many women, like Faye and Joyce at the conference, today. Their numbers are still huge if their proportions are declining. They are most apt to be: mothers of more than three children, wives of affluent men and women without a high-school degree who have meager opportunities in the job market.)

Pattern B: Following essentially the same career pattern as men, in that you remain in the paid labor force continuously and full-time throughout all the years between leaving school and retirement. (Most likely to be following this pattern today are women without children, black women and women in professional and managerial jobs.)

Pattern C: Working until you have children, then staying home

262

for a certain amount of time (typically between five and ten years but the amount of time out is now getting shorter) and then returning or trying to return to the paid labor force on a basis that won't conflict with your remaining family responsibilities. Of the three patterns this is now the dominant one, the fastest growing one, and the one that is having far greater consequences than I ever understood before starting out.

Bea, a homemaker returning to work at night at the Wisconsin data processing center: "They offered $2 an hour for beginners, $2.50 for experienced data processors, which was just about what I was making four years before. I thought, goodness, nothing has progressed in all this time, what's going on?"

Joan, a waitress in her forties, working different shifts: "Diners and coffee shops are where waitresses often start out, where they work while they're raising their kids, and where they return to when they're too old to get the sexpot jobs."

Lillian, who has worked on and off in department stores since her first child was born: "It wasn't like it was before when I was single and had nothing else to worry about, I can tell you that. And then when you work part-time or temporary they treat you differently, they don't take you as seriously, I think."

Nora, before getting her job at the insurance company: "The employment agencies, God bless them, warned me not to expect too much at my age. All my past experience counted for very little."

Are these women exceptions? Are their experiences unusual? It would be less worrisome to think so. One could just shake her/his/its head and hope that personal solutions will soon be found. In fact, however, a landmark study of the work histories of more than 18,000 women between ages 30 and 44 indicates that the reception Bea, Joan, Lillian and Nora received upon returning to the job market is now the rule.* Conducted for the Department of Labor by Ohio State University's Center for Human Resource Research, the study found:

*Dual Careers: A Longitudinal Study of the Labor Market Experiences of Women, Manpower Research Monograph No. 21, Volume 1, Manpower Administration, U.S. Department of Labor, 1970.

Nearly a third of American women 30 to 44 years of age are serving in the same . . . occupation in which they began their careers . . . Marriage and childbearing increase the chances that a woman will experience downward mobility from first job to current (or last) job. A larger proportion of ever-married white women moved down than up. Among such women who have had at least one child 15 percent were upwardly mobile, while 20 percent experienced downward shifts. It is worth noting that on average, never-married white women without children moved up . . . suggesting that . . . strong attachment to the labor force enhances career prospects. In the case of ever-married women with children . . . upward mobility is less frequent and downward mobility more frequent among the blacks than among the whites.

The solution? If you don't want to find yourself in a lower level job at age forty than you had at age twenty-two, what should you do? Apparently there are three main choices today. Don't get married. Or, don't have children. Or, don't interrupt your paid work life if you do have children. In other words, follow Pattern B, which is just what many professional women in the women's movement have been doing and advocating. And if you're married or living with a man get him to share the homemaking tasks too. The trouble, as I was to hear again and again from women I met, is that for those who are not interested in professions and careers, Pattern B may not sound so terrific. May not sound like a step ahead. For Joyce in Wisconsin, the opportunity to at last stop worrying about jobs when her husband finally earned enough to make it possible was "What a relief! You can't imagine what a relief that is. Don't tell me about how liberating other jobs are." Another woman I talked with expressed it this way: "I think you'd have to be very unusual to prefer sitting behind a typewriter all day to being around when your children are small and growing. I know I would have hated to have to work then." As it happened this woman's children were grown and she was realizing the cost of her decision to stay home twenty years ago every time she received her paycheck for the clerical job she had recently taken. Her salary was exactly the same as that of her twenty-one-year-old daughter. But still this woman insisted: "I wouldn't have missed those years for anything." And if the homemakers at the Wisconsin conference are correct, most American mothers, at least most mothers in nonprofessional jobs, feel the same way, too.

But doesn't the surge of mothers returning to the paid labor force when their children are younger and younger prove that this attitude is now changing? Not necessarily. First of all, study after study shows that economic necessity is the main reason most mothers of preschool children seek outside work. Second of all, when you begin to look more closely at the When of their labor force participation, the situation begins to take on a slightly different cast. A decidedly pinker cast.

When over the course of the day and year do most women work outside the home?

When over the course of the day and year do most women *want* to work outside the home?

What difference does it all make?

Once again there are three major patterns:

1. Working full-time throughout the year-round, as do most men.

2. Working part-time throughout the year-round or for part of the year.

3. Working temporarily during the year, either on a part-time or full-time basis.

Amid all the current hoopla about the new working woman, I was amazed to find out that less than a third of American females are now working full-time all year. According to the *1975 Economic Report of the President:* "Although more than half . . . were in the labor force at some time in 1973, only 31 percent were in the labor force for 50-52 weeks." (For males aged 25 to 54 the figure was 87 percent.)

Of those women who were in the labor market at all, only 41.8 percent worked full-time year-round. Here was the exact breakdown, again reported in the 1975 *Handbook on Women Workers:*

Worked full-time (35 hours or more) and full year (50 to 52 weeks):   41.8 percent
Worked full-time for 27 to 49 weeks (teachers would be included here):   12.3 percent
Worked full-time for one to 26 weeks: 14.0 percent

Worked part-time (less than 35 hours a week) for the full year: 10.7 percent
Worked part-time for 27 to 49 weeks: 7.6 percent
Worked part-time for one to 26 weeks: 13.7 percent

Most likely to be working full-time year-round were the same women most likely to remain in the paid labor force continuously throughout their working years; Pattern B women. In other words, women without children, black women and women in managerial jobs and in professions not dominated by women. (Most female-dominated professions—teachers, nurses, librarians, medical technologists—included heavy numbers of part-time and part-year workers.)

Strikingly, although white married women have lately been moving into the work force at a faster pace than black wives (who were already there in high proportions) the ratio of white women working full-time has been *dropping* recently while the proportion of black women doing so has been moving up. (Only a decade ago or so, in 1965, more white than black women were working full-time; 76 and 71 percent respectively. In 1974 the figures were more than reversed; 71 percent of white women working full-time as opposed to 80 percent of black women. If we added the changing proportions of those working on temporary jobs, the white-black shifts would no doubt be present there as well.)

Among black women the change is largely due to the drop in the proportion engaged in domestic work and the higher percentage now in clerical and other full-time fields. Among white women the change is largely due to the increased proportion of mothers with young children in the labor force. Of all workers they are the most likely to be in search of part-time and temporary opportunities.

And where are such jobs to be found? In which of the three labor markets—the mainly male one, the mainly female one or the integrated one—are part-time and temporary jobs most prevalent? Ah, now the plot thickens. The pink collar tightens. Exactly. It is in precisely the occupations where women predominate, pink-collar occupations, that such opportunities can be found. Very few jobs are available for part-time managers. Very few openings exist for pilots, butchers, machinists to work over the Christmas vacation. At the same time four out of five waitresses work less than a full year. Department store saleswork, as we saw, is becoming an increasingly part-time operation. As already discussed, offices are turning more and more to part-timers and temps. Beauty shops always have. In hospitals and the health field generally, where women comprise 75 percent of the workforce (except at the top), shift work and part-time arrangements are traditionally the rule of thumb. In New York full-time teachers have recently begun complaining about the growing use of part-timers in schools, too, thus reducing the already reduced demand for their labor. In contrast, in the industries dominated by men—transportation, steel, mining, public administration, etc.—part-time and temporary work (not counting seasonal layoffs) is virtually unknown.

Thus the When of a woman's work often determines the What. "In the face of the demands on her time," economist Juanita Kreps has noted, "the young wife is likely to find that the scheduling of her job is the most important single consideration. Her immediate job choice is dictated in large measure by the time constraints imposed in the short run, and this choice in turn directs her subsequent career development."

The most important single consideration. The rub of course is that later when those time constraints diminish so will the full-time outside job opportunities available to her. And later still (as Margie at the store, and Edna at Schrafft's and Nora at the insurance company all noted) when her family responsibilities are at last just about over, she will more than likely be asked to leave the work force entirely, although her job may now be the main social world she has left.

The ironies are, to say the least, strong. On the one hand young mothers like Diane and Nancy, with scarcely a free moment for themselves, are having to take outside jobs because of economic necessity and wishing they could be home, while on the other hand women like Nora, who have more time of their own than ever before, are being pushed out. Diane at the insurance company: "It's too bad my mother and I can't change places with each other for a few years, isn't it?" And she and her mother nodded. How many other women would nod? Although there are inestimable rewards to be gotten from doing useful work and getting paid for it—assuming one can find such work—how many women—or men—wouldn't like to have the opportunity to do something else for a while? Even teachers take sabbaticals, or used to. "It takes time to love, but who's got time on their hands?" went an old Jefferson Airplane song. It also takes time to think. It has often been noted that upper middle-class intellectuals have typically been the ones to ferment social revolutions; the presumption apparently being that they are the only ones with the abstract and conceptual tools at their disposal. It occurs to me after seeing these young mothers slicing themselves into five pieces to get everything done that the real distinction is that the intellectuals have the time to do the thinking. Not only to think but to go to all those meetings. Bea, running from the data processing center at midnight to have five minutes with her husband before he goes to sleep, so that tomorrow she can be up with her children at seven, is not about to sit down and write *Das Kapital.* Time is money, the saying goes. Money is also time.

To stop the hyperbole, are we really sure that Pattern B is the grail we all should be reaching for? Although for many people it may be ideal, the increasing and disquieting paradox of our time is that while certain women have been fighting for the right not to be "forced" to stay home, an even larger number are increasingly being forced—by inflation, taxes, the insufficient wages of their husbands, those that have husbands—to leave their homes to take jobs they often never wanted. And then later when they do want them, more than ever, they are forced to retire.

"It's too bad my mother and I can't change places with each for a few years." How many older women would agree? Obviously, many women, as do many men, *want* to retire. Wait excitedly for the day. But it was a revelation for me to meet so many who didn't. Margie at the department store: "It's my first home, not my second." The representative of the United Storeworkers: "We hold preretirement classes for our older workers and time and time again we hear them say, they don't want to retire, they would miss their friends at the store." Moreover, in a British study of semiskilled workers in their fifties, Dan Jacobson found that women viewed retirement much less favorably than did men.* Only 41 percent of the women as against 62.1 percent of the men preferred to retire at the pensionable age. What both sexes overwhelmingly agreed upon was that in the question of retirement, "flexibility" would be the best answer.

Flexibility. An individual choice for women on the question of when to enter, when to interrupt, when to return, when to retire. What could make more sense? What could now be more difficult? "An individual choice? This is a business not a country club."

WHY

When the facts come home to roost, let us try at least to make them welcome. Let us try not to escape into some utopias . . . or sheer follies.

—Hannah Arendt

There used to be a television commercial, perhaps it is still shown, that opened with a radiant woman, blonde hair flowing, strolling through sylvan fields, while the entranced man hurrying toward her murmured: *The . . . closer . . . you get . . . the better she looks.* In the case of the blatant undervaluing of the work the majority of American women still do—both the work at home and the work outside—the closer you get the more interrelated it all looks. The more deeply embedded. The more of a boon to the business structure of this country.

"In the real struggle between wife-mother and career-woman," Sebastian de Grazia wrote, "each side has had its violent advocates. What few suspect is that the fluctuation back and forth

*Human Relations, Vol. 27, No. 5, pp. 427–92.

serves a purpose. It creates a labor reservoir ready to man the pumps at home or [outside] depending on the economic barometer."

Today, as we have seen, this labor reservoir is being drawn upon in a very special way. The fluctuation of women back and forth over the course of their lives, over the course of their days and weeks and children, serves an even more profitable purpose than ever before. Not only does it provide management with readily available labor but with readily available cheap labor. Not only with readily available cheap labor but readily available cheap *and* skilled labor. The best that the least amount of money could possibly buy. A businessman's dream. In her study, *The Female Labor Force in the United States*, Valerie Oppenheimer notes:

> Once recourse has been made to female labor to provide quality labor at a low price, employers tend to get used to relatively well-educated workers (standards have been going up not down) who have been working for much less than men who have received a comparable education. To substitute men to any considerable extent would require either a rise in the price paid for labor or a decline in the quality of the labor, or both. Unless there are some very compelling reasons for it, it seems unlikely that many female occupations of this type will radically change their sex composition.

Once in the era of twelve- and sixteen-hour work days, the standard procedure for squeezing the last drop of energy from your workers was to keep them on the job until they were ready to collapse. Today in the age (thanks, give the chauvinists their important due, to male-dominated labor unions) of minimum wage; eight and seven hour work days; premium pay for overtime; Saturdays as well as Sundays off; coffee breaks; benefits (health, pensions, vacations) that are said now to add twenty percent to the average worker's annual pay—all possible methods of cutting labor costs are constantly explored. In heavy manufacturing (in male manufacturing) the major method continues to be newer and speedier machines to reduce the amount of human la-

270

bor (unionized, higher priced labor) needed. In light manufacturing (mainly female and/or nonwhite) the contest is between exporting for cheaper and mechanizing for fewer. In service and office jobs, where bodies are still needed, female bodies, inexpensive female bodies, the temporary and part-time worker is increasingly the answer in addition to new machines.

"Organizations exhibit quite contrary needs for both stability and flexibility," Marcia Freedman writes in her book, *Labor Markets: Segments and Shelters.* Occupying two-thirds of all part-time jobs today, women constitute the bulk of the flexible work force. The other major occupants are students. But while male students typically mature into the primary jobs (with all the benefits and access to promotions) women—particularly noncollege women—"remain the mainstay of the flexible work force at all ages."

Rushing from her non-paying job at home to her low-paying job at the Wisconsin data processing firm, Bea commented: "You're probably going to think I'm unliberated or something." Bea, I don't know about liberated or unliberated. I frankly don't understand what those words mean. But I have come to see that the difficulties you and other mothers of young children face could not be of more benefit to the cost-conscious businesses you work for. Could not be more capitalized upon. Especially if you are working part-time. And for those mothers who try to go the full-time, full-year route, the Pattern B route, there immediately are all the problems that Norma Briggs discussed with me after the homemaker conference:

> Now as a job-holding parent, I really feel the schizophrenia of our society toward working mothers. Here, in Wisconsin, a state employee gets two weeks vacation, her child gets all summer off. Our school system, which believes it's responsible to the needs of the community, doesn't provide alternate care during the summer. Likewise our medical system. It's impossible to get a dental appointment, for example, for your child outside of working hours. So what can you do? What's the answer? An honest recognition that it's impossible and beyond the capacity of the nuclear family—which is more and more a

271

two-earner family—to take the full responsibility for the growth of American children. We need more flexibility on the part of employers, more responsibility on the part of public agencies, must have some coordination between work and school scheduling.

In fact, while the male-breadwinner, female-homemaker family is still being portrayed as the typical American family, another family type has quietly been moving into the neighborhood. While the country's major educational, health, employment and social security policies continue to be based on the assumption that father is out there carrying the whole economic load on his overworked shoulders while mama stays home like a good woman should, the new family has been steadily taking over more and more of the territory. Bye-bye male breadwinner. Welcome to our little community, new American family.

What is the new family like? It would be splendid to announce that it is the equalitarian family of many (although still far from all) women's dreams, with women and men sharing equally in both the homemaking and breadwinning roles. But that, outside of a once again privileged minority (who can afford to hire outside help if it doesn't work out) is far from the case. The new family type is Linda, the beautician, with a husband who refuses to be inconvenienced. The new family type is Diane at the insurance company with "no time of my own" although unlike Linda's, her husband does share many of the chores around the house. The new family type is what the Census Bureau poetically describes as a husband-primary-earner, wife-secondary-earner family.

A quarter of a century ago, 56 out of 100 American husband-wife families were (officially) supported by the husbands' earnings alone. In 1973 that tally had dropped to only 31 out of 100. In contrast by then in 47 percent of husband-wife families, both husband and wife toiled for pay. "The most obvious conclusion," according to Harold Hayge of the Bureau of Labor Statistics, "is that American families have undergone a fundamental change in the manner in which they provide for their economic welfare." Meaning the manner in which the wife provides.

Secondary worker outside the home, still the primary worker

inside, her earnings from her outside, usually pink-collar, job contribute on the average 26 percent of the family income. If she works outside full-time and full-year, her contribution increases to 37.5 percent, still less than half of his. What does it matter how little she makes? the unbiased male bosses and male union members used to say. After all, she's only working for pin money. Aside from the fact that 40 percent of women in the labor force today are either divorced, single or separated, here is what a mother of three at the department store told me she did with the pin money (less than $90 a week) she took home after forty hours of work: "I spend it all on food and carfare. I take the check and leave it all at the supermarket before I even get home." As Harold Hayge put it: a fundamental change in the manner in which Americans provide for their economic welfare has taken place. But whether it adds up to progress or not depends not only on who's defining the situation but on who's living *in* it. And who's living *off* it.

And so the pink collar appears now to be closed. To reduce a richly complex human world into a one-dimensional summary:

Who: The majority of American women.

What: 878's, among others. Often the most socially useful of all jobs rated at the lowest level. Particularly if they are filled by noncollege, nonunionized women. A convenient explanation for the fact that they are also often paid at the lowest level.

Where: Home first of all. Then offices. Then restaurants, stores, hospitals, beauty shops, small electronics factories, garment factories, schools, all kinds of workplaces, large and small, where women are working in jobs predominately filled by women and seldom having entree to other jobs within the organization.

When: Part-time and temporary and full-time. Before and during and after marriage. When the children are small and when they are pimply and when they are grown. Whenever the jobs are available. Whenever a woman can juggle her other responsibilities at home. Except when she's 65 and has the most time of all.

Why: If in their need for cheap and skilled and flexible labor, the members of our American business structure didn't plan it this way, they couldn't have come up with a more ingenious solu-

273

tion, could they? Although a host of publishers are still selling their textbooks showing why the male-breadwinner, female-homemaker family is the most "functional" for the country and the economy, another family type has moved to center stage. What the Census Bureau calls a male primary earner, female secondary earner family. A female secondary earner to work (along with unmarried and divorced and separated women) at secondary jobs. At secondary pay. To work in pink-collar jobs. It all seems to fit, doesn't it? Maybe a little too neatly. In the old sociologist's catch phrase, it appears to be No Accident.

Beyond the five W's, most reporters have the good sense not to go. There are other W's of course, What-to-do. What-next. Before her death Hannah Arendt warned in a very different context against escaping into utopias when the "facts come home to roost." Should these be the facts (they are of course only one interpretation of them) then there is also a danger, it seems to me, of escaping into attitudes of gloom and doom. So many issues, so many obstacles, so many different levels of concern—it is easy to feel overwhelmed, immobilized by the realization.

Big things, bigger things, little things.

Big things: A full employment program that will mean adequate and decent opportunities for all people, college and noncollege, outside the pink-collar zone should they want it, particularly in the crowded labor market coming up. Unionization, flexible hours, affirmative action, equal education, particularly equal vocational education, paid maternity leaves, quality child care, all the middle-range issues women are now working on.

Bigger things: A deeper understanding of how this economic system capitalizes on the conflicts of women in dual roles. A fresh look at how women still engaged in traditional work, within and outside the home, can be awarded the recognition and economic protection they need, without falling back into the stereotyped roles of the 1950s. An attack on a lockjaw work world that says there is only one way—Pattern B—to move ahead through a system that kicks you out when you may have the most to give.

And chairs. Lockers. Little things. I have personally become

274

obsessed about the issue of chairs for store workers. (I felt it first where it pinched the most.) Although deep in my bones I am convinced that we will have female astronauts on the moon before we have New York supermarket cashiers in chairs, I find myself badgering the managers near my home. ("The customers wouldn't like it," the last said to me. Which customer? I'm a customer.)

Big things, bigger things, little things. "It's depressing," the magazine editor said. Maybe that's what she really meant. A nice warm optimistic article about the successes and triumphs of individual women moving up the career ladder is one thing. An unblinking look at the structural reasons most women are, and for the foreseeable future will continue to be, locked into a low-paying pink collar work world is quite another matter.

If that's the case I know how she feels. I don't know about you, but my frame of mind, my outlook on these matters, seem to vary widely lately. One day I'm reading about the newest field opening up, and I feel, goddamn it, we're really moving ahead, aren't we? Another day I get a call from a friend who desperately wants a teaching job after twenty years in the home and can't find it; or I'm reading the latest statistics on the massive and barely moving unemployment rate of black teenage females; or I'm reading of the amazing and short-lived triumphs of women at the beginning of this century, and I feel—what's the use; nothing really changes, does it? At those times, at some of those times when I'm doing my flip-flops, I think of something S. M. Miller once wrote about another issue, the issue of ending poverty in this country. High optimism, he wrote, discourages analysis. High pessimism discourages the pressure and action that is needed to bring about change. That seems to me to be the hard truth in this matter, too. What is needed is neither optimism nor pessimism, neither exaggerated breakthroughs nor exaggerated breakdowns, but continued pressure and action on the middle-range issues that have begun to be attacked, and continued analysis, deeper analysis, on the obdurate issues that remain.

It has been said that the best part of an uprising is always in the beginning. The winds are strong. The outlook is clear. Every day in every way things are getting better and better. Then the clouds start to appear. Phase Two. The obstacles are tougher than anyone knew. The conditions, the permutations, the reality are all more complex. Some of the troops begin to tire. Some of the troops begin to despair. According to a recent article in the *Washington Post*, feminism is no longer "in" among high school females. (Personally, I hadn't realized it was ever in.) At dinner parties it is no longer fashionable to discuss the women's movement. (*That* again?) It seems to me that all of this is not necessarily a bad sign. The really necessary work was never fashionable. Just vital. Just basic. Just political, in the deepest sense.

Big things, bigger things, little things. It's inescapable, isn't it? Women's work has still just begun.

"Naturally," Peggy would say.

Appendix:

The Female Labor Force/
A Statistical Portrait

CHART A

The Number of Women Workers Doubled between 1950 and 1974 ~ And They Now Account for Nearly Two-fifths of All Workers

Number and proportion of women workers in the civilian labor force, April 1950-1974

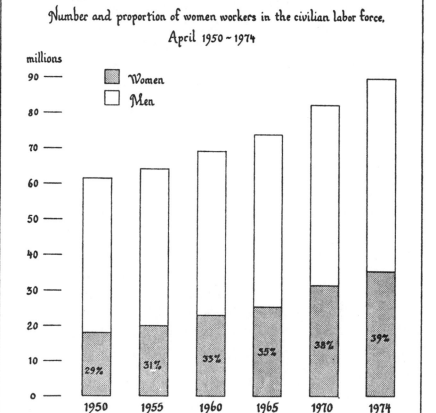

millions

Women
Men

Source: U.S. Department of Labor, Bureau of Labor Statistics.

More Than Half of All Women 18 ~ 64 Years of Age Are in the Labor Force

Women's civilian labor force participation rates by age ~ April 1974

percent ~ 0   10   20   30   40   50   60

Age
18 - 64 years old
18 - 19 years old
20 - 24 years old
25 - 34 years old
35 - 44 years old
45 - 54 years old
55 - 64 years old
65 years and over

Source: U.S. Department of Labor, Bureau of Labor Statistics.

CHART C

In the 1960 ~ 1974 Period the Greatest Increase in Labor Force Participation Rates Was Among Women 20-34 Years of Age: In the 1950's the Largest Increase Was among Women 45 ~ 64.

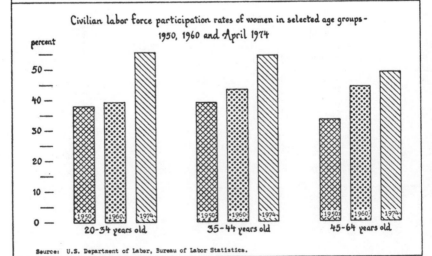

Civilian labor force participation rates of women in selected age groups ~ 1950, 1960 and April 1974

percent

50 —
40 —
30 —
20 —
10 —
0 —

1950 1960 1974   1950 1960 1974   1950 1960 1974
20 - 34 years old   35 - 44 years old   45 - 64 years old

Source: U.S. Department of Labor, Bureau of Labor Statistics.

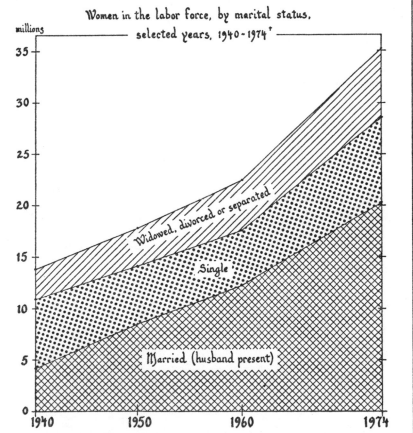

CHART D

The Number of Married Women in the Labor Force Has Expanded Dramatically

Women in the labor force, by marital status, selected years, 1940-1974 [†]

millions

Widowed, divorced or separated

Single

Married (husband present)

[†] Data cover March of each year and are for females 14 years of age and over except 1974 which are for 16 and over.
Source: U.S. Department of Labor, Bureau of Labor Statistics.

281

CHART E

Mothers Are More Likely To Work Than Ever Before. More Than Half of All Mothers of School Age Children Were in the Labor Force in 1974.

Civilian labor force participation rates of ever-married women, by age of children, selected years 1948-1974[†]

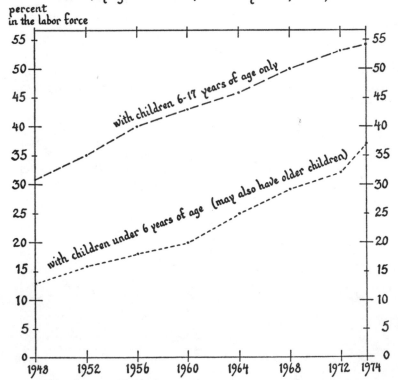

percent in the labor force

with children 6-17 years of age only

with children under 6 years of age (may also have older children)

[†] Data cover March of each year except for April 1948 and 1952, and are for females 14 years of age and over except in 1968, 1972 and 1974, which are for 16 years and over.

Source: U.S. Department of Labor, Bureau of Labor Statistics.

CHART F

7 out of 10 Employed Women Work Full-Time

Distribution of women employed in nonagricultural industries
by full- or part-time status, April 1974

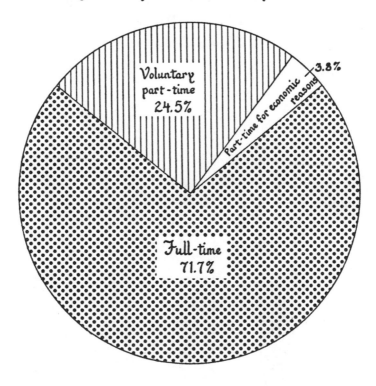

Voluntary
part-time
24.5%

Part-time for economic reasons

3.8%

Full-time
71.7%

Source: U.S. Department of Labor, Bureau of Labor Statistics.

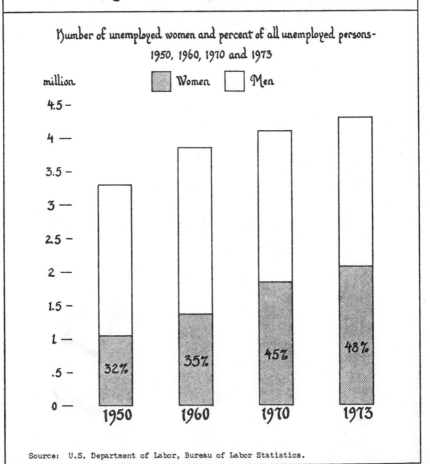

CHART G

The Number of Unemployed Women Has Increased Greatly, and Women Account for an Increasing Proportion of All Unemployed Persons

Number of unemployed women and percent of all unemployed persons—
1950, 1960, 1970 and 1973

million

Women   Men

4.5 –

4 —

3.5 –

3 —

2.5 –

2 —

1.5 –

1 —

.5 –

0 —

1950   1960   1970   1973

32%   35%   45%   48%

Source: U.S. Department of Labor, Bureau of Labor Statistics.

CHART H

Unemployment Rates Are Highest for Teenage and Minority Race Women

Unemployment rates for white and minority race women
16-19 and 20-64 years of age ~ April 1974

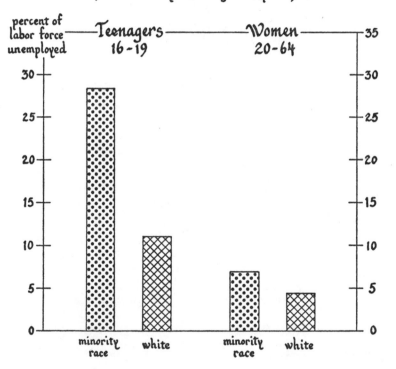

Source: U.S. Department of Labor, Bureau of Labor Statistics.

CHART I

Employment in Different Occupation Groups Varies by Sex

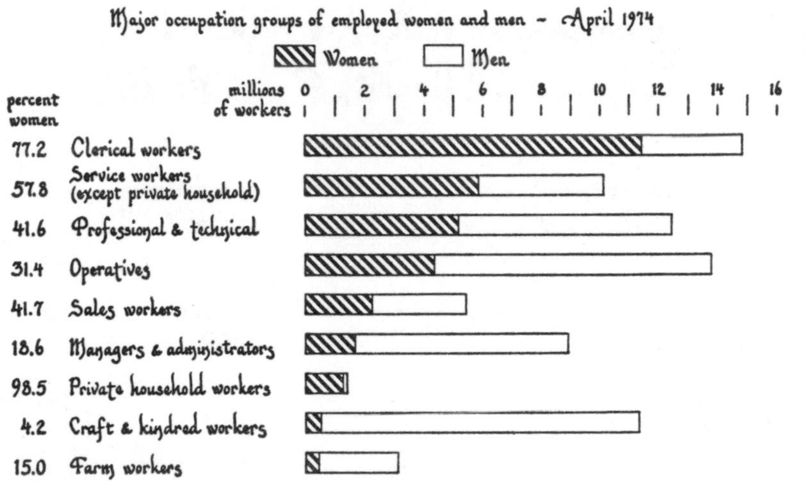

Major occupation groups of employed women and men – April 1974

🟦 Women   ⬜ Men

percent women	millions of workers	Occupation
77.2		Clerical workers
57.8		Service workers (except private household)
41.6		Professional & technical
31.4		Operatives
41.7		Sales workers
18.6		Managers & administrators
98.5		Private household workers
4.2		Craft & kindred workers
15.0		Farm workers

millions of workers: 0 2 4 6 8 10 12 14 16

Source: U.S. Department of Labor, Bureau of Labor Statistics.

There Are Differences in the Distribution of Minority Race and White Women by Occupation, but the Differences Are Narrowing

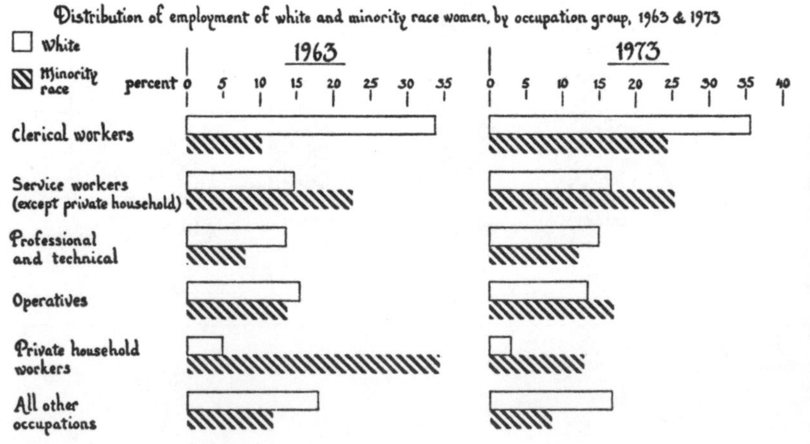

Distribution of employment of white and minority race women, by occupation group, 1963 & 1973

⬜ White
🟦 Minority race

1963   1973

percent 0 5 10 15 20 25 30 35   0 5 10 15 20 25 30 35 40

- Clerical workers
- Service workers (except private household)
- Professional and technical
- Operatives
- Private household workers
- All other occupations

Source: U.S. Department of Labor, Bureau of Labor Statistics.

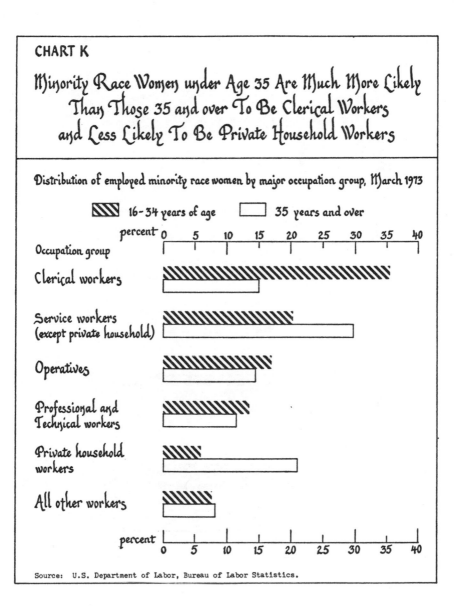

CHART K

Minority Race Women under Age 35 Are Much More Likely Than Those 35 and over To Be Clerical Workers and Less Likely To Be Private Household Workers

Distribution of employed minority race women by major occupation group, March 1973

▧ 16-34 years of age   ☐ 35 years and over

percent 0   5   10   15   20   25   30   35   40

Occupation group

Clerical workers

Service workers (except private household)

Operatives

Professional and Technical workers

Private household workers

All other workers

percent 0   5   10   15   20   25   30   35   40

Source: U.S. Department of Labor, Bureau of Labor Statistics.

CHART L

Most Women Work Because of Economic Need

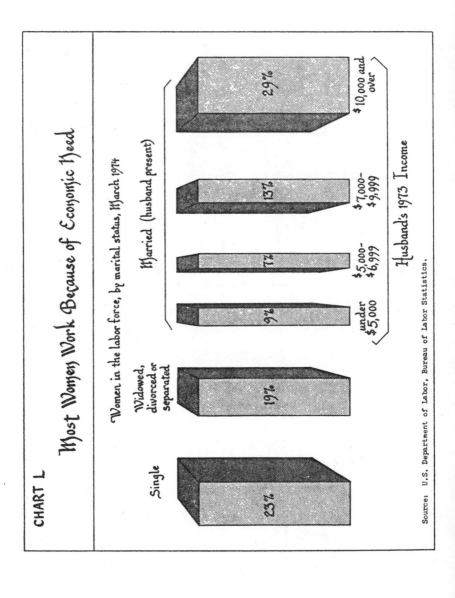

Women in the labor force, by marital status, March 1974

Married (husband present)

Single — 23%

Widowed, divorced or separated — 19%

under $5,000 — 9%

$5,000–$6,999 — 7%

$7,000–$9,999 — 13%

$10,000 and over — 29%

Husband's 1973 Income

Source: U.S. Department of Labor, Bureau of Labor Statistics.

288

CHART M

The Earnings Gap between Women and Men Continues To Widen

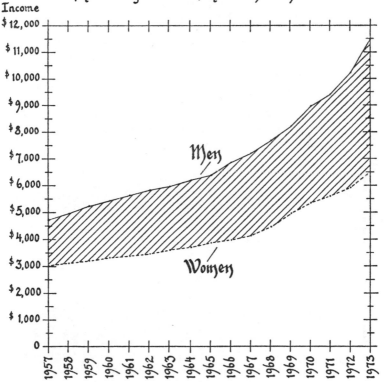

Median earnings of full-time year-round workers, 14 years of age and over, by sex, 1957-1973

Income

Note: Data for 1967-1973 are not strictly comparable with those for prior years, which are for wage and salary income only and do not include earnings of self-employed persons.

Source: U.S. Department of Commerce, Bureau of the Census.

Percentage of Female Workers in Selected Occupations,

(Numbers in thousands)

Occupations	Total employed	Percent Female
Total	84,783	39.6
White-collar workers	42,227	49.9
Professional and technical	12,748	41.3
Accountants	782	24.6
Architects	70	4.3
Computer specialists	363	21.2
Computer programmers	223	25.6
Computer systems analysts	122	14.8
Engineers	1,150	1.1
Aeronautical and astronautical engineers	51	.
Civil engineers	160	1.3
Electrical and electronic engineers	290	1.4
Industrial engineers	187	2.7
Mechanical engineers	200	1.0
Lawyers and judges	392	7.1
Lawyers	374	7.2
Librarians, archivists, and curators	190	78.4
Librarians	180	81.1
Life and physical scientists	277	14.4
Biological scientists	54	31.5
Chemists	131	14.5
Operations and systems researchers and analysts	124	15.3
Personnel and labor relations workers	326	36.5
Physicians, dentists and related practitioners	647	11.3
Dentists	110	1.8
Pharmacists	119	17.6
Physicians, medical and osteopathic	354	13.0
Nurses, dieticians, and therapists	1,126	91.8
Registered nurses	935	97.0
Therapists	157	60.5
Health technologists and technicians	397	72.3
Clinical laboratory technologists and technicians	177	74.6
Radiologic technologists and technicians	79	69.6

Occupations	Total employed	Percent Female
White-collar workers—Continued		
Managers and administrators—Continued		
Managers and superintendents, building	148	48.6
Office managers, n.e.c.	302	54.3
Officials and administrators, public administration n.e.c	361	22.4
Officials of lodges, societies and unions	102	20.6
Restaurant, cafeteria and bar managers	501	33.3
Sales managers and department heads, retail trade	315	33.7
Sales managers, except retail trade	305	3.9
School administrators, college	103	28.2
School administrators, elementary and secondary	263	28.1
All other managers and administrators	5,282	13.1
Sales workers	5,460	42.5
Advertising agents and sales workers	78	28.2
Demonstrators	92	93.5
Hucksters and peddlers	179	74.3
Insurance agents, brokers and underwriters	504	14.3
Newspaper carriers and vendors	81	25.9
Real estate agents and brokers	414	40.1
Stock and bond sales agents	104	13.5
Sales workers and sales clerks, n.e.c	4,002	45.2
Sales representatives, manufacturing industries	366	9.3
Sales representatives, wholesale trade	761	5.8
Sales clerks, retail trade	2,307	70.0
Sales workers, except clerks, retail trade	442	17.6
Sales workers, services and construction	126	31.0
Clerical workers	15,128	77.8
Bank tellers	350	91.1
Billing clerks	144	86.8
Bookkeepers	1,689	87.8
Cashiers	1,180	87.1

1975 annual averages

Religious workers	304	11.8
Social scientists	189	24.3
Economists	99	13.1
Psychologists	61	42.6
Social and recreation workers	402	58.5
Social workers	296	60.8
Recreation workers	107	51.4
Teachers, college and university	543	31.1
Teachers, except college and university	3,022	70.6
Adult education teachers	56	46.4
Elementary school teachers	1,332	85.4
Prekindergarten and kindergarten teachers	214	98.6
Secondary school teachers	1,184	49.2
Teachers except college and university, n.e.c.	234	76.1
Engineering and science technicians	896	11.8
Chemical technicians	76	14.5
Drafters	301	9.3
Electrical and electronic engineering technicians	177	5.6
Surveyors	70	
Technicians, except health, engineering and science	154	11.7
Airplane pilots	60	
Vocational and educational counselors	144	48.6
Writers, artists, and entertainers	1,055	34.4
Athletes and kindred workers	106	32.1
Designers	125	25.6
Editors and reporters	177	44.6
Musicians and composers	139	31.7
Painters and sculptors	146	46.6
Photographers	76	17.1
Public relations specialists and public writers	115	32.2
Research workers not specified	95	32.6
All other professional and technical workers	100	28.0
Managers and administrators, except farm	8,891	19.4
Bank officials and financial managers	518	23.6
Buyers and purchasing agents	370	25.1
Buyers, wholesale and retail trade	146	38.4
Credit and collection managers	57	38.6
Health administrators	152	45.4
Inspectors, except construction and public administration	112	7.1
Clerical supervisors, n.e.c	226	66.4
Collectors, bill and account	71	52.1
Counter clerks, except food	327	75.8
Dispatchers and starters, vehicle	92	18.5
Estimators and investigators, n.e.c	383	44.9
Expediters and production controllers	211	28.0
File clerks	264	86.4
Insurance adjusters, examiners, and investigators	150	48.0
Library attendants and assistants	144	80.6
Mail carriers, post office	252	8.7
Mail handlers, except post office	143	46.2
Messengers and office helpers	76	26.3
Office machine operators	714	69.5
Bookkeeping and billing machine operators	59	91.5
Computer and peripheral equipment operators	295	44.4
Key punch operators	250	92.8
Payroll and timekeeping clerks	199	74.9
Postal clerks	290	30.0
Receptionists	460	96.7
Secretaries	3,245	99.1
Secretaries, legal	133	99.2
Secretaries, medical	78	98.7
Secretaries, n.e.c.	3,035	99.1
Shipping and receiving clerks	428	17.1
Statistical clerks	326	74.5
Stenographers	100	93.0
Stock clerks and storekeepers	473	30.2
Teachers aides, except school monitors	288	91.3
Telephone operators	344	93.3
Ticket, station and express agents	136	39.0
Typists	1,025	96.6
All other clerical workers	1,402	74.1
Blue-collar workers	27,962	17.0
Craft and kindred workers	10,972	4.6
Carpenters	988	0.6
Brickmasons and stonemasons	160	0.6
Cement and concrete finishers	82	-
Electricians	534	0.6
Excavating, grading, and road machinery operators	397	0.8
Painters, construction and maintenance	420	3.8

See note at end of table.

[Numbers in thousands]

Occupations	Total employed	Percent Female
Blue-collar workers—Continued		
Craft and kindred workers—Continued		
Plumbers and pipefitters	386	
Structural metal craft workers	75	.
Roofers and slaters	80	.
Blue-collar worker supervisors, n.e.c.	1,393	8.6
Machinists and job setters	557	2.5
Job and die setters, metal	96	4.2
Machinists	461	2.2
Metal craft workers, excluding mechanics, machinists, and job setters	594	1.9
Millwrights	79	.
Molders, metal	52	7.7
Sheetmetal workers and tinsmiths	144	1.4
Tool and die makers	174	0.6
Mechanics, automobiles	1,102	0.5
Automobile body repairers	164	0.6
Mechanics, automobiles	937	0.4
Mechanics, except automobiles	1,795	1.2
Airconditioning, heating, and refrigeration mechanics	171	.
Aircraft mechanics	120	1.8
Data processing machine repairers	57	.
Farm implement mechanics	60	.
Heavy equipment mechanics, including diesel	756	0.9
Household appliances and accessory installers and mechanics	141	0.7
Office machine repairers	58	1.7
Radio and television repairers	124	2.4
Railroad and car shop mechanics	53	.
Printing craft workers	375	17.6
Compositors and typesetters	154	21.4
Printing press operators	146	10.3
Blue-collar workers—Continued		
Operatives, except transport—Continued		
Shoemaking machine operatives	67	68.7
Furnace tenders and stokers, except metal	72	1.4
Textile operatives	302	56.3
Spinners, twisters, and winders	112	62.5
Welders and flame cutters	654	4.4
Winding operatives, n.e.c	60	45.0
All other operatives, except transport	2,646	31.4
Transport equipment operatives	3,219	5.7
Busdrivers	310	37.7
Delivery and route workers	583	4.5
Fork lift and tow motor operatives	314	1.6
Railroad switch operators	53	.
Taxicab drivers and chauffeurs	161	8.7
Truck drivers	1,694	1.1
All other transport equipment operatives	105	1.9
Nonfarm laborers	4,134	8.6
Animal caretakers	101	38.6
Construction laborers including carpenters' helpers	765	1.4
Freight and material handlers	721	8.6
Garbage collectors	87	.
Gardeners and groundskeepers, except farm	579	4.7
Timber cutting and logging workers	79	.
Stockhandlers	815	19.3
Vehicle washers and equipment cleaners	161	11.8
Warehouse laborers, n.e.c	204	3.4
All other nonfarm laborers	623	5.5
Service workers	11,657	62.3

1975 annual averages

Occupation	Number	Percent
Bakers	123	40.7
Cabinetmakers	77	2.6
Carpet installers	61	1.6
Crane, derrick, and hoist operators	169	1.2
Decorators and window dressers	95	66.3
Electric power line and cable installers and repairers	116	.
Inspectors, n.e.c.	134	4.5
Locomotive engineers	56	.
Stationary engineers	190	.
Tailors	51	35.3
Telephone installers and repairers	314	4.8
Telephone line installers and repairers	60	1.7
Upholsterers	63	27.0
All other craft workers	525	11.0
Operatives, except transport	9,637	38.4
Assemblers	1,015	49.7
Checkers, examiners, and inspectors, manufacturing	652	49.2
Clothing ironers and pressers	141	78.0
Cutting operatives, n.e.c	200	28.5
Dressmakers and seamstresses, excluding factory	121	96.7
Drillers, earth	50	2.0
Dry wall installers and lathers	59	.
Filers, polishers, sanders, and buffers	113	23.9
Furnace tenders, smelters, and pourers, metal	62	1.6
Garage workers and gas station attendants	450	4.7
Laundry and dry cleaning operatives, n.e.c	192	65.6
Meat cutters and butchers, excluding manufacturing	207	5.8
Meat cutters and butchers, manufacturing	100	27.0
Mine operatives, n.e.c.	183	1.1
Mixing operatives	91	2.2
Packers and wrappers, excluding meat and produce	592	62.5
Painters, manufactured articles	129	11.6
Photographic process workers	78	46.2
Precision machine operatives	360	10.6
Drill press operatives	61	23.0
Grinding machine operatives	132	7.6
Lathe and milling machine operatives	118	6.8
Punch and stamping-press operatives	130	27.7
Sawyers	108	9.3
Sewers and stitchers	803	95.8
Private households	1,171	97.4
Child care workers	435	98.4
Cleaners and servants	599	97.3
Housekeepers	87	97.7
Service workers, except private households	10,486	58.3
Cleaning workers	2,210	34.6
Lodging quarters cleaners	191	96.3
Building interior cleaners, n.e.c	750	56.3
Janitors and sextons	1,269	12.5
Food service workers	3,640	69.6
Bartenders	247	35.2
Waiters' assistants	164	17.7
Cooks	1,001	58.7
Dishwashers	222	34.7
Food counter and fountain workers	372	86.3
Waiters	1,183	91.1
Food service workers, n.e.c	451	78.7
Health service workers	1,718	88.9
Dental assistants	126	100.0
Health aides and trainees, excluding nursing	219	83.6
Nursing aides, orderlies, and attendants	1,001	85.8
Practical nurses	370	96.8
Personal service workers	1,628	74.3
Attendants	236	46.2
Barbers	124	8.1
Child care workers	422	93.8
Hairdressers and cosmetologists	504	90.5
Housekeepers, excluding private households	105	75.2
Welfare service aides	62	87.1
Protective service workers	1,290	6.3
Fire fighters	221	.
Guards	492	6.7
Police	473	2.7
Sheriffs and bailiffs	51	7.8
Farm workers	2,936	15.7
Farm and farm managers	1,593	6.4
Farmers (owners and tenants)	1,560	6.4
Farm laborers and supervisors	1,343	26.7
Farm laborers, wage workers	935	14.2
Farm laborers, unpaid family workers	367	61.0

NOTE: N.E.C. is an abbreviation for "not elsewhere classified" and designates broad categories of occupations which cannot be more specifically identified.

Source: Employment and Earnings report, January 1976, U.S. Department of Labor.

Readings

ABBOTT, EDITH. *Women in Industry.* New York: Appleton and Company, 1910. Reprinted by Arno Press, 1969.

ARNOWITZ, STANLEY. *False Promises: The Shaping of American Working Class Consciousness.* New York: McGraw-Hill, 1973.

BAKER, ELIZABETH FAULKNER. *Technology and Women's Work.* New York: Columbia University Press, 1964.

BANNER, LOIS W. *Women in Modern America: A Brief History.* New York: Harcourt Brace Jovanovich, 1974.

BELL, DANIEL. *The Coming of Post-Industrial Society.* New York: Basic Books, 1973.

BENET, MARY KATHLEEN. *The Secretarial Ghetto.* New York: McGraw-Hill, 1972.

BERG, IVAR. *Education and Jobs: The Great Training Robbery.* New York: Praeger, 1970.

BERGER, PETER, ed. *The Human Shape of Work.* New York: Macmillan, 1964.

BIRD, CAROLINE. *Born Female.* New York: David McKay Company, Inc., 1968.

BLUM, ALBERT A., ESTEY, MARTEN, KUHN, JAMES W., WILDMAN, WESLEU A., TROY, LEO. *White Collar Workers.* New York: Random House, 1971.

BRAVERMAN, HARRY. *Labor and Monopoly Capital:* The *Degradation of Work in the Twentieth Century.* New York: Monthly Review Press, 1974.

BROWNLEE, W. ELLIOT and MARY M. *Women in the American Economy: A Documentary History, 1675 to 1929.* New Haven, Conn.: Yale University Press, 1976.

CAIN, GLEN G. *Married Women in the Labor Force.* Chicago: University of Chicago Press, 1968.

CHAFE, WILLIAM HENRY. *The American Woman: Her Changing Social, Economic and Political Roles, 1920–1970.* New York: Oxford University Press, 1972.

COOK, ALICE H. *The Working Mother.* New York State School of Industrial and Labor Relations. Ithaca, N.Y.: Cornell University Press, 1975.

CURTIN, EDWARD B. *White Collar Unionization.* New York: National Industrial Conference Board, Personnel Policy, Study No. 220, 1970.

DAVIS, REBECCA HARDING. *Life in the Iron Mills.* New York: The Feminist Press, 1972.

DE GRAZIA, SEBASTIAN. *Of Time, Work, and Leisure.* New York: Twentieth-Century Fund, 1962; Anchor books, 1964.

DURKHEIM, EMILE. *The Division of Labor in Society.* New York: Macmillan, 1933; Free Press Paperback, 1964.

EPSTEIN, CYNTHIA FUCHS. *Woman's Place; Options and Limits in Professional Careers.* Berkeley: University of California Press, 1971.

FAIRFIELD, ROY P., ed. *Humanizing the Workplace.* New York: Prometheus Books, 1974.

FLEXNER, ELEANOR. *A Century of Struggle.* Cambridge, Mass.: Harvard University Press, 1959.

FREEDMAN, MARCIA. *Labor Markets: Segments and Shelters.* Montclair, N.J.: Allan Held, Osmun, 1976.

GARSON, BARBARA. *All the Livelong Day:* The *Meaning and De-meaning of Routine Work.* New York: Doubleday, 1975.

GILMAN, CHARLOTTE PERKINS. Carl Degler, ed. *Women and Economics.* New York: Harper and Row, 1966.

GROSS, EDWARD. *"Plus Ça Change. . . .* The Sexual Structure of Occupations Over Time." *Social Problems.* XIV (Fall 1968).

GUTMAN, HERBERT G. *Work, Culture and Society.* New York: Knopf, 1976.

HALL, RICHARD H. *Occupations and the Social Structure.* New Jersey: Prentice-Hall, 1969.

HOWE, LOUISE KAPP, ed. *The Future of the Family.* New York: Simon and Schuster, 1973; Touchstone Paperback, 1974.

HUBER, JOAN, ed. *Changing Woman in a Changing Society.* Chicago: University of Chicago Press, 1973.

JAFFE, A.J. and FROOMKIN, JOSEPH. *Technology and Jobs.* New York: Praeger, 1968.

JARMON, CAROLYN GROO. "Relationship Between Homemakers' Attitudes Toward Specific Household Tasks and Family Composition, Other Situational Variables and Time Allocation," Unpublished Master's Dissertation. Ithaca, N.Y.: Cornell University, 1972.

JENCKS, CHRISTOPHER. *Inequality: A Reassessment of the Effect of Family and Schooling in America.* New York: Basic Books, 1972.

JENKINS, DAVID. *Job Power.* New York: Doubleday, 1973.

KREPS, JANITA. *Sex in the Marketplace: American Women at Work.* Baltimore: Johns Hopkins Press, 1971.

LEVISON, ANDREW. *The Working-Class Majority.* New York: Coward, McCann & Geoghegan, 1974.

LIFTON, ROBERT, ed. *The Woman in America.* Boston: Houghton Mifflin, 1967.

LLOYD, CYNTHIA B., ed. *Sex, Discrimination, and the Division of Labor.* New York: Columbia University Press, 1975.

LOPATA, HELENA Z. *Occupation: Housewife.* New York: Oxford University Press, 1971.

MAHER, JOHN R., ed. *New Perspectives in Job Enrichment.* New York: Van Nostrand Reinhold., 1971.

MAUPIN, JOYCE. *Working Women and their Organizations.* Berkeley, Calif.: Union Wage Educational Committee, 1975.

MILLS, C. WRIGHT. *White Collar.* New York: Oxford University Press, 1953.

National Manpower Council. *Womanpower.* New York: Columbia University Press, 1957.

NYE, F. IVAN AND HOFFMAN, LOIS WLADIS. *The Employed Mother in America.* Chicago: Rand McNally, 1963.

OAKLEY, ANN. *Woman's Work: The Housewife Past and Present.* New York: Pantheon, 1974.

O'NEILL, WILLIAM L. *Everyone Was Brave.* Chicago: Quadrangle, 1971.

OPPENHEIMER, VALERIE KINCADE. *The Female Labor Force in the United States*. Population Monograph Series, No. 5, Berkeley, Calif.: Institute of International Studies, University of California, 1970.

PARKER, CORNELIA STRATTON. *Working with the Working Woman*. New York: Harper and Brothers, 1922.

PETERSON, DEENA, ed. *Practical Guide to the Women's Movement*. New York: Women's Action Alliance, 1975.

PRICE, COLETTE. "New Ways of Keeping Women Out of Paid Labor." *Feminist Revolution,* New York: Redstockings, 1975.

REZLER, JULIOUS. *Automation and Industrial Labor*. New York: Random House, 1969.

RICHARDSON, DOROTHY. *The Long Day* and LANGER, ELINOR. *Inside the New York Telephone Company: Women at Work*. New York: Quadrangle, 1972.

ROSSOW, JEROME M., ed. *The Worker and the Job: Coping with Change*. New Jersey: Prentice Hall, 1974.

ROWBOTHAM, SHEILA. *Hidden From History*. New York: Pantheon, 1974.

SAMUELS, CATHERINE. *The Forgotten Five Million: Women in Public Employment: A Guide to Eliminating Sex Discrimination*. Women's Action Alliance, Inc., 1975.

SENNET, RICHARD and COBB, JONATHAN. *The Hidden Injuries of Class*. New York: Knopf, 1973.

SHEA, JOHN R. RODERICK, ROGER D. ZELLER, FREDERICK A. and KOHEN, ANDREW I. *Years for Decision*. U.S. Department of Labor Manpower Research Monograph 20, Washington, D.C.: U.S. Government Printing Office, 1971.

SHOSTAK, ARTHUR B. and GOMBERG, WILLIAM, eds. *Blue Collar World*, New Jersey: Prentice Hall, 1964.

Signs, Journal of Women in Culture and Society, Volume 1, Number 3, Part 2, "Women and the Workplace, The Implications of Occupational Segregation." Entire issue.

SMUTS, ROBERT W. *Women and Work in America.* New York: Columbia University Press, 1959, Shocken Books, 1971.

STURMTHAL, ADOLPH, ed. *White-Collar Trade Unions.* Urbana: University of Illinois Press, 1966.

TEPPERMAN, JEAN. *Not Servants, Not Machines: Office Workers Speak Out.* Boston: Beacon Press, 1976.

TERKEL, STUDS. *Working.* New York: Pantheon, 1974.

United States Department of Labor, *Dual Careers,* Volume 1, 2 and 3, Manpower Research Monograph Number 21, Manpower Administration, Washington, D.C.: 1970, 1973 and 1975.

U.S. Department of Labor, *1975 Handbook on Women Workers.* Washington, D.C.: Women's Bureau, Bulletin 297, 1975.

U.S. Department of Labor, *Occupational Outlook Handbook, 1974-75 Edition,* Bureau of Labor Statistics, Bulletin 1785, Washington, D.C.: 1974.

U.S. Department of Labor, *Years for Decision,* Volumes 1 and 2, Manpower Research Monograph No. 24, Manpower Administration, Washington, D.C.: 1971.

WALKER, KATHRYN E., "Household Work: Can We Add It to the GNP?" *Journal of Home Economics.* October, 1973.

WERTHEIMER, BARBARA M. and NELSON, ANNE H., *Trade Union Women.* New York: Praeger, 1975.

WITT, MARY and NAHERNY, PATRICIA K. *Women's Work—Up from 878: Report on the DOT Research Project.* Women's Education Resources, University of Wisconsin, Extension.

READINGS

Work in America: Report of a Special Task Force to the Secretary of Health, Education and Welfare. Cambridge, Mass.: MIT Press, 1973.